**Peterson Institute for
International Economics**

FACING UP TO LOW PRODUCTIVITY GROWTH

Adam S. Posen and
Jeromin Zettelmeyer, editors

Peterson Institute for International Economics

FACING UP TO LOW PRODUCTIVITY GROWTH

Adam S. Posen and
Jeromin Zettelmeyer, editors

Washington, DC
February 2019

Adam S. Posen has been president of the Peterson Institute for International Economics since January 2013, after first joining in July 1997. He has written on macroeconomic stabilization policy, the long-term effects of and recovery from financial crises, and the political economy of growth in the G7 economies.

Jeromin Zettelmeyer has been a senior fellow at the Peterson Institute for International Economics since September 2016 and was a nonresident senior fellow during 2013–14. From 2014 until September of 2016, he served as director-general for economic policy at the German Federal Ministry for Economic Affairs and Energy.

**PETERSON INSTITUTE FOR
INTERNATIONAL ECONOMICS**
1750 Massachusetts Avenue, NW
Washington, DC 20036-1903
+1.202.328.9000 www.piie.com

Adam S. Posen, *President*
Steven R. Weisman, *Vice President for
Publications and Communications*

Cover Photo by ©Sue Smith—Fotolia
Printing by Versa Press

For reprints/permission to photocopy please contact the APS customer service department at Copyright Clearance Center, Inc., 222 Rosewood Drive, Danvers, MA 01923; or email requests to: info@copyright.com

Printed in the United States of America
21   20   19   5   4   3   2   1

**Library of Congress
Cataloging-in-Publication Data**
Names: Posen, Adam S., editor. | Zettelmeyer, Jeromin, editor. Title: Facing up to low productivity growth / Adam S. Posen and Jeromin Zettelmeyer, editors. Description: Washington, DC : Peterson Institute for International Economics, [2018] | Includes index. Identifiers: LCCN 2018035919 | ISBN 9780881327311. Subjects: LCSH: Industrial productivity. | Debts, Public—Econometric models. | Fiscal policy. | Equality. Classification: LCC HC79.I52 F33 2018 | DDC 331.11/8—dc23

This publication has been subjected to a prepublication peer review intended to ensure analytical quality. The views expressed are those of the authors. This publication is part of the overall program of the Peterson Institute for International Economics, as endorsed by its Board of Directors, but it does not necessarily reflect the views of individual members of the Board or of the Institute's staff or management.

The Peterson Institute for International Economics is a private nonpartisan, nonprofit institution for rigorous, intellectually open, and indepth study and discussion of international economic policy. Its purpose is to identify and analyze important issues to make globalization beneficial and sustainable for the people of the United States and the world, and then to develop and communicate practical new approaches for dealing with them. Its work is funded by a highly diverse group of philanthropic foundations, private corporations, and interested individuals, as well as income on its capital fund. About 35 percent of the Institute's resources were provided by contributors from outside the United States.

A list of all financial supporters is posted at https://piie.com/sites/default/files/supporters.pdf.

Contents

Preface

Since the mid-2000s, productivity growth has slowed markedly in almost all the advanced economies, by roughly the same order of magnitude. The decline was particularly spectacular in the United States, because it was preceded by a temporary boom in the decade before and no obvious precipitating event (since the slowdown clearly set in well before the global financial crisis). In other high-income economies, the decline has come on more slowly but has been steady, picking up speed in the aftermath of the global financial crisis. In the last few years, productivity growth appears to have stabilized at around 0.5 to 1 percent per annum at the technological frontier, in many cases half or less of its former rate of growth.

An enormous literature explores possible causes of the now evident productivity slowdown. It ranges from poor measurement to changes in the nature and effects of technological progress, to a sense that the low-hanging fruit from greater educational attainment rates have been picked, to explanations emphasizing declining business dynamism and the spillovers from international trade rolling back. Far less research, however, has been done on the consequences for long-term economic policymaking of a productivity slowdown, should the slowdown persist. *Facing Up to Low Productivity Growth* addresses this gap, based on the contributions of 12 leading scholars, under the guidance of Peterson Institute for International Economics (PIIE) Senior Fellow Jeromin Zettelmeyer and myself.

A possible reason why there is so little research to date on the consequences of lower productivity growth may be that they appear obvious: Lower productivity growth means slower improvement of living standards than we have experienced in past decades and were counting on for the future. Economists then could straightforwardly update their forecast assumptions for their aggregate projections. This simple aggregate characterization misses significant implications for specific countries, sectors, and population groups, depending on a given economy's existing institutions. The productivity slowdown has not and will not be felt equally everywhere, even if the downshift in growth is relatively uniform across advanced economies.

Lower productivity growth will lead to a widening of productivity gaps along some dimensions (e.g., between leading and new firms) and to a narrowing along others (e.g., between some countries, depending upon their adaptability). These differential impacts will have meaningful consequences for the development of inequality, capital flows, and political economy. There are clearly some negative fiscal implications, but where and how much they bite are heavily dependent upon the nature of tax systems, the structure of pension and insurance frameworks, and their interaction with a country's demography. And to the extent that a lower long-term growth rate prolongs the current period of very low interest rates, it will have implications for financial stability and monetary policy, as well.

The contributions in this volume explore some of these policy-relevant and realistic consequences of lower productivity growth, which must be faced by policymakers. Neil Mehrotra (chapter 1) focuses on the impact of slower productivity growth on the ability of countries to pay off public debts. Elena Duggar (chapter 2) looks at the potential impacts on sovereign risk through several channels, including quasi-fiscal liabilities and financial stability. Karen Dynan (chapter 3) asks whether adapting to lower productivity growth requires changes in tax policy in the United States. Louise Sheiner (chapter 4) examines the impact via revenues and expenditures in the United States on its long-term fiscal commitments. Axel Börsch-Supan (chapter 5) explores the effects on pension systems around the world, and how their differences in provision influence the impact of the slowdown. José De Gregorio (chapter 6) examines the link between productivity growth in advanced and emerging-market countries, and the potentially substantial implications for cross-border capital flows. Filippo di Mauro, Bernardo Mottironi, Gianmarco Ottaviano, and Alessandro Zona-Mattioli (chapter 7) study the implications of a sustained slowdown in productivity growth for exports, including global supply chains, and the feedback on growth in trade and thus productivity itself. Anna Stansbury and Lawrence Summers (chapter 8) investigate the extent to which productivity continues to exert an influence on wages, and how this will affect wage trends in a low-inflation, low-growth environment. Jason Furman and Peter Orszag (chapter

9) look at the link between productivity growth, corporate competition, and inequality, especially in an age of increasing number of network and winner-takes-all industries. Finally, Daniel Drezner (chapter 10) explores the potential impact of lower productivity growth in the United States on its electoral politics.

Two main messages emerge from our research program. First, the effects of slower productivity growth will be largely negative, as expected, but not always in the ways and through the channels expected. For example, in most fiscal systems, revenues and most expenditures are indexed to average wages. As a result, slower productivity growth is much less of a threat to the sustainability of these systems than, for example, population aging. At the same time, slower productivity growth will have destructive consequences through previously overlooked channels. Persistent low productivity encourages overborrowing by corporations and households; private debt crises, in turn, represent a big risk to economies and fiscal systems. A similar logic applies to the social and political impact of low productivity growth. As long as it remains positive, slower productivity growth cannot in itself create new social problems. This conclusion can change radically, however, if productivity growth goes along with higher inequality or if voters find past promises and expectations disappointing. Unfortunately, this seems to be the case.

The second message concerns policy implications. To use a climate change concept, the contributions in this volume by intent are focused on *adaptation* to persistent lower productivity growth than on *mitigation* of the productivity trend downshift itself. For some this is an overdue recognition of reality, while for others this is a defeatist approach. For the most part, however, there turns out to be no tension between seeking to mitigate and to adapt. We find that a wide range of policies are available that are good for addressing both challenges. These dual purpose policies stress enhancing economic dynamism, and include doing so by increasing business entry and competition, facilitating mobility of workers, strengthening education, building fiscally robust universal healthcare systems, and reducing tariff and nontariff barriers to trade.

The priorities among such policy responses, however, are different when lower productivity growth is taken as unlikely to be significantly reversed any time soon than when one assumes that one can rapidly improve the productivity growth trend. One contribution of this volume and the underlying research project is to show that simply marking down fiscal projections is incorrect—design of pension and tax systems matter. Another contribution is to bring out the sizable international implications of the slowdown in the advanced economies, which have been largely overlooked to date. The differential impact across high-income economies, and more importantly the channels linking that to developing-economy growth, will shape trade, investment, and capital flows and thus prospects for global growth (including for safe higher returns for advanced-economy savers to offset slower domestic growth).

This project thus relates to the work done simultaneously on the volume that the PIIE published jointly with the International Monetary Fund's Asia Pacific Department in December 2018, *Sustaining Economic Growth in Asia*. A major conference exploring the causes of the decline in productivity growth, "Making Sense of the Productivity Slowdown," was held at the Institute in November 2015. A second major conference, "Policy Implications of Sustained Low Productivity Growth," followed two years later, in November 2017. This latter conference included presentations of early drafts of a number of the contributions that have been published in this volume; most have been significantly revised and extended for this publication. As all PIIE publications, these contributions seek to extend the frontier of research relevant for policymaking.

This volume, and the conference on which it is based, would not have been possible without the generous support of the Robert D. Ziff Foundation. Beyond the Foundation's financial support, the Peterson Institute for International Economics and Jeromin Zettelmeyer and I, as editors of this volume, are indebted to Robert and Daniel Ziff for their constant encouragement and many stimulating conversations that inspired and continue to improve our work in this area.

***

The Peterson Institute for International Economics is a private nonpartisan, nonprofit institution for rigorous, intellectually open, and indepth study and discussion of international economic policy. Its purpose is to identify and analyze important issues to making globalization beneficial and sustainable for the people of the United States and the world and then to develop and communicate practical new approaches for dealing with them.

The Institute's work is funded by a highly diverse group of philanthropic foundations, private corporations, and interested individuals, as well as income on its capital fund. About 35 percent of the Institute resources in our latest fiscal year were provided by contributors from outside the United States. A list of all our financial supporters for the preceding year is posted at https://piie.com/sites/default/files/supporters.pdf.

The Executive Committee of the Institute's Board of Directors bears overall responsibility for the Institute's direction, gives general guidance and approval to its research program, and evaluates its performance in pursuit of its mission. The Institute's President is responsible for the identification of topics that are likely to become important over the medium term (one to three years) that should be addressed by Institute scholars. This rolling agenda is set in close consultation with the Institute's research staff, taking input from its distinguished Board of Directors and other stakeholders.

The President makes the final decision to publish any individual Institute study, following independent internal and external review of the work. Interested readers may access the data and computations underlying Institute publications for research and replication by searching titles at www.piie.com. The Institute hopes that its research and other activities will contribute to building a stronger foundation for international economic policy around the world. We invite readers of these publications to let us know how they think we can best accomplish this objective.

ADAM S. POSEN
President
Peterson Institute for International Economics

Facing Up to Low Productivity Growth: Introduction

ADAM S. POSEN AND JEROMIN ZETTELMEYER

Since the mid-2000s, virtually all economies in the Organization for Economic Cooperation and Development (OECD) have experienced a decline in average productivity growth, compared with both the preceding decade and long-term postwar averages (OECD 2015). In the United States, the decline began after the end of a temporary boom in total factor productivity (TFP) growth that began in the mid-1990s (figure I.1). In most other major economies, it reflected a continuation of a trend that started in the early 1970s.

The reduction in recorded productivity growth does not mainly appear to reflect poor measurement. GDP and, by extension, productivity are indeed mismeasured—because quality improvements or intangible investment in training, reorganization, and advertising are not adequately counted, for example. But mismeasurement cannot explain the productivity slowdown in the United States, because it was even worse between 1996 and 2004, when productivity boomed (Byrne, Fernald, and Reinsdorf 2016). Free digital services—online searches, social networks, and entertainment—have been on the rise since the mid-2000s, but including them as part of household final consumption has only a small impact on growth (Nakamura and Soloveichik 2015; Byrne, Fernald, and Reinsdorf 2016). Furthermore, the productivity slowdown across countries does not appear to be correlated with cross-country differences in the production or use of information tech-

Adam S. Posen is the president of the Peterson Institute for International Economics. Jeromin Zettelmeyer is senior fellow at the Peterson Institute for International Economics. The authors gratefully acknowledge suggestions from Olivier Blanchard and Jason Furman and research assistance by Colombe Ladreit and Alvaro Leandro.

1

Figure I.1 Productivity growth in the United States and other advanced economies

a. Total factor productivity growth in the United States, 1950–2017

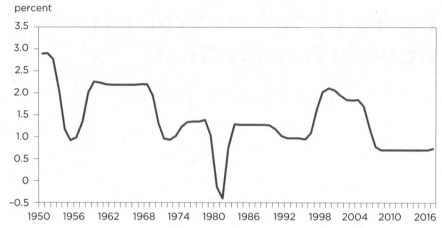

b. Growth of GDP per hour worked, constant prices (five-year moving averages), 1975–2017

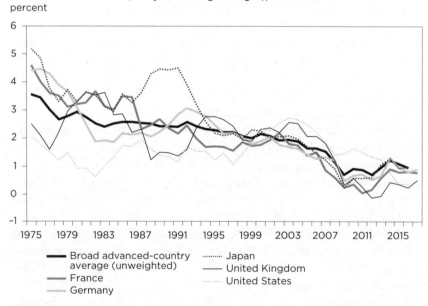

Sources: Data in panel A are from CBO (2018, supplemental table 1); data in panel B are from OECD.Stat.

nology (IT), suggesting that mismeasurement of IT services cannot be the reason for the slowdown (Syverson 2017). Although the data are imperfect, the phenomenon of lower productivity hence needs to be taken seriously.

A substantial body of literature explores the possible causes of the productivity slowdown. The most influential explanations focus on technology. Gordon (2012) conjectures that the slowing of growth across the industrial world since the 1970s mainly reflects the absorption of the main inventions of the late 19th century—electricity, the telephone, and the internal combustion engine. Fernald (2014) provides evidence that the US slowdown since 2004 was the "flip-side of the mid-1990s speed-up" linked to IT. Additional explanations include educational plateauing (no further rises in years of schooling); expansion in global labor supply as China and Eastern Europe were integrated into the global economy in the 1990s and early 2000s; end of a temporary productivity boom related to outsourcing and creation of global value chains; and decline in new business creation, business dynamism, and technology diffusion (Fernald and Jones 2014; Gordon 2010, 2014; Goodhart and Pradhan 2017; OECD 2015; Andrews, Criscuolo, and Gal 2016; Decker et al. 2017).

In contrast, very little work has been done on the consequences of the slowdown, in part because the first-order impact (lower growth and lower standards of living) seems obvious. There is also a view that the productivity slowdown will not persist. The Congressional Budget Office (CBO) projects a rise in TFP growth from about 0.7 percent a year (its level since 2008) to a long-run rate of 1.2 percent (its average level during 1972–2017). "Techno-optimists" predict a return to TFP growth closer to 2 percent, in line with the experience in 1950–1972 and 1996–2004, arguing that recent and future digital innovations will eventually accelerate productivity growth (Brynjolfsson and McAfee 2014; Mokyr 2014; Mokyr, Vickers, and Ziebarth 2015; Branstetter and Sichel 2017).

The premise of this volume is that it is important to explore the economic and social consequences of a sustained period of slower productivity growth in advanced economies, for two reasons. First, one does not have to be a techno-pessimist to believe that slower productivity growth may persist for some time. Even if the digital revolution does, at some point, translate into higher productivity growth, that point may be some way off. In the meantime, various headwinds are likely to hold back productivity growth.[1] Some, such as the educational plateau in advanced economies

---

1. Studies that speak to one or several of these arguments include Jorgenson and Vu (2010), Gordon (2012, 2014), German Council of Economic Experts (2015), Fernald and Jones (2014), and Summers (2014).

and a leveling off in trade integration, are to blame for the slowing that has already occurred. And following the decision of the United Kingdom to leave the European Union and the election of a protectionist president in the United States, there is concern that trade integration and cross-border value chains, which have been a source of productivity gains in the past, could be reversed rather than just level off.

Second, the first-order effect of slower productivity growth—lower than expected future living standards—masks more granular consequences that could have significant welfare implications for specific countries, sectors, and population groups and could both influence and be influenced by public policy. Slowing productivity does not mean that productivity slows everywhere in tandem. As a result, it could lead to either a widening (e.g., between firms) or a narrowing (e.g., between some countries) of productivity gaps, with potential consequences for inequality, capital flows, and politics. For related reasons, the slowdown may not affect government revenues and expenditures one for one and hence have fiscal implications. To the extent that lower productivity prolongs the current period of very low interest rates, it could also have implications for financial stability.

The contributions in this book explore some of these more granular consequences. The common assumption is that productivity growth remains at the low average level of the past decade, about 0.5 percent a year lower than currently expected by forecasters such as the CBO. The chapters analyze the implications of this sustained drop for fiscal sustainability, including the sustainability of pension systems and tax policy; wages and income distribution; international trade; and growth in emerging-market economies.

Fiscal Implications

The first five chapters focus on fiscal implications. Neil Mehrotra (chapter 1) focuses on the impact of slower productivity growth on the ability of countries to pay off their public debts, analyzing both the relevant macroeconomic mechanisms and the international evidence. Elena Duggar (chapter 2) takes a broad view of the potential impacts on sovereign risk through several channels, including quasi-fiscal liabilities and financial stability. Karen Dynan (chapter 3) asks whether adapting to lower productivity growth requires changes in tax policy. Louise Sheiner (chapter 4) looks at the impact on revenues and expenditures at all three levels of government (federal, state, and local) in the United States. Axel Börsch-Supan (chapter 5) explores the effects of lower productivity growth on pension systems around the world.

As Mehrotra explains, the impact of lower productivity growth on debt sustainability—defined as a stable or declining ratio of public debt to GDP—is prima facie ambiguous. For a fixed primary (noninterest) deficit, debt sustainability depends on the real interest rate (r), which affects the numerator of the debt-to-GDP ratio, and real growth (g), which affects the denominator. Lower than expected productivity growth will lower g, but according to most macroeconomic models—and the broad data trends documented in chapter 1—it would also be expected to translate into lower real interest rates. Depending on the strength of the relationship, debt sustainability may deteriorate, stay about the same (if r and g decline by the same amount), or even improve. Small open economies, whose interest rates are determined by world interest rates rather than domestic growth, may even benefit from a productivity slowdown in the United States and other large advanced economies, because it would tend to lower their borrowing costs and they might be able to buck the trend toward lower productivity growth.

This relatively sanguine assessment could change if productivity growth affects not only r and g but also the noninterest deficit. Sheiner concludes in chapter 4 that slower productivity growth is likely to lead to a deterioration of the US fiscal balance, particularly at the federal level, by (1) reducing real bracket creep (the tendency for productivity growth to raise tax rates by shifting up real income); (2) gradually raising inflation-indexed expenditures, such as social security benefits and certain discretionary outlays as a share of GDP; and (3) increasing poverty and hence poverty-related social spending.

The impact of these effects is small in any given year but adds up over time. According to Sheiner, a 0.6 percentage point reduction in annual productivity growth compared with the CBO's baseline would raise the projected federal primary deficit in 2042 from 3.2 to 5.1 percent and the projected federal debt level from 130 to 159 percent of GDP. The projection for the federal debt assumes that lower productivity growth would lead to a correspondingly lower rise in the interest rate path compared with current projections. If it does not—that is, if the CBO's baseline interest rate assumptions are maintained—the 2042 debt-to-GDP ratio could rise by more than 40 percentage points, to 173 percent of GDP. If the interest rate path reacts to the lower productivity baseline by more than one-for-one, the debt-to-GDP ratio would rise by less compared with the baseline, but for plausible parameter ranges it would still rise. Assuming a two-for-one reaction of interest rates to the reduction in productivity growth, for example, Sheiner projects a rise in the 2042 debt-to-GDP ratio to 146 percent, 16 points above the latest CBO baseline projection.

One of the drivers of the deterioration of US fiscal accounts that would accompany lower productivity is an increase in spending on social security (pensions). Could lower productivity growth also put pressure on other pension systems, particularly in Europe? As Axel Börsch-Supan shows in chapter 5, the answer depends on the system, but the results are generally less alarming that one might expect. The reason is that while US social security benefits are linked to the price level, pension benefits in most other pay-as-you-go systems are indexed to current wages.[2] In such systems, slower productivity growth will induce slower growth in both wages and pensions—and hence keep benefits stable relative to the contributions of the current working-age generation.

In contrast, fully funded systems adjust benefits in line with either accumulated savings (in defined-contribution systems) or preretirement wages (in defined-benefit systems). In both cases, a decline in productivity growth leads to reduced benefits, via lower interest rates or lower wages. The reduction is bad for the retiree, but the solvency of the system generally remains unaffected. The only exception would be a situation in which interest rates react more sharply to a drop in productivity growth than wages, reducing the assets of a fully funded system relative to its liabilities.

To summarize the flavor of these contributions, slower productivity growth will have a negative impact on the fiscal position of the US federal government and on some pension systems. These impacts need to be understood and addressed, but they appear manageable. In particular, Sheiner's analysis implies that a cumulative fiscal adjustment of just 1 percent of GDP over the next 25 years would be enough to offset the deterioration of the primary fiscal balance caused by slower productivity growth. This adjustment is much smaller than the fiscal adjustment needed to offset the adverse fiscal effects of population aging or the effects of President Trump's recent tax cuts.

This relatively reassuring conclusion is likely to understate the threat that slower productivity growth presents to fiscal stability—and economic stability more broadly—for at least two reasons, however. First, persistent low productivity tends to go along with persistent low interest rates and flat yield curves. It creates financial sector risks by encouraging overborrowing by corporations and households, by making it harder for banks and life insurance companies to make profits, and by encouraging riskier or leveraged investments (IMF 2016a). As Duggar points out in chapter 2, financial sector crises have historically represented the biggest single risk to

---

2. Pension benefits and current average wage levels are linked both in flat-benefit (Beveridgean) pay-as-you-go systems, in which the level of benefits does not depend on individual lifetime contributions, and in earnings-related (Bismarckian) systems. In Bismarckian systems, lifetime earnings determine the level of benefits relative to current average wages, not their absolute level.

sovereign balance sheets. Through this channel, slower productivity growth could create fiscal problems even when its direct fiscal sustainability implications are modest.

Second, both Sheiner and Börsch-Supan explicitly or implicitly assume that low productivity growth translates into low wage growth but does not affect the distribution of wages. Suppose, however, that wages become more dispersed as productivity and average wages grow more slowly (a well-founded concern, as shown below). According to Sheiner, greater dispersion would magnify the impact of lower productivity growth on social spending and hence on the primary fiscal balance. It could also translate into negative real pension growth at the bottom of the earnings distribution. Such an erosion of benefits may not be feasible socially or politically, particularly in systems in which replacement rates are already declining because of population aging, creating pressures to subsidize the system.

The discussion so far carries several policy implications. A "low-for-long" environment calls for regulatory and supervisory policies, including macroprudential policies, that identify and contain emerging financial sector risks. It also requires policies that create fiscal space to accommodate and offset inevitable spending pressures. These policies could focus on the efficiency of spending, on the revenue side, or both.

Beyond the need to create or preserve fiscal space, sustained low productivity growth may have implications for tax policy. In chapter 3, Dynan points to three. First, in a low growth, low interest rate environment, monetary policy will find it harder to stabilize economic fluctuations. This calls for strengthening tax-based automatic stabilizers. Second, lower wage growth may weaken incentives for work participation, which could further reduce per capita income growth. This argues for improved tax incentives for work. Finally, slower income growth may suggest raising savings, including through higher tax subsidies for individual retirement savings, particularly to encourage well-designed workplace retirement savings plans.

International Dimensions

Two chapters look at the implications of slowing productivity growth for emerging-market economies and international trade. In chapter 6, José De Gregorio asks how slowing productivity growth in advanced economies might affect emerging-market economies. The results are not encouraging. Although the GDP per capita gap has narrowed between emerging-market economies and the United States, it is explained by faster accumulation of physical and human capital. In contrast, TFP growth in most emerging-market economies has been slower than in the United States. This is bad news, because it is difficult to imagine sustained catchup in living standards without an acceleration of TFP: As De Gregorio shows, TFP growth rather than factor accumulation tends to drive growth accelerations in emerging-market economies. He also shows that productivity growth in emerging-market economies is correlated with that of advanced economies and that this correlation has increased in recent years, perhaps as a result of increased trade-related spillovers. Hence a slowdown in productivity growth in advanced economies could make an already bleak picture in emerging markets even bleaker.

In chapter 7, Filippo di Mauro, Bernardo Mottironi, Gianmarco Ottaviano, and Alessandro Zona-Mattioli examine the implications of a sustained slowdown in productivity growth for exports. Using a large firm-level database, they show that an economy's export performance depends on its share of highly productive firms—that is, it is not just average productivity that matters, but the size of the right tail of the productivity distribution of firms. They also show that export competitiveness of countries depends not only on average TFP growth—which both shifts the productivity distribution of firms and increases its dispersion—but also on an economy's allocative efficiency, which measures the extent to which employment is located in the most productive firms. Their main conclusion is that a sustained slowdown in TFP growth by about 0.4 percentage point relative to the baseline would reduce the annual increase in export competitiveness from 0.5 to 0.3 percent. Di Mauro et al. also show that an improvement in allocative efficiency can go some way toward offsetting this effect. For example, a reform that moves a country from the average allocative efficiency case to the top 10 percent could offset the impact of slowing productivity growth on export competitiveness for as long as three and a half years.

Wages and Inequality

One premise underlying virtually all thinking about the consequences of lower productivity growth is that lower growth in labor productivity implies lower real wage growth. Consequently, efforts to reverse productivity growth are often motivated by the need to restore growth in average or median wages. But as an empirical matter, is there a link? Raw data suggest that the link may be broken. Since 1973, US median compensation grew by only 11 percent in real terms, while labor productivity rose 75 percent.

However, as Lawrence Summers and Anna Stansbury show in chapter 8, productivity continues to exert a strong influence on wages. All else equal, a 1 percentage point increase in productivity growth has been associated with 0.65 to 1.0 percentage point higher median real compensation growth since 1973. Hence the divergence between wage and productivity trends observed since then does not reflect a weakening of the relationship between productivity growth and wage growth but rather third factors that have partly offset the impact of higher productivity on wages, lowering the labor share of GDP.

What could these factors be? One possibility is technological progress, in the form of capital-augmenting technological change that leads to the automation of production. Another could be related to the increasing concentration and market power of firms. As Furman and Orszag argue in chapter 9, this hypothesis could potentially explain not just the decline in the labor share—why wages have fallen relative to profits—but also observed increases in earnings inequality, as the incomes of top earners have continued to rise while those of most Americans have stagnated. It could also be contributing to the productivity slowdown. In other words, it is possible—indeed, plausible, according to the evidence presented by Furman and Orszag—that the increase in inequality and the slowdown in productivity growth observed since the early 2000s have a common cause—namely, a reduction in competition and firm dynamism, reflecting both "natural" trends, like the increased importance of network externalities in the internet economy, and increased regulatory barriers to entry.

The increase in the concentration and dispersion of firm-level profitability lowered innovation and investment and led to rising inequality, of two varieties: (1) lower wages and higher profits, as a result of increased employer leverage and reduced worker mobility and (2) increasingly disparate wages, as increasingly disparate firm-level success is passed on to firms' employees. If Furman and Orszag are correct, a scenario of sustained low productivity growth in the future would be expected to go along with continued high—and possibly increasing—earnings inequality.

Policy Implications

One useful way of thinking about the policy implications of the analysis is to transpose the distinction between mitigation and adaptation familiar from the climate change literature. Policies that are mainly adaptive—in the sense that they seek to minimize the economic and social costs of the productivity slowdown—include defending or freeing up fiscal space, strengthening automatic stabilizers, preventing financial crises, and rebalancing tax incentives in a way that encourages labor force participation. Other policies in this category include strengthening the redistributive capacity of the tax and transfer system, to reduce the extent to which a widening dispersion of market earnings increases inequality of disposable incomes.

If, however, slower productivity growth and higher inequality have common causes, as Furman and Orszag argue, policies should not stop here but rather attempt to address these causes directly. Policies of this type could both mitigate and help countries adapt to the productivity slowdown. Based on the chapters by Furman and Orszag, Di Mauro et al., and De Gregorio, these policies include the following:

- Enhancing entry and competition among firms (through, for example, vigorous enforcement of antitrust policies, limits on the scope of intellectual property protections, and efforts to reduce regulation that creates barriers to entry) would both benefit innovation and investment and reduce rents, which increase inequality.

- Facilitating the mobility of workers (by, for example, reducing occupational licensing and land use restrictions) would enhance allocative efficiency (and hence aggregate productivity) and strengthen the bargaining power of workers.

- Strengthening education and universal healthcare would increase labor productivity and allocative efficiency by making it easier for workers to move across firms.

- Reducing tariff and nontariff trade barriers would help offset the adverse impact of the productivity slowdown and mitigate the productivity slowdown itself, as the decline in trade since the Great Recession—which reflects increasing "micro protectionism" (Hufbauer and Jung 2016, IMF 2016b)—contributes to slower productivity growth.

Depressingly, many governments—not least in the United States—have recently been implementing policies that seem to head in the opposite direction.

References

Andrews, D., C. Criscuolo, and P.N. Gal. 2016. *The Best versus the Rest: The Global Productivity Slowdown, Divergence across Firms and the Role of Public Policy*. OECD Productivity Working Paper 05. Paris: Organization for Economic Cooperation and Development.

Branstetter, L., and D. Sichel. 2017. *The Case for an American Productivity Revival*. PIIE Policy Brief 17-26. Washington: Peterson Institute for International Economics.

Byrne, D. M., J. G. Fernald, and M. B. Reinsdorf. 2016. *Does the United States Have a Productivity Slowdown or a Measurement Problem?* Working Paper 2016-03. Federal Reserve Bank of San Francisco.

Brynjolfsson, E., and A. McAfee. 2014. *The Second Machine Age: Work, Progress and Prosperity in Times of Brilliant Technologies*. New York: W.W. Norton & Company.

CBO (Congressional Budget Office). 2018. *The Budget and Economic Outlook: 2018 to 2028*. Congressional Budget Office Report (April). Washington.

Decker, R., J. Haltiwanger, R. Jarmin, and J. Miranda. 2017. Declining Dynamism, Allocative Efficiency, and the Productivity Slowdown. *American Economic Review* 107, no. 5 (May): 322–26.

Fernald, J. 2014. Productivity and Potential Output before, during, and after the Great Recession. *NBER Macroeconomics Annual 2014*, volume 29. Cambridge, MA: National Bureau of Economic Research.

Fernald, J., and C. I. Jones. 2014. *The Future of US Economic Growth*. NBER Working Paper 19830. Cambridge, MA: National Bureau of Economic Research.

German Council of Economic Experts. 2015. *Annual Report on the German Economy*. Wiesbaden.

Goodhart, C., and M. Pradhan. 2017. *Demographics will reverse three multi-decade global trends*. BIS Working Paper No 656. Basel: Bank for International Settlements.

Gordon, R. J. 2010. *Revisiting US Productivity Growth over the Past Century with a View of the Future*. NBER Working Paper 15834. Cambridge, MA: National Bureau of Economic Research.

Gordon, R. J. 2012. *Is US Economic Growth Over? Faltering Innovation Confronts the Six Headwinds*. NBER Working Paper 18315. Cambridge, MA: National Bureau of Economic Research.

Gordon, R. J. 2014. *The Demise of US Economic Growth: Restatement, Rebuttal, and Reflections*. NBER Working Paper 19895. Cambridge, MA: National Bureau of Economic Research.

Hufbauer, G. C., and E. Jung. 2016. Why Has Trade Stopped Growing? Not Much Liberalization and Lots of Micro-Protection. Trade and Investment Policy Watch Blog, March 23. Washington: Peterson Institute of International Economic.

IMF (International Monetary Fund). 2016a. Financial Stability Challenges in a Low-Growth, Low-Rate Era. *Global Financial Stability Report* (October): 1–48. Washington.

IMF (International Monetary Fund). 2016b. Global Trade: What's behind the Slowdown? *World Economic Outlook* (October): 63–119. Washington.

Jorgenson, D., and K. Vu. 2010. Potential growth of the world economy. *Journal of Policy Modeling* 32, no. 5: 615–31.

Mokyr, J. 2014. The Next Age of Invention: Technology's Future Is Brighter than Pessimists Allow. *City Journal* (Winter): 14–20. New York: Manhattan Institute.

Mokyr, J., C. Vickers, and N.L. Ziebarth. 2015. The History of Technological Anxiety and the Future of Economic Growth: Is This Time Different? *Journal of Economic Perspectives* 29, no. 3: 31–50.

Nakamura, L., and R. Soloveichik. 2015. *Valuing 'Free' Media Across Countries in GDP*. Working Paper no. 15-25. Federal Reserve Bank of Philadelphia.

OECD (Organization for Economic Cooperation and Development). 2015. *The Future of Productivity*. Paris.

Summers, L. 2014. U.S. Economic Prospects: Secular Stagnation, Hysteresis, and the Zero Lower Bound. *Business Economics* 49, no. 2.

Syverson, C. 2017. Challenges to Mismeasurement Explanations for the US Productivity Slowdown. *Journal of Economic Perspectives* 31, no. 2: 165–86.

I

FISCAL IMPLICATIONS

Implications of Low Productivity Growth for Debt Sustainability

NEIL R. MEHROTRA

A decade after the onset of the Great Recession, advanced economies remain mired in slow growth and saddled with higher levels of public debt. Despite hope that productivity growth would accelerate as the impact of the financial crisis abated, it has fallen in the United States and other advanced economies in recent years. The decline in trend productivity growth alongside increased levels of public debt has prompted concern about the medium- and long-run sustainability of public debt in many advanced economies.

Most of the Organization for Economic Cooperation and Development (OECD) countries shown in figure 1.1 exhibited a substantial increase in debt-to-GDP ratios between 2000 and 2015. Japan nearly doubled its debt-to-GDP ratio to nearly 200 percent. The increase was even starker in the United States and the United Kingdom, where debt-to-GDP ratios rose from 33 and 43 percent to 98 and 108 percent of GDP, respectively.[1] By historical standards, many advanced economies hold high levels of public

Neil R. Mehrotra is assistant professor of economics at Brown University. He thanks participants at the Peterson Institute's "Policy Implications of Sustained Low Productivity Growth" conference, held in November 2017, and Jeromin Zettelmeyer for extensive discussions and editorial assistance. He also thanks Mark Aguiar, Manuel Amador, Cristina Arellano, Javier Bianchi, Anmol Bhandari, Elena Duggar, Karen Dynan, Gauti Eggertsson, Jason Furman, Kyle Herkenhoff, Juan-Pablo Nicolini, Fabrizio Perri, Adam Posen, Louise Sheiner, and Mark Wright for helpful comments and gratefully acknowledges the Brookings Institution and the Peterson Institute for International Economics for financial support.

1. In the United States, these figures include public debt owed to the Social Security Trust Fund. The rise is similarly stark if the calculation is restricted to debt held by the public.

Figure 1.1 Debt-to-GDP ratios, 2000 and 2015

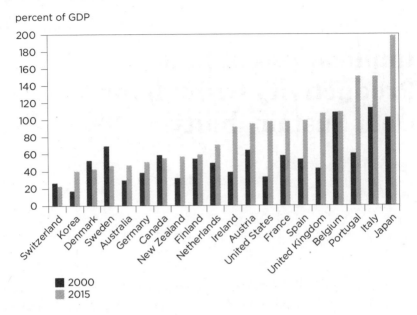

percent of GDP

■ 2000
▨ 2015

Source: Central government debt data for 2000 from OECD government series, https://stats.oecd.org; 2015 data from World Bank, *World Development Indicators*, http://wdi.worldbank.org/tables.

debt. For the countries shown in figure 1.1, the median level of debt rose from 45 percent of GDP in 2005 to 81 percent of GDP in 2015.

These elevated levels of public debt come alongside a marked slowdown in productivity growth. In the same group of countries, the median level (across countries) of labor productivity growth fell from 1.9 percent in the decade ending in 2000 to 0.9 percent in 2010–16 (figure 1.2). The slowdown was particularly pronounced for larger advanced economies, such as the United States, Japan, the United Kingdom, and Italy.

Figure 1.2 also shows substantial variability in the decline in productivity growth across economies, with productivity growth falling well below 0.5 percent in some countries, and other economies maintaining healthier growth rates above 1 percent. Multifactor productivity also declined markedly, with the average median value falling from 0.9 percent in 1990–99 to 0.47 percent in the aftermath of the Great Recession.

At face value, high debt levels and low rates of productivity growth (and hence GDP growth) would seem to be problematic for debt sustainability. The typical metric adopted for judging debt sustainability is the difference between the cost of paying interest on the debt and the overall growth rate of the economy, $r - g$. This difference represents the unit cost of keeping the

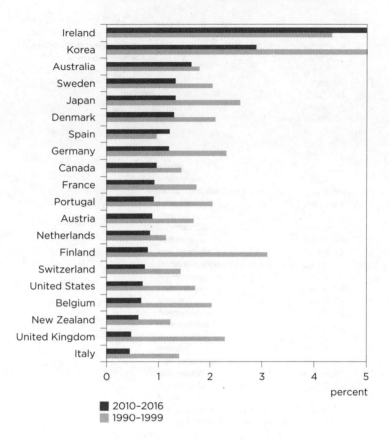

Figure 1.2 Average labor productivity growth in selected advanced economies, 1990–99 and 2010–16

■ 2010–2016
▨ 1990–1999

Source: Derived from GDP per hour worked indices from OECD productivity series, https://stats.oecd.org.

debt-to-GDP ratio constant.[2] A fall in productivity growth directly affects g. But the current economic environment is also characterized by a depressed r—very low real interest rates on government debt. In fact, for the United States and many other advanced economies, $r - g$ is actually negative.

Figure 1.3 shows both the unit cost of maintaining a stable debt-to-GDP ratio ($r - g$) and the total cost of servicing the debt.[3] For the United States, real rates on 10-year government bonds averaged about 0.5 percent

---

2. The implicit assumption is that the relevant object for debt sustainability is the debt-to-GDP ratio.

3. The latter is simply the unit cost multiplied by the debt-to-GDP ratio; it represents the real resources devoted to paying interest on the public debt in steady state.

Figure 1.3 Debt servicing costs in selected advanced economies, 2012–17

a. Unit cost: (r − g)

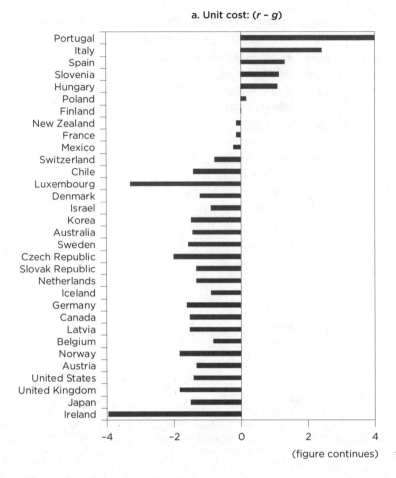

(figure continues)

between 2012 and 2017, and real GDP growth rates averaged 1.5–2 percent. Thus $r < g$. Holding $r - g$ constant and keeping the debt-to-GDP ratio stable, a higher level of public debt actually raises fiscal resources for the government.

The United States is not the only country in which $r < g$. In the rest of the G-7, this unit cost is negative for all economies except Italy.[4]

Given that low productivity growth appears to coincide with even lower real interest rates, the implications for debt sustainability appear

---

4. To measure r for the G-7, I use nominal interest rates on benchmark government securities, as reported by the OECD, less average consumer price inflation rates for 2012–17. Given that the maturity of government debt is typically less than 10 years, this measure is a conservative one for keeping the debt-to-GDP ratio stable.

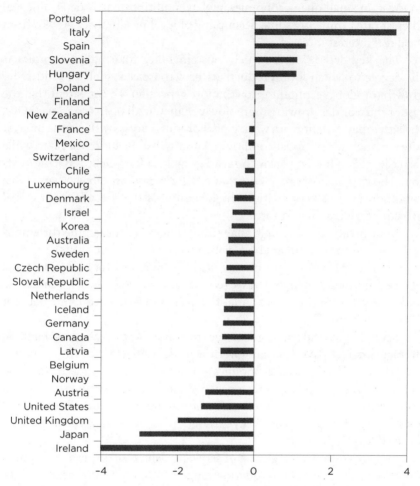

b. Debt servicing cost: $(r - g)B/Y$

Source: Author's calculations based on long-term nominal interest rates (quarterly, 2012–17) from OECD finance series, https://stats.oecd.org; consumer prices, all items (quarterly, 2012–17) from OECD price series, https://stats.oecd.org; GDP—expenditure approach (quarterly, year over year, 2012–17) from OECD national accounts series, https://stats.oecd.org.

ambiguous. This chapter investigates the relationship between productivity growth and interest rates theoretically and empirically to offer some lessons for debt sustainability.

Standard macroeconomic models posit a tight relationship between real interest rates and underlying productivity growth. For closed economies, productivity growth transmits to real interest rates via consumption growth. When households expect slower consumption growth, the real interest rate falls. The magnitude of the fall in real interest rates is governed by a key parameter: the elasticity of intertemporal substitution (EIS). In contrast, in small open economies, global conditions partly determine real interest rates, implying some decoupling of local productivity growth from local real interest rates.

The key determinant of debt sustainability for small economies is the degree to which local productivity growth exceeds global productivity growth (or global economic growth more generally). To the extent that the rest of the world is growing more slowly than a small open economy (SOE), the latter may benefit from weak global productivity growth via the interest rate channel. Weak global conditions lower global real interest rates, while faster local productivity growth raises growth to keep debt servicing costs low. The reverse holds for SOEs that are growing more slowly than global conditions; $r - g$ is kept relatively high because of the effect of faster global growth on global interest rates.

Informed by these simple analytical frameworks, I examine the empirical evidence on government borrowing rates and economic growth to assess some of the key factors determining debt sustainability for both closed and open economies. A macro dataset recently assembled by Jordà, Schularick, and Taylor (2016) provides annual financial and macroeconomic data for 17 advanced economies for 1870–2013.

Several empirical findings emerge from analysis of these data. First, on average, interest payments on government debt are close to the economic growth rate of advanced economies (on average $r = g$). Indeed, for long periods of time, $r < g$, implying a negative unit cost of keeping the debt-to-GDP ratio stable. These findings are not unique to the United States, and they are not driven by historically extreme episodes, such as the world wars or the Great Depression.

Despite the low average cost of servicing debt, $r - g$ displays substantial variation over time. Its interquartile range is roughly 5 percentage points, implying a potentially large swing in the real resources needed to stabilize the debt-to-GDP ratio, particularly for countries with a large stock of debt. To examine the probability of reversions to conditions of $r > g$, I estimate a series of probit regressions. They exhibit some persistence in $r - g$ over time; periods of $r < g$ tend to be followed by periods of $r < g$, but future debt servicing costs are not well explained by current levels of $r - g$. Moreover, factors such as current population growth, productivity growth, and the debt-to-GDP ratio do not have substantial predictive power for the probability of switching to a regime of $r > g$ over the subsequent 5- or 10-year period. I also find that, historically, GDP per capita growth is negatively correlated with $r - g$; periods of slow growth (likely driven by slow underlying productivity growth) are periods when this unit cost rises. Overall, these findings suggest that periods of negative debt servicing cost are not uncommon but that carrying a large stock of public debt is risky in such an environment given the reversion probabilities.

For economies other than the United States, I document several additional facts that are relevant for assessing debt sustainability. First, I find evidence that a strong common component drives real interest rates across countries. I provide more formal statistical evidence of cointegration of country interest rates with US interest rates in line with the findings of Holston, Laubach, and Williams (2017). GDP per capita growth rates across countries (a proxy for productivity growth) exhibit greater idiosyncratic variation: Principal components analysis reveals that the first principal component accounts for only 28 percent of the variation in annual GDP per capita growth. By contrast, the first principal component accounts for 60 percent of overall variation in real rates.

Consistent with the analytical framework, I find evidence that low US real rates induce a real appreciation of foreign currencies and a deterioration of the current account. These effects may carry indirect implications for fiscal policy by affecting the tax base. I also find evidence of spillovers from low US real rates to total loan growth, mortgage loan growth, and housing price growth, potentially highlighting risks to financial stability that may eventually be problematic for fiscal policy. The empirical evidence suggests that low productivity growth should benefit fast-growing small economies, given the strong common component in global rates. However, low global rates affect the external balance and financial stability in ways that carry implications for medium-run debt sustainability.

I provide statistical projections for the real interest rate and debt servicing costs for the G-7 economies. I use a simple time series approach by estimating a vector error correction model (VECM), which is necessary because of the nonstationarity of real interest rates. I estimate a VECM on US real rates and GDP per capita using data for 1950–2015. For other countries, I assume that local rates and GDP growth are cointegrated with US real rates.[5]

In the G-7 countries other than the United States, the cointegration coefficient on US rates is large and significant, with the point estimate close to 1. The error correction terms indicate that local rates typically adjust more than US rates when the cointegration relationship is unbalanced. For all countries except Italy, the standard Johansen cointegration test rejects the null hypothesis of no cointegration relationship at the 5 percent level.

---

5. I also consider a more general four-country VECM, to allow for cointegration of real rates in the United States, Japan, the United Kingdom, and Germany.

I use the VECM estimates to construct dynamic forecasts for the real interest rate and GDP per capita growth for the remaining G-7 countries. For Canada, Germany, and Japan, real rates are projected to remain negative; they are projected to rise somewhat in France, Italy, and the United Kingdom. Overall, real rates remain low. The uncertainty bands around these estimates are large and rise over the projection horizon.

I combine the real interest rate forecasts with GDP per capita forecasts and population growth averages to forecast $r - g$. Eurozone economies are expected to revert to conditions of $r > g$. In contrast, this relationship remains negative over the next decade in Canada, Japan, the United Kingdom, and the United States. These findings suggest that $r - g$ is somewhat lower for economies that borrow in their own currency and control their own monetary policy.

I present a model-based analysis of the relationship between the real interest rate and productivity growth for the United States along with estimates of alternative productivity scenarios. I find that for an EIS of 0.5 (the baseline calibration), lower productivity growth is actually beneficial from a debt sustainability perspective. Slower productivity growth lowers real interest rates more than one-for-one with economic growth, increasing fiscal resources when the debt-to-GDP ratio is held constant. This finding depends on a key parameter: For an EIS close to or above unity, lower productivity growth is no longer beneficial. However, a substantial body of literature in finance and macroeconomics finds evidence for an EIS of less than 1. I also show that under the baseline calibration, the tax-minimizing level of debt is actually slightly lower than current levels. This result stems from the fact that a lower stock of government debt lowers the real interest rate. From a tax-minimizing point of view, there is an optimal level of debt that trades off the benefits from lower unit costs $r - g$ and a higher stock of debt, which in the steady state raises more fiscal resources when $r < g$.

The chapter is organized as follows. The first section describes related literature. Section 2 provides the analytical framework for debt sustainability and the relationship between r and g for both closed and open economies. Section 3 presents basic statistics on $r - g$, evidence on reversions to conditions of $r > g$ over the medium term (5–10 years), and evidence of spillovers of low US real rates to other economies. Section 4 provides formal evidence of a common component in real rates and empirical projections of r and g for the G-7 economies. Section 5 uses a richer quantitative lifecycle model to assess the connection between real rates, productivity growth, and the debt-to-GDP ratio for a model calibrated to key US moments. Section 6 summarizes the chapter's main findings.

Related Literature

This chapter contributes to several strands of the literature, including work on debt sustainability, an emerging body of literature on low interest rates and secular stagnation, and an extensive body of work on sovereign debt crises and public debt in SOEs. Research conducted in the late 1980s and early 1990s examines the sustainability of public debt in the United States. Auerbach (1994) discusses large US deficits in the late 1980s and provides a medium-term outlook. Woodford (1990) and Ball, Elmendorf, and Mankiw (1998) show that higher deficits and public debt need not be problematic, based on theoretical and historical considerations, respectively. Aiyagari and McGrattan (1998) use a quantitative model to show that the level of public debt in the late 1990s may not have exceeded the optimal level. More recently, Elmendorf and Sheiner (2016) and Mehrotra (2017) consider US debt sustainability given low interest rates and low growth (this chapter draws in part on some of the findings in Mehrotra 2017).

The secular stagnation literature has been resurrected by Summers (2013) and formalized by Eggertsson and Mehrotra (2014), who incorporate the zero lower bound and downward nominal wage rigidities in a three-period overlapping generations model. This literature emphasizes the possibility that the natural rate of interest (the interest rate consistent with full employment) may be low for an extended period, leading to chronic zero lower-bound episodes. Caballero and Farhi (2017) shows how a flight to safety may account for low safe interest rates and secular stagnation. Eggertsson, Mehrotra, and Robbins (2017) extend the analysis of Eggertsson and Mehrotra (2014) to provide quantitative estimates of the drivers of low US interest rates. Laubach and Williams (2016) and Hamilton et al. (2016) provide estimates of the US natural rate of interest. Holston, Laubach, and Williams (2017) extend these natural rate estimates to the United Kingdom and eurozone. All of these authors find some evidence of a depressed natural rate of interest, weak links between productivity growth and the real interest rate, and a common component in global rates.

Caballero, Farhi, and Gourinchas (2015) and Eggertsson et al. (2016) extend the secular stagnation framework to an open economy setting. This work considers the policy implications and spillovers of low natural rates across large open economies. Corsetti et al. (2016) consider the implications for SOEs of low world interest rates, emphasizing the possibility of multiple steady states and the role of exchange rates in transmitting secular stagnation to SOEs.

The analytical framework considered here draws in part on this literature and more standard SOE models along the lines of Schmitt-Grohe and Uribe (2003). Gourinchas and Rey (2016) and Farhi and Maggiori (2016) provide empirical and theoretical discussion of safe asset provision and draw implications for global interest rates and capital flows.

Analytical Framework

I start by introducing a basic analytical framework for thinking about debt sustainability and the channels through which slow productivity growth affects debt sustainability. A standard metric used to assess debt sustainability is the difference between the real interest rate on government debt r and real GDP growth g. This difference represents the unit cost of maintaining a stable debt-to-GDP ratio.

The logic for $r - g$ as a debt sustainability measure can be ascertained by inspecting the government's flow budget constraint:

$$T_t + B_{t+1}^g = G_t + (1 + r_t)B_t^g \tag{1.1}$$

where T_t is real tax revenue (net of any transfers), G_t is real government expenditures, B_t^g is real government debt, and r_t is the effective real interest rate paid on government debt. For any variable X_t, $\tilde{x}_t = \frac{X_t}{A_t N_t}$ is the variable X_t detrended by output per capita (A_t) and population (N_t). Along the balanced growth path, GDP will grow at g (where $1 + g = A_{t+1} N_{t+1}/A_t N_t$), and the debt-to-GDP ratio will remain stable as long as debt grows at this rate.

Equation 1.2 is obtained by dividing through using A_t and N_t:

$$\tilde{t}_t + \tilde{b}_{t+1}^g \frac{A_{t+1}}{A_t} \frac{N_{t+1}}{N_t} = \tilde{g}_t + (1 + r_t) \tilde{b}_t^g. \tag{1.2}$$

Equation 1.3 is the steady state obtained by dropping time subscripts:

$$\tilde{t} = \tilde{g} + \big((1 + r) - (1 + g)\big) \tilde{b}_g. \tag{1.3}$$

The difference between the gross return on public debt $r = 1 + r$ and $(1 + g)$ represents the real resources the government must raise to keep the debt-to-GDP ratio stable. If $r > g$, the government must raise taxes in excess of government spending to finance interest payments. If $r < g$, the public debt can be kept stable with tax revenues below government spending, and higher levels of public debt reduce the tax revenues needed to finance a given level of government spending.[6] Effectively, public debt raises a type of seigniorage revenue akin to resources raised by the monetary authority when printing money that carries a zero nominal return. In deriving the $r - g$ criterion for debt sustainability, no behavioral assumptions are imposed on the government, households, or firms.

---

6. Equivalently, a government could borrow more, spend the proceeds, and see the debt-to-GDP ratio return to its original level.

Closed Economy

Along the balanced growth path, GDP growth is the sum of GDP per capita growth and population growth. The growth rate of GDP per capita is therefore just the growth rate of productivity (A_t/A_{t-1}). Taking productivity growth as exogenous, the key question for debt sustainability is the relationship between the real interest rate and productivity growth.

The standard neoclassical growth model delivers strong predictions for the relationship between real interest rates and productivity growth. It features a representative household maximizing lifetime discounted utility subject to the economy's resource constraint:

$$\max \sum_{t=0}^{\infty} \beta^t u(C_t)$$

$$F(K_t, A_t L) = K_{t+1} - (1 - \delta)K_t + C_t L$$

where L is the labor force, assumed to be constant and perfectly inelastic (no wealth effects on labor supply). Productivity (A_t) is labor augmenting and growing at rate g. With constant relative risk aversion utility, given by $u(c) = \frac{c^{1-\frac{1}{\sigma}}}{1-\frac{1}{\sigma}}$, and a Cobb-Douglas production, given by $F(K, AL) = K^\alpha (AL)^{1-\alpha}$, equilibrium can be summarized by a resource constraint and an Euler equation that governs the household's optimal consumption/saving decision.

With a Cobb-Douglas production, the economy's resource constraint and Euler equation can be expressed in detrended per capita terms (for variable X_t, $\tilde{x}_t = \frac{X_t}{A_t L}$):

$$\tilde{k}_t^\alpha = \tilde{k}_{t+1}(1 + g) - (1 - \delta)\tilde{k}_t + \tilde{c}_t \tag{1.4}$$

$$\frac{1}{\beta} = \left(\frac{\tilde{c}_{t+1}}{\tilde{c}_t}\right)^{-\frac{1}{\sigma}} (1 + g)^{-\frac{1}{\sigma}} \left(\alpha \tilde{k}_t^{\alpha-1} + 1 - \delta\right). \tag{1.5}$$

As can be seen from the resource constraint, consumption per capita along the balanced growth path will be maximized if the return to capital (the marginal product of capital plus undepreciated capital) equals the gross productivity growth rate (as seen by computing $\frac{d\tilde{c}}{d\tilde{k}}$ in equation 1.4). A standard no-arbitrage condition requires that the net return on capital be equal to the return on government debt:

$$r_t = \alpha \tilde{k}_t^{\alpha-1} - \delta.$$

Plugging this expression into equation (1.5), rearranging the terms, and considering a steady state with $\tilde{c}_t = \tilde{c}_{t+1}$ reveals a simple relationship between the real interest rate and productivity growth:

$$1 + r = \frac{1}{\beta}(1 + g)^{\frac{1}{\sigma}}. \tag{1.6}$$

It can be easily shown that the elasticity of the real interest rate to productivity growth in the steady state is $1/\sigma$. A low value of the EIS (σ) means that real interest rates are sensitive to changes in productivity growth. As discussed in section 5, typical estimates of this parameter place the EIS at less than unity. In that section, I also examine the elasticity of the real interest rate to productivity growth in a richer quantitative lifecycle model. In that setting, the EIS remains an important determinant of the response of the real interest rate to productivity growth, but it will no longer be the sole determinant of that elasticity. In the standard model, for an EIS close to 1, it must be the case that $r > g$, the standard criterion for dynamic efficiency.[7]

Open Economy

For economies with an open capital account, the link between rates of return on assets and the underlying growth rate of productivity may be attenuated or completely broken in the absence of any barriers to capital flows. To think through the channels through which slow productivity growth both at home and abroad affects an SOE, I consider a standard open economy model with a representative agent.

The standard SOE model features a representative household maximizing lifetime discounted utility subject to the economy's resource constraint:

$$\max \sum_{t=0}^{\infty} \beta^t u(C_t)$$

$$F(K_t, A_t) = (1 + r_t)D_{t-1} - D_t + T_t + K_{t+1} - (1 - \delta)K_t + C_t$$

where D_t are the household's foreign borrowings that must be repaid at interest rate r_t, and T_t are the lump-sum taxes levied by the government. In the event of autarky and assuming no government debt or government spending, these equations simplify to the closed economy case.

The only difference in the open economy is the presence of an optimality condition governing borrowing from overseas. To the household's optimality conditions, I add the government's budget constraint (equa-

---

7. To the extent that government debt provides liquidity services or eases intermediation costs, the return on government debt may be sufficiently depressed so that $r < g$. The analysis to this point does not incorporate risk premia, which may also depress the return on safe assets (see Abel et al. 1989).

tion 1.1) and a debt-elastic interest spread. This equation relates domestic borrowing rates r_t and the foreign interest rate r_t^*:

$$r_t = r_t^* + \frac{\kappa}{\gamma} D_t^\gamma$$

where $\gamma > 0$ is a parameter governing the elasticity of the interest spread to borrowing by the private sector. With constant productivity growth, in the steady state the spread will adjust so that the interest rate faced by the representative household r_t is equal to equation (1.6), as in the closed economy case. However, the global interest rate need not satisfy this equation.[8]

The main difference relative to the closed economy case is the decoupling of global interest rates and domestic productivity growth. The debt-elastic interest rate spread faced by households ensures stationarity for an SOE (see Schmitt-Grohe and Uribe 2003). It is possible that the government could borrow at a lower rate than households' r_t^g as long as $r_t^* < r_t^g < r_t^*$.[9] Given a sufficiently low world real rate and a moderate debt-to-GDP ratio, the SOE would enjoy a situation in which $r_t^g < g$.

Given this framework, what are the effects of low global productivity growth for an SOE? A fall in global productivity growth would lower r_t^*; holding constant the level of foreign debt, the domestic real interest rate r_t would also fall. Households would increase their foreign borrowing, and the current account would deteriorate. This increased foreign borrowing would likely take the form of growth in various types of domestic loans, including mortgages. Eventually, the net foreign asset position would deteriorate sufficiently such that the domestic rate r_t satisfies equation (1.6). To the extent that $r_t^g \approx r_t^*$, a fall in global rates would also reduce the cost of servicing the public debt and, holding the debt-to-GDP ratio constant, lower the taxes needed to fund a given level of government expenditure.

The key determinant of debt sustainability is therefore the deviation of local productivity growth from global productivity growth and other determinants of global real interest rates. If, for example, an SOE has a 1 percent growth rate of productivity but the global productivity growth is 0.5 percent, the SOE is likely to enjoy favorable debt financing condi-

---

8. Along a balanced growth path, to maintain the SOE assumption, it must be the case that productivity growth in the SOE is less than or equal to global productivity growth ($g \leq g'$). If this were not the case, eventually the SOE would become large and influence global rates.

9. In this case, households would have no incentive to hold government debt; indeed, they would seek to sell government bonds short. Only foreign households would hold domestic public debt. If households can hold only positive levels of government debt, governments could potentially borrow at a rate between the world rate and the domestic rate faced by households. To ensure stationarity, it would have to be the case that at high debt-to-GDP levels, $r_t^g \to r_t$.

tions, as global rates will be depressed. By contrast, if an SOE has 0 percent productivity growth against global growth of 0.5 percent, real rates may be high relative to local productivity growth.

This framework specifies a single global consumption good (so that the real exchange rate is constant and equal to one). Changes in global productivity growth would likely have demand effects on the good produced by the SOE. For example, in a world with a home and a foreign good, a slowdown in global productivity growth would have an effect on the size of the foreign market, diminishing foreign demand and causing a real appreciation for the SOE currency. This real appreciation would have an effect on domestic production that could trigger changes in the debt-to-GDP ratio by affecting the denominator. The real exchange rate thus represents an additional channel through which low global real rates can affect debt sustainability.

Empirical Evidence

In this section I use historical data on government interest rates, inflation rates, GDP growth, and public debt-to-GDP ratios to examine empirically the behavior of $r - g$ over a long time horizon. Several lessons emerge.

First, current conditions of $r < g$ are not a historical anomaly; among advanced economies, the average unit cost has been close to zero since 1870. However, $r < g$ has little predictive value for the debt servicing cost over the medium term (5–10 years). The likelihood of reverting to a scenario in which $r > g$ is substantial. Furthermore, historically, periods of weak GDP per capita growth (a proxy for productivity growth) are periods in which $r - g$ is high.

For SOEs a key finding is that real rates across countries exhibit less idiosyncratic variation than GDP growth rates. This means that relatively fast-growing SOEs will benefit fiscally in an otherwise slow-growth, low–interest rate global economy. (The opposite holds for relatively slow-growing small economies.) However, for advanced economies other than the United States, periods of low US rates are periods in which the current account deteriorates and the real exchange rate appreciates, which may indirectly affect debt sustainability. Similarly, financial stability risks can be magnified when US rates are low as a result of faster credit and housing price growth.

Dataset

To analyze the behavior of $r - g$, I draw on the dataset of Jordà, Schularick, and Taylor (2016), which provides macroeconomic and financial variables for 17 advanced economies, including the United States, from 1870

Table 1.1 Summary statistics (percentage points)

Variable	17 advanced countries			United States		
	Median	25th percentile	75th percentile	Median	25th percentile	75th percentile
Long-term nominal interest rate	4.61	3.62	6.38	3.92	3.32	5.48
Inflation rate	2.14	0.11	4.39	1.75	0	3.51
Real interest rate	2.71	1.17	4.82	2.66	1.52	4.29
Real GDP per capita growth	2.01	0.28	3.82	1.89	−0.45	3.75
Population growth	0.80	0.44	1.17	1.39	0.97	1.91
Debt-to-GDP ratio	44.2	24.3	68.6	36.4	15.1	59.0
Number of observations	2,145			134		

Note: The real interest rate is the long-term nominal interest rate less a three-year moving average of inflation rates. Statistics are based on a data set that excludes observations with fiscal costs greater than 10 percent or less than –10 percent.

Sources: Long-term nominal interest rate, CPI, real GDP growth, and population growth from Jordà, Schularick, and Taylor (2016) Macrohistory Database; author's calculations.

to 2013.[10] I use annual data on real GDP growth, inflation rates, population growth, long-term interest rates on government debt, housing price indices, and various measures of borrowing.

Measuring the cost of servicing the debt requires a measure of the ex ante real interest rate. I use a three-year moving average of inflation as a proxy for expected inflation, in line with the approach in Hamilton et al. (2016). Real interest rates are the nominal long-term interest rate measured in Jordà, Schularick, and Taylor (2016) less expected inflation. When using annual data, I winsorize extreme observations of r at +/–10 percent to eliminate outliers.[11] The resulting dataset is an unbalanced panel of 2,107 observations (slightly fewer for debt-to-GDP ratios).

Table 1.1 provides basic summary statistics. For all countries, the median nominal long-term interest rate is 4.6 percent, with a median inflation rate of 2.1 percent. For the United States, both interest and inflation rates are slightly lower than the global median. Population growth is somewhat higher in the United States than for the sample of 17 advanced economies.

---

10. The dataset is available at www.macrohistory.net/data.

11. The Jordà, Schularick, and Taylor (2016) dataset provides both a short-term and a long-term interest rate measure. I take the conservative approach of using the long-term measure, which typically exceeds the short-term interest rate and likely better represents the interest expense faced by the fiscal authority.

Table 1.2 Moments of fiscal cost measure

Variable	17 advanced countries			United States		
	1870–2016	1870–1914 and 1946–2016	1946–2016	1870–2016	1870–1914 and 1946–2016	1946–2016
Net fiscal cost ($r - g$)						
25th percentile	-2.69	-1.83	-3.04	-2.24	-2.16	-2.23
Median	0.09	0.23	-0.75	-0.34	-0.40	-1.00
75th percentile	2.46	2.35	1.35	1.69	1.69	0.85
Percent of years with negative net fiscal cost	48.7	46.6	57.6	51.7	54.5	71.4
Percent of years with net fiscal cost of less than –2 percent	29.7	24.4	34.0	31.0	27.3	35.7
Number of observations	491	373	238	29	22	14

Note: The real interest rate is the long-term nominal interest rate less a three-year moving average of inflation rates. Statistics are based on a dataset that excludes observations with fiscal costs greater than 10 percent or less than –10 percent.

Sources: Long-term nominal interest rate, CPI, real GDP growth, and population growth from Jordà, Schularick, and Taylor (2016) Macrohistory Database, www.macrohistory.net/data; author's calculations.

Debt Servicing Cost and Reversion Risk

Table 1.2 presents statistics on the unit cost of stabilizing the debt-to-GDP ratio for both the United States and the full dataset. I average $r - g$ over five-year, nonoverlapping periods to smooth out business cycle variations and capture the medium-term cost of servicing the debt.

For the period 1870–2016 in the full dataset of countries, the median unit cost is just 9 basis points, with an interquartile range from –2.69 percent to 2.46 percent. In the postwar period for the full sample of countries, this range narrows somewhat and the median cost falls to –0.34 percent. In the typical five-year period, governments thus face zero debt servicing cost. The table also shows that in nearly a third of these five-year periods, the debt servicing cost is very negative (below –2 percent). As the second column shows, these findings are not driven by historically extreme periods, such as the world wars or the Great Depression/interwar years.

For the United States, the cost of servicing the debt is negative and exhibits a somewhat narrower range than the full 17-country sample. The interquartile range is approximately 4 percentage points, falling to slightly over 3 percentage points in the postwar period. Remarkably, in the postwar period, over 70 percent of the five-year periods are ones in which the unit cost of keeping the debt-to-GDP ratio stable are negative. Only over the 1980s and 1990s did the United States experience a sustained period in which $r > g$. The US debt-to-GDP ratio fell from 120 percent of GDP to 35

Table 1.3 Probit regressions of fiscal cost

Variable	5-year forward ($r > g$)			10-year forward ($r > g$)		
	(1)	(2)	(3)	(4)	(5)	(6)
Current value: $r - g$	14.913*** (1.209)	14.546*** (1.169)	22.193*** (4.330)	8.183*** (1.231)	7.841*** (1.208)	12.004*** (3.770)
Debt-to-GDP ratio	-0.040 (0.170)	-0.120 (0.182)	-0.163 (0.306)	-0.123 (0.188)	-0.212 (0.197)	-0.198 (0.320)
Population growth		-23.041*** (7.514)	-61.035*** (19.036)		-26.163*** (8.463)	-58.900*** (17.865)
Constant	0.075 (0.080)	0.313*** (0.126)	0.579** (0.226)	0.067 (0.092)	0.339 (0.140)	0.660*** (0.229)
McFadden pseudo R-squared	0.130	0.137	0.269	0.045	0.055	0.145
Number of observations	449	449	218	431	431	201

Note: The dependent variable is a dummy variable that takes a value of 1 if the fiscal cost measure is positive ($r > g$) in the next period (1–5 years forward) or the subsequent period (6–10 years forward). Columns (1) and (4) do not include population growth; columns (3) and (6) limit the sample to the postwar period. Each column presents a separate regression. Standard errors are clustered at the country level. *** and ** significant at the 1 and 5 percent level, respectively.

Sources: Long-term nominal interest rate, CPI, real GDP growth, and population growth from Jordà, Schularick, and Taylor (2016) Macrohistory Database, www.macrohistory.net/data; author's calculations.

percent of GDP by 1980 because of strong US GDP growth, particularly from 1945 to 1970.

Given these findings, a natural question is how persistent periods of $r < g$ are and whether governments can take advantage of these periods by postponing debt reduction or possibly further increasing the debt-to-GDP ratio to raise additional revenues. As table 1.2 suggests, debt servicing costs display a substantial degree of variation, which was somewhat attenuated in the postwar era. To quantify the possibility of ending up in an $r > g$ economic environment, I estimate the 5- or 10-year probability of reverting to conditions of $r > g$. Specifically, I estimate the following probit specification:

$$P(fisc_{i,t+j} > 0 | X) = \Phi(c + \beta_f fisc_{i,t} + \beta_p popgrwth_{i,t} + \beta_d dgdp_{i,t} + \epsilon_{i,t})$$

where $fisc_{i,t} = r_{i,t} - g_{i,t}$ in country i and period t; $popgrwth_{i,t}$ is population growth in country i in period t; $dgdp_{i,t}$ is the public debt-to-GDP ratio in country i in period t; and $\Phi(\cdot)$ is the standard normal cumulative distribution function. Table 1.3 shows coefficient estimates obtained using maximum likelihood methods.[12]

---

12. Given the time series component to this regression, I also use Newey-West standard errors with one or two lags. The standard errors are similar to those obtained by clustering.

The probit regression reveals that the value of $r - g$ (defined as $fisc_{i,t}$) enters significantly in both the 5- and 10-year reversion probabilities. The positive and significant coefficient implies some degree of persistence: Five-year periods of negative unit cost are more likely to be followed by periods of negative unit cost, for example. Columns (2) and (5) include population growth as an additional covariate. The point estimates suggest that higher population growth lowers the probability of $r > g$, but this coefficient is insignificant in the postwar period (shown in columns 3 and 6). Across all specifications, the debt-to-GDP ratio does not predict future periods of $r > g$; the point estimate is slightly negative but statistically insignificant.

One way to make the probit estimates more tangible is to evaluate them at current values of the covariates. Using more recent values for real interest rates and GDP growth rates (2014–16) and debt-to-GDP ratios (2015) for the 17 economies in this dataset, I estimate the probability of reverting to conditions of $r > g$ in the next five years. The current median interest rate is –0.90 percent, the debt-to-GDP ratio is 72 percent, and population growth is 0.68 percent. Given these values for the covariates, the probit models estimate a probability of 38–45 percent of a reversion to $r > g$ in the next five years. The 10-year reversion probabilities range from 44 percent to 48 percent. These probabilities are fairly close to the share of periods in which $r > g$ in table 1.2 (in other words, the conditional probabilities are close to the unconditional probabilities). The relatively low McFadden R-squared values show the limited ability of current $r - g$ and other covariates to predict future fiscal cost.

Figure 1.4 plots real GDP per capita growth against $r - g$ (averaged over five-year periods). It shows that the cost of servicing public debt tends to be high precisely in the periods when productivity growth is low. Periods in which governments wish to increase the debt-to-GDP ratio to engage in expansionary fiscal policy or increase government spending in productivity-enhancing projects (such as building infrastructure and other public capital or investing in basic research) are periods in which fiscal space is somewhat more constrained, because of relatively high financing costs. Debt servicing costs are relatively high in periods during which governments may wish to further increase the debt-to-GDP ratio.

Global Component of Rates and Growth

The link between productivity growth and real interest rates is greatly attenuated in open economies. To the extent that large economies—namely, the United States—determine global rates, small open economies will benefit in terms of debt sustainability from slow productivity growth in the United States, as it keeps world interest rates lower than they might have been under autarky.

**Figure 1.4   Correlation between productivity growth and net
fiscal cost**

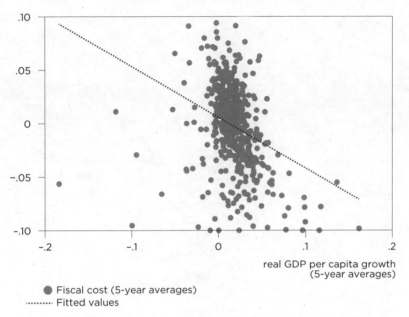

● Fiscal cost (5-year averages)
········· Fitted values

Source: Author's calculations based on data in Jordà, Schularick, and Taylor
(2016).

Figure 1.5 shows postwar real interest rates and per capita GDP growth
rates for the 17 advanced economies in the dataset. The comovement of real
interest rates is evident.

One way to measure the importance of a common component is
through principal components analysis (PCA). Using annual data over
the entire period (1870–2013), I find that the first principal component
explains nearly 60 percent of the variation in real interest rates—a high
degree of explanatory power for the most important principal component.
The second principal component explains only 12 percent of total variation.

In contrast, for per capita GDP growth, the first principal component
explains only 28 percent of total variation; the second component explains
18 percent. The loadings on the first principal component are larger on
average for country real interest rates than for country GDP per capita
growth rates. If one restricts the analysis to five-year averages of real interest
rates and GDP per capita growth, the differences are less stark. However,
the first principal component still explains 64 percent of total variation; it
explains 52 percent of total variation for real rates relative to GDP per capita
growth. The variation in productivity growth across the full set of OECD
countries is substantial (see figure 1.2).

Figure 1.5 Real interest and GDP per capita growth rates in the 17 advanced economies in the dataset, 1950–2013

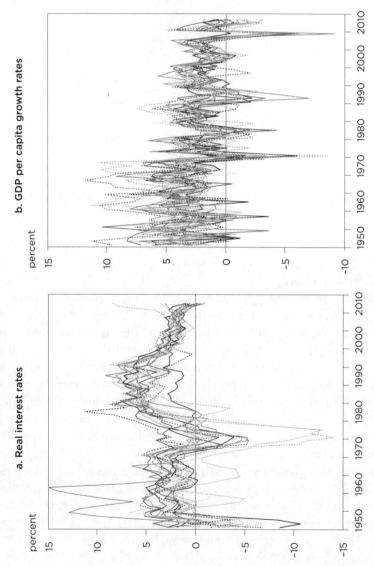

a. Real interest rates

b. GDP per capita growth rates

Note: Figure shows postwar real interest rates and per capita GDP growth rates for the 17 advanced economies in the dataset. The comovement of real interest rates is evident.

Source: Long-term nominal interest rate, CPI, and GDP per capita from Jorda, Schularick, and Taylor (2016) Macrohistory Database, www.macrohistory.net/data; author's calculations.

Table 1.4 Fixed-effect regressions of low spillovers from the US rate

	External		Financial		
Dependent variable	Current account (1)	Real exchange rate (2)	Loan growth (3)	Mortgage loan growth (4)	Housing prices (5)
US real rate (<1 percent)	−0.001 (0.004)	−0.014*** (0.004)	0.004 (0.007)	−0.006 (0.009)	0.013 (0.008)
US real rate (<1 percent, five-year lag)	−0.013*** (0.004)	0.009 (0.006)	0.035*** (0.006)	0.035*** (0.009)	0.018 (0.011)
Null hypothesis: Sum of current and lagged effects	−0.014** (0.006)	−0.005 (0.005)	0.039*** (0.006)	0.029*** (0.008)	0.030** (0.008)
Country fixed effects	Yes	Yes	Yes	Yes	Yes
Number of observations	208	208	208	208	190

Note: The dependent variable is described in the first row. The independent variable is a dummy variable that is equal to 1 when US real interest rates are below 1 percent. Each column presents a separate regression. Standard errors in parentheses are clustered at the country level. *** and ** significant at the 1 and 5 percent level, respectively.

Sources: Current account, nominal exchange rate, CPI, total loan growth, mortgage loan growth, and house price growth from Jordà, Schularick, and Taylor (2016) Macrohistory Database; author's calculations.

Spillovers from Low US Rates

A decline in global interest rates should generate a capital inflow into SOEs, holding other factors constant. These capital flows may flow to both the public and private sectors, worsening the current account along the transition path and causing an appreciation in the real exchange rate.

To examine how low US rates may spill over, I estimate a fixed-effects regression on five-year averaged data from 1950–2013 of various external and financial indicators on a dummy for low US real interest rates:

$$y_{i,t} = c_i + \delta \mathbb{I}_t + \delta_{lag} \mathbb{I}_{t-1} + \epsilon_{i,t}$$

where c_i is a country fixed effect, δ is the contemporaneous effect of low US rates, δ_{lag} is the one-period (five-year) lagged effect of low US rates, and $\mathbb{I}_t$ is a dummy variable that takes the value of 1 if the US real interest rate falls below 1 percent. In effect, this regression estimates the difference in conditional means when current or lagged US real rates are above or below 1 percent.

Table 1.4 shows the results of a fixed-effects regression for the 16 advanced countries other than the United States. For external indicators, there is evidence that low US rates trigger a contemporaneous decline in real exchange rate growth (a real appreciation for the foreign currency) and a lagged deterioration of the current account. The sum of the coefficients on the current and lagged dummy variable is significant in both cases and consistent with the channels described above. On average, when current or lagged US rates are low, the current account falls by 1.4 percent of GDP relative to periods of higher US rates. Real exchange rate growth slows, with the foreign currency experiencing a real appreciation, when US rates are low. These changes in the external balance may also carry fiscal or growth implications, particularly for less advanced economies that rely on growth in the tradables sector. Overall, however, the magnitudes appear to be modest.

Columns (3)–(5) also show how low US rates may trigger financial stability concerns. Total loan growth and mortgage loan growth increase with a five-year lag, and the overall effect of low US real interest rates is statistically significant. Total loan growth increases 3.9 percentage points a year when US rates are low relative to the baseline period of rates above 1 percent; for mortgage loans, the growth rate is 2.9 percentage points higher. Housing price growth, estimated for a slightly smaller sample, also increase by 3 percentage points a year on average when current and lagged US rates are below 1 percent. The debt sustainability implications are indirect: Low US rates may trigger a credit and/or housing boom that, if excessive, could trigger substantial fiscal consequences if it leads to a financial crisis. The indirect effect of low US (and global) real rates may be important in a fuller assessment of the effects of low global rates on medium-term debt sustainability.

Country Scenarios

In this section I estimate a statistical model for real interest rates and GDP per capita growth for the G-7 economies. I use the model to generate forecasts for country real interest rates and the unit cost of servicing the public debt.

For the six G-7 economies other than the United States (Canada, France, Germany, Italy, Japan, and the United Kingdom), I construct empirical estimates of real interest rates and GDP per capita growth using historical data for 1950–2015. World real interest rates appear to share a strong common component (as discussed in the previous section). Given the importance of the United States in global output and capital markets, I assume that foreign and US interest rates are cointegrated. I estimate a VECM for each country's interest rates of the following form:

$$\Delta y_t = \gamma + \alpha \beta y_{t-1} + \sum_{j=1}^{J} \Pi_j \Delta y_{t-j} + \varepsilon_t \tag{1.7}$$

where y_t is a vector including the local country interest rate, the local country GDP per capita growth rate, and the United States real interest rate. The vector α is a 3 × 1 vector of short-run error adjustment coefficients, β is a 1 × 3 cointegration vector, Π_j are 3 × 3 matrixes of lag parameters, and ε_t is a vector of mean zero innovations. I maintain the assumption of the presence of a single cointegrating vector, in which domestic interest rates are cointegrated with US interest rates and local GDP per capita growth. Interest rates for all countries are computed annually as the difference between the benchmark interest rate on government debt (as collected by Jordà, Schularick, and Taylor 2016) and a three-year, centered moving average of the inflation rate (defined as the growth rate of the consumer price index).

For the United States, I also estimate a VECM with only two variables: the US real interest rate and the US GDP per capita growth for 1950–2015. In addition to this parsimonious specification, I estimate a four-country VECM using real interest rates from the United States, the United Kingdom, Japan, and Germany (the largest, most advanced, and most open economies in the postwar period). As with the individual country specification, I test for and impose a single cointegration relationship. The VECM four-country model that is shown in the projections in this section is from this specification (shown as a dark gray dotted line in figure 1.6). With the exception of Japan, the interest rate projections do not meaningfully differ between the bilateral and four-country specifications.

Table 1.5 presents the estimates for the three-variable VECM for each of the G-7 countries. Estimates are shown for a subset of the adjustment coefficients α and the cointegration vector β; they are obtained via maximum likelihood methods. Table 1.5 also shows the Johansen trace statistic testing the null hypothesis of no cointegration. Except in Japan and Italy, the trace statistic is significant at the 1 percent level. For Japan the trace statistic is significant at the 5 percent level; it is marginally below the 5 percent level for Italy. In some cases, the trace statistic suggests more than one cointegrating relationship.[13] For consistency, I impose the presence of a single cointegration relationship in the estimation for all six countries other than the United States. For the four-country VECM, the Johansen trace statistic rejects the null hypothesis of no cointegrating equation and confirms the null hypothesis of one cointegrating equation.

For the United States, interest rate and unit debt servicing costs are obtained from a two-equation VECM. The null hypothesis of no cointegrating relationship is rejected; the coefficient on GDP per capita growth is large and statistically significant (see table 1.5).[14] The adjustment coef-

---

13. Given the mixed evidence for the right number of cointegrating relationships, I also consider a vector autoregression (VAR) in levels with a time trend. This specification has the largest impact for Canada and Japan, resulting in higher fiscal cost forecasts. Real interest rate forecasts remain within the (large) confidence intervals shown in figure 1.6.

14. Taken at face value, the cointegrating equation suggests a very low elasticity of intertemporal substitution.

Figure 1.6   Real interest rates and unit costs in the G-7 countries (*r – g*)

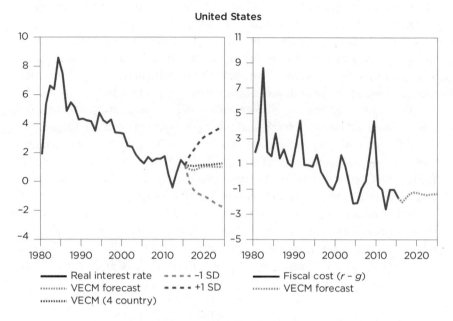

United States

Real interest rate
VECM forecast
VECM (4 country)
– – – –1 SD
– – – +1 SD

Fiscal cost (*r – g*)
VECM forecast

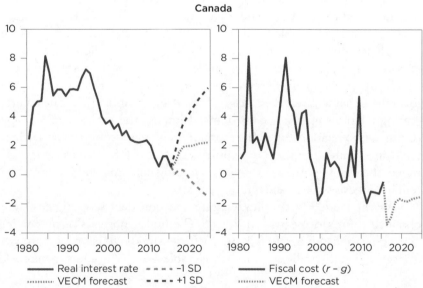

Canada

Real interest rate
VECM forecast
– – – –1 SD
– – – +1 SD

Fiscal cost (*r – g*)
VECM forecast

VECM = vector error correction model; SD = standard deviation

Figure 1.6   Real interest rates and unit costs in the G-7 countries (*r – g*)
(continued)

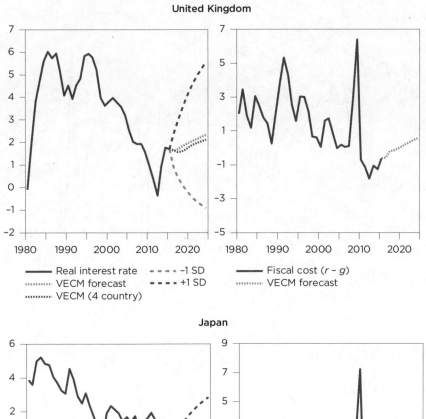

United Kingdom

Real interest rate
VECM forecast
VECM (4 country)
–1 SD
+1 SD

Fiscal cost (*r – g*)
VECM forecast

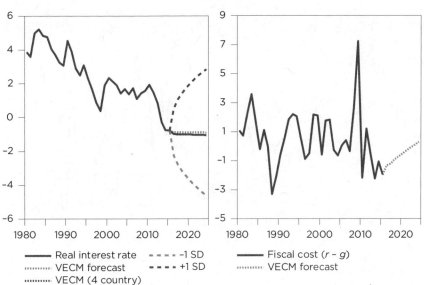

Japan

Real interest rate
VECM forecast
VECM (4 country)
–1 SD
+1 SD

Fiscal cost (*r – g*)
VECM forecast

VECM = vector error correction model; SD = standard deviation

(figure continues)

Figure 1.6   Real interest rates and unit costs in the G-7 countries (*r – g*)
(continued)

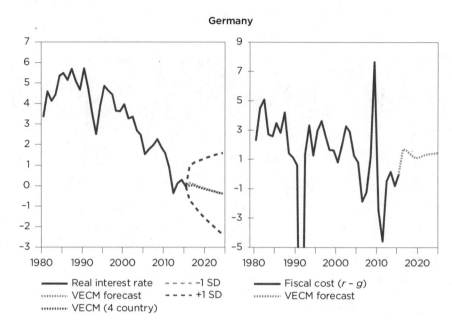

Germany

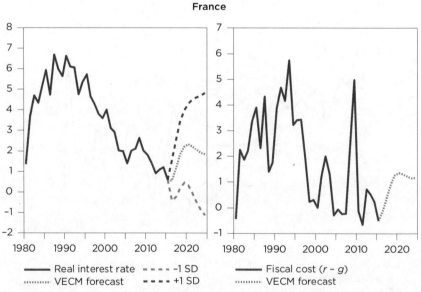

France

VECM = vector error correction model; SD = standard deviation

(figure continues)

Figure 1.6 Real interest rates and unit costs in the G-7 countries (*r* – *g*)
(continued)

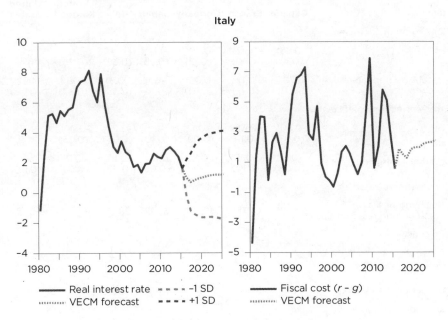

Italy

VECM = vector error correction model; SD = standard deviation

Sources: Author's calculations based on OECD data underlying figure 1.1 and interest rate/growth data from Jordà, Schularick, and Taylor dataset (see tables 1.1 and 1.2).

ficient is also weak, ensuring that US rates do not move quickly when the cointegrating relation is unbalanced. The coefficients for the four-country VECM are not shown, but the dynamic forecast is presented in the interest rate projections of figure 1.6 as a dark gray dotted line. Both the single-country and four-country models project a flat trajectory for the US real interest rate at approximately 1 percent through 2025. The one standard deviation error bands show that this real rate forecast comes with a high degree of uncertainty.[15]

Given a flat real interest rate projection of 1 percent for the United States and assuming population growth of 0.7 percent, the statistical model projects that *r* – *g* will remain negative over the forecast horizon. A negative unit cost of between –1.5 and –2 percent yields fiscal resources of 1.0 to 1.4 percent of GDP per year holding the debt-to-GDP ratio at 70 percent. The United States is in a somewhat more favorable position in terms of debt servicing costs relative to the rest of the G-7. These estimates of real rates do

15. The grey one standard error bands are shown only for the baseline two-equation model; the standard error bands are suppressed for the four-country VECM.

Table 1.5 Estimated interest rates in the G7 countries

Item	Canada	France	Germany	Japan	Italy	United Kingdom	United States
Cointegration coefficients							
US real interest rate	−0.88** (0.10)	−0.92** (0.10)	−0.70** (0.12)	−1.12** (0.26)	−0.40 (0.38)	−1.22** (0.29)	n.a. n.a.
Local GDP per capita growth	0.70** (0.11)	0.12 (0.12)	−0.68** (0.10)	−0.12 (0.14)	−0.31 (0.33)	2.09** (0.37)	−4.92** (0.89)
Error-correction coefficients							
Local real interest rate	−0.30** (0.07)	−0.61** (0.11)	−0.12 (0.08)	−0.11 (0.10)	−0.21** (0.07)	−0.09** (0.03)	n.a. n.a.
US real interest rate	−0.17* (0.08)	−0.10 (0.10)	0.12 (0.08)	0.16** (0.06)	−0.10* (0.05)	−0.05 (0.03)	0 (0.02)
Johansen trace statistic							
Null hypothesis: No cointegrating relationship	67.02**	43.77**	42.75**	30.12*	28.27	61.68**	39.11**
Lag specification							
Criterion	AIC	AIC	AIC	AIC	AIC	AIC	AIC
Lag length	2	3	2	2	3	2	3
Number of observations	64	63	64	64	63	64	63

n.a. = not applicable

Note: Each column presents a separate estimation of a vector error correction model assuming one cointegration vector consisting of the local long-term real interest rate, the long-term US real interest rate, and local GDP per capita growth. Data are for 1950–2015. They present cointegration coefficients and error correction coefficients for local and US rates (error correction term for GDP per capita and lag coefficients are suppressed). The real interest rate is the long-term nominal interest rate less the inflation rate (three-year moving average). The Akaike information criterion (AIC) was used for all lag specifications. Estimates via maximum likelihood and Johansen trace statistic critical values are 29.68 and 35.6 at the 5 and 1 percent levels, respectively. Standard errors are in parentheses. ** and * significant at the 5 and 10 percent level, respectively.

Sources: Long-term nominal interest rate and GDP per capita growth from Jordà, Schularick, and Taylor (2016) Macrohistory Database, www.macrohistory.net/data; author's calculations.

not take into account technological factors or inequality trends highlighted by the secular stagnation literature, which may put further downward pressures on the real rate.

Figure 1.6 shows the dynamic interest rate forecasts from a three-equation VECM for the United Kingdom and Canada—two countries that borrow in their own currency and control their own monetary policy. The United Kingdom and Canada display a marked decline in real interest rates from 6 and 8 percent, respectively, in the 1980s. In both cases, real interest rates are projected to rise somewhat toward 2 percent by 2025. However, the uncertainty bands are large in both cases, with the one standard deviation bands ranging from –2 percent to 6 percent. The cointegration relation with US real rates is significant in both cases and, unsurprisingly in the case of Canada, close to 1 (–0.88 in the β vector). The error correction term shows somewhat faster adjustment of Canadian rates when the cointegration equation is unbalanced.

The statistical model estimates that $r - g$ will gradually converge back to zero in the United Kingdom. For Canada the forecast is more negative, with r projected to remain roughly 2 percent less than g. At 55 percent of GDP, Canada's public debt is toward the lower end of the OECD; with a negative cost, its public debt appears sustainable over the medium term. The primary risks to this outlook include any financial instability caused by a correction in housing prices (which have increased rapidly in cities like Vancouver), renewed weakness in commodity markets, or a rapid rise in US real interest rates that spill over to Canada. By contrast, the United Kingdom's debt-to-GDP ratio is relatively high, and the fiscal and growth implications of Brexit remain unclear.

Japan, another country that borrows in its own currency, displays a persistent decline in real interest rates, from 4 percent to approximately –1 percent over the past 30 years. Real interest rates remain low for Japan through 2025 under both the two- and four-country VECM projections, but the uncertainty bands are wide. Japan's real rates are estimated to be cointegrated with US rates, with more than a one-for-one movement in Japanese rates in response to US rates. The error correction coefficient is insignificant for Japanese real rates and significant for US rates, reflecting the fact that the decline in Japanese real rates preceded the decline in the United States.

VECM estimates of GDP per capita growth also weaken over this period; combined with negative Japanese population growth, $r - g$ for Japan is projected to slowly rise over the next decade. In contrast to the other G-7 economies, $r - g$ in Japan was low over nearly the entire period since 1980, probably because of the impact of the Japanese financial crisis in the mid-1990s and reductions in nominal rates to the zero bound. The debt-to-GDP ratio for Japan is the worst among the G-7; even small movements in $r - g$ will have significant fiscal consequences. With a debt-to-GDP ratio near 200 percent, a 1 percentage point increase in $r - g$ for Japan would require a 2 percent of GDP fiscal consolidation. The high level of Japanese debt and significant uncertainty over the path of the real interest rate point to the need for debt reductions over the medium term. However, despite the unfavorable debt dynamics, there remains little evidence of inadequate demand for Japanese government bonds. Japan's ability to borrow in its own currency would appear to be critical in keeping rates low.

For the three largest eurozone economies (Germany, France, and Italy), the VECM estimates for real interest rates and GDP per capita growth suggest that the unit cost $r - g$ is likely to rise between now and 2025. The increase is most pronounced in France and Italy; it is more muted in Germany, where a continued decline in real interest rates is projected through 2025. Real rates in Germany fell below zero after 2010. The VECM forecasts real rates continuing to drift downward, with somewhat tighter uncertainty bands than for other countries. German real rates are forecast to approach –0.5 percent by 2025. By 2020 real rates are forecast to rise above 2 percent in France and to 1.5 percent in Italy.

In contrast to the United States and Canada, r is forecasted to rise above g in the United Kingdom and Japan, implying a positive and increasing fiscal cost of keeping the debt-to-GDP ratio stable. The forecast for $r - g$ is worse among the eurozone economies than in the rest of the G-7, because of unfavorable growth forecasts. For France and Italy, the situation is complicated by the elevated levels of the debt-to-GDP ratio. With population growth averaging only 0.5 percent since 2000, $r - g$ is forecasted to approach 2 percent. With public debt at more than 100 percent of GDP, the cost of keeping the debt-to-GDP ratio stable is projected to exceed 2 percent of GDP. For Italy $r - g$ rises to nearly 3 percent. Given a debt-to-GDP ratio of 150 percent of GDP, debt servicing costs would balloon to nearly 5 percent of GDP, a clearly unsustainable level. In sharp contrast, with a debt-to-GDP ratio of only 50 percent, a slightly positive $r - g$ for Germany does not represent a major fiscal expenditure. Of the major European economies, Germany appears best placed in terms of debt sustainability.

Lifecycle Model

The previous section presents empirical estimates of real interest rates and the cost of servicing the public debt based on a simple statistical model. A disadvantage of that approach is the difficulty of separating the contribution of slow productivity growth from other factors that may account for low real interest rates over the short and medium term.

In this section, I present some insights on how productivity growth affects the real interest rate and $r - g$ using a basic quantitative lifecycle model that matches key moments of the US economy. Two insights emerge. First, the richer lifecycle model confirms the possibility that slower productivity growth improves debt sustainability. Second, even though $r < g$, the revenue-maximizing level of US public debt is actually lower than the current level.

For brevity I present the quantitative model used to think about debt sustainability only in words (for full details of the model and its calibration, see Mehrotra 2017). In the model, households live for 56 periods (from ages 25 to 81), choose consumption and saving plans, and face escalating mortality risk. Households inelastically supply labor to a representative intermediate good firm that produces using a Cobb-Douglas production function. Markups and pure profits are introduced via the presence of retailers that costlessly differentiate the product and sell it to households at a markup. I introduce an intermediation wedge to reflect risk premia and intermediation costs that increases the cost of capital relative to the cost of government debt.

The model is calibrated either directly (using data on demographic parameters like the fertility rate and survival probabilities, for example) or by matching key moments of the US economy. The rate of time preference is chosen to target a real interest rate of 0.54 percent, the average for 2012–17 of the US 10-year government bond rate less the inflation rate, as measured by the core personal consumption expenditure index (PCE). The parameter determining retailers' market power is set to target a labor share of 60 percent, as documented in Karabarbounis and Neiman (2014). The size of the intermediation wedge is set to target a credit spread between Aaa corporate debt and the 10-year rate of 1.79 percent (the average between 2012 and 2017). The capital share parameter in the production function is chosen to target an investment-to-output ratio of 16.7 percent, matching the post-2000 average investment rate. Under this calibration, the level of capital accumulation remains dynamically efficient—that is, the economy does not overaccumulate capital.[16]

The key parameter determining the relationship between the real interest rate and productivity growth is the EIS. I consider three different values: 0.5, 1.0, and 2.0. An extensive body of literature has attempted to measure the EIS by examining how households' consumption growth responds to changes in the real interest rate they face. The consensus in this literature is that the EIS is less than unity, with some estimates suggesting that it is substantially less than 1.

Figure 1.7 shows how the real interest rate in the model varies with the growth rate of productivity (which in the model is equivalent to the growth rate of GDP per capita) and how this relationship changes with different elasticities of intertemporal substitution. For an EIS of 1 or 2, the response of the real interest rate with respect to productivity growth is less than 1; in the vicinity of the calibrated value of $r = 0.54$ percent, the real interest rate

---

16. The economy does not overaccumulate capital because the intermediation wedge (and the presence of markups) places a wedge between the return on government debt and the return on capital (and the return on capital and the marginal product of capital, respectively). See Abel et al. (1989) for a discussion of why low real interest rates on safe assets should not necessarily be interpreted as evidence of dynamic inefficiency.

Figure 1.7   US lifecycle model estimates of real interest rates, productivity growth rates, cost of debt servicing, and debt-to-GDP ratio

a. Real interest rate and growth rate of productivity

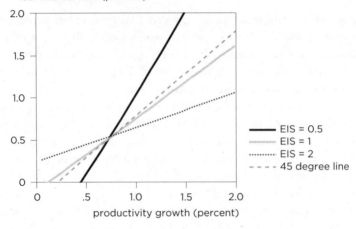

b. Cost of servicing public debt and debt-to-GDP ratio

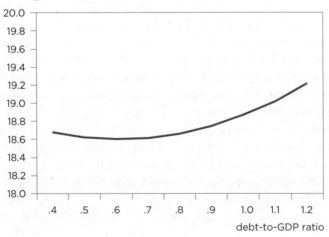

Sources: Author's calculations; Mehrotra (2017, table 5).

varies less than one-for-one with productivity growth.[17] Thus when productivity growth rises, the real interest rate rises by less and the unit cost of servicing the public debt falls. Conversely, if productivity growth falls, the real interest rate falls by less and the cost of servicing the debt rises. In these cases, faster productivity growth improves debt sustainability and slower productivity growth worsens debt sustainability.

However, most estimates of the EIS are somewhat below unity.[18] As the solid black line in figure 1.7 shows, when the EIS = 0.5, the real interest rate moves by more than one-for-one with productivity growth. In this case, slower productivity growth is actually beneficial for debt sustainability, as the real interest rate falls by more than the growth rate of productivity. The reverse holds true for higher productivity growth. With $r = 0.54$ percent, a debt-to-GDP ratio for the United States of about 70 percent of GDP (excluding public debt held by the Social Security Trust Fund), and underlying productivity growth of 0.7 percent per year, the current annual cost of servicing the public debt is –0.6 percent of GDP. In other words, keeping the debt-to-GDP ratio constant, the US government raises real resources of 0.6 percent of GDP, because interest rates are below the growth rate of the economy. With an EIS of 0.5, a return to 1990s productivity growth of 1.5–2 percent would raise real rates sufficiently to ensure that $r > g$. To keep the debt-to-GDP ratio stable, a fiscal consolidation of 0.6 percent of GDP would be needed. By contrast, a collapse in US productivity growth to zero would actually increase fiscal resources to the US government from the current 0.6 percent of GDP to 1.1 percent of GDP, by further lowering the real interest rate on government debt.

Figure 1.7 illustrates how the cost of servicing the public debt in the United States varies with the debt-to-GDP ratio. The debt servicing cost in steady state is given by

$$(r-g)\frac{B_g}{Y}.$$

As the debt-to-GDP ratio rises, the real interest rate r also changes. At the current debt-to-GDP ratio of 70 percent, the United States is above the taxation-minimizing level of public debt. Even though $r < g$ in the calibrated

---

17. The elasticity of the real interest rate with respect to productivity growth is not exactly the EIS, because the precise relationship between g and r from the representative agent model breaks down in a lifecycle model.

18. Rios-Rull (1996) estimates a range for the EIS of 0.25–1.0. Kaplan (2012) estimates a narrower range of 0.54–0.62. Krueger and Kubler (2006); Glover et al. (2011); and Constantinides, Donaldson, and Mehra (2002) all find that the EIS is below 1. Gourinchas and Parker (2002) estimate the EIS at 0.71–2.0.

steady state, a further reduction in the debt-to-GDP ratio increases fiscal resources to the government by further lowering the real interest rate. The taxation-minimizing level of debt is roughly 60 percent of GDP. Over a fairly large range of the debt-to-GDP ratio, the cost of servicing the public debt is fairly stable. For example, a rise in the ratio to 120 percent requires a fiscal consolidation of only 0.7 percent of GDP—roughly the same order of magnitude as the effects of a reversion to 1990s levels of productivity growth.

This quantitative model suggests two counterintuitive findings. First, slower productivity growth may be beneficial from a debt sustainability perspective; the unit cost of keeping the debt-to-GDP ratio constant falls, because the indirect effect of productivity growth on real interest rates dominates the direct effect on economic growth. Second, even though $r < g$ currently, the level of public debt that minimizes taxes (holding constant government expenditures) is actually lower than current debt levels, because of the endogenous response of the real interest rate to the debt-to-GDP ratio.

Conclusion

This chapter examines the consequences of low productivity growth for debt sustainability, as measured by $r - g$. The difference between r and g multiplied by the debt-to-GDP ratio represents the real resources a government must raise to keep the debt-to-GDP ratio constant.

Advanced economies emerged from the Great Recession with high levels of public debt and low levels of productivity growth—a potentially troublesome combination for debt sustainability. However, real interest rates on government debt are low, meaning the cost of servicing the debt is low or even negative.

The simple analytical framework shows how declines in productivity growth can lower the real interest rate for both closed and open economies and may therefore have an ambiguous impact on debt servicing costs. The empirical evidence shows that real interest rates on government debt frequently fall below the growth rate of the economy but that, in the medium run, the likelihood of reverting to conditions of $r > g$ remains high. Interest rates for many countries appear to be cointegrated with US real interest rates. Low real interest rates in the United States may therefore benefit SOEs, particularly faster-growing ones, by keeping the cost of servicing the debt low.

For the G-7 economies, I provide interest rate estimates using a VECM. Confidence bands are wide, but for faster-growing economies like the United Kingdom, Germany, and Canada, the fiscal cost of servicing the debt is likely to remain substantially depressed. For slow-growing economies like Italy, the fiscal cost of servicing the debt is substantial and likely to remain so absent a pronounced acceleration in productivity or population growth.

On the theoretical side, I use a standard representative agent model to show how, for closed economies, the real interest rate is closely tied to the growth rate of productivity, with the EIS governing the response of real interest rates to productivity growth. Crucially, if the EIS is less than unity, slower productivity growth can be beneficial for debt sustainability, because the indirect effect of slower productivity growth on the real interest rate dominates its direct effect on GDP growth. A substantial body of literature in finance and macroeconomics estimates this elasticity to be less than 1. For the United States, for a benchmark EIS of 0.5, a decline in productivity growth from 0.7 to 0 would raise fiscal resources of 0.5 percent of GDP, given the current debt-to-GDP ratio. Conversely, a return to mid-1990s levels of productivity growth (g = 1.5–2.0 percent) would imply an additional fiscal cost of 0.6 percent of GDP to keep the debt-to-GDP ratio constant.

References

Abel, Andrew B., N. Gregory Mankiw, Lawrence H. Summers, and Richard J. Zeckhauser. 1989. Assessing Dynamic Efficiency: Theory and Evidence. *Review of Economic Studies* 56, no. 1: 1–19.

Aiyagari, S. Rao, and Ellen R. McGrattan. 1998. The Optimum Quantity of Debt. *Journal of Monetary Economics* 42, no. 3: 447–69.

Auerbach, Alan J. 1994. The U.S. Fiscal Problem. *NBER Macroeconomics Annual* 9: 141–75.

Ball, Laurence, Douglas W. Elmendorf, and N. Gregory Mankiw. 1998. The Deficit Gamble. *Journal of Money, Credit and Banking* 30, no. 4: 699–720.

Caballero, Ricardo J., and Emmanuel Farhi. 2017. The Safety Trap. *Review of Economic Studies* 85, no. 1: 223–74.

Caballero, Ricardo J., Emmanuel Farhi, and Pierre-Olivier Gourinchas. 2015. *Global Imbalances and Currency Wars at the ZLB*. NBER Working Paper 21670. Cambridge, MA: National Bureau of Economic Research.

Constantinides, George M., John B. Donaldson, and Rajnish Mehra. 2002. Junior Can't Borrow: A New Perspective on the Equity Premium Puzzle. *Quarterly Journal of Economics* 117, no. 1: 269–96.

Corsetti, Giancarlo, Eleonora Mavroeidi, Gregory Thwaites, and Martin Wolf. 2016. Step Away from the Zero Lower Bound: Small Open Economies in a World of Secular Stagnation. Unpublished manuscript. Department of Applied Economics, Cambridge University.

Eggertsson, Gauti B., and Neil R. Mehrotra. 2014. *A Model of Secular Stagnation*. NBER Working Paper 20574. Cambridge, MA: National Bureau of Economic Research

Eggertsson, Gauti B., Neil R. Mehrotra, and Jacob Robbins. 2017. A Model of Secular Stagnation: Theory and Quantitative Evaluation. Unpublished manuscript. Department of Economics, Brown University, Providence, RI.

Eggertsson, Gauti B., Neil R. Mehrotra, Sanjay R. Singh, and Lawrence H. Summers. 2016. A Contagious Malady? Open Economy Dimensions of Secular Stagnation. *IMF Economic Review* 64, no. 4: 581–634.

Elmendorf, Douglas W., and Louise Sheiner. 2016. *Federal Budget Policy with an Aging Population and Persistently Low Interest Rates*. Hutchins Center Working Paper 18. Washington: Brookings Institution.

Farhi, Emmanuel, and Matteo Maggiori. 2016. *A Model of the International Monetary System*. NBER Working Paper 22295. Cambridge, MA: National Bureau of Economic Research

Glover, Andrew, Jonathan Heathcote, Dirk Krueger, and José-Victor Rios-Rull. 2011. *Intergenerational Redistribution in the Great Recession*. NBER Working Paper 16924. Cambridge, MA: National Bureau of Economic Research.

Gourinchas, Pierre-Olivier, and Jonathan A. Parker. 2002. Consumption over the Life Cycle. *Econometrica* 70, no. 1: 47–89.

Gourinchas, Pierre-Olivier, and Hélène Rey. 2016. *Real Interest Rates, Imbalances and the Curse of Regional Safe Asset Providers at the Zero Lower Bound*. NBER Working Paper 22618. Cambridge, MA: National Bureau of Economic Research.

Hamilton, James D., Ethan S. Harris, Jan Hatzius, and Kenneth D. West. 2016. The Equilibrium Real Funds Rate: Past, Present, and Future. *IMF Economic Review* 64, no. 4: 660–707.

Holston, Kathryn, Thomas Laubach, and John C. Williams. 2017. Measuring the Natural Rate of Interest: International Trends and Determinants. *Journal of International Economics* 108, no. S1: S59–S75.

Jordà, Oscar, Moritz Schularick, and Alan M. Taylor. 2016. Macrofinancial History and the New Business Cycle Facts. *NBER Macroeconomics Annual* 31.

Kaplan, Greg. 2012. Inequality and the Life Cycle. *Quantitative Economics* 3, no. 3: 471–525.

Karabarbounis, Loukas, and Brent Neiman. 2014. The Global Decline of the Labor Share. *Quarterly Journal of Economics* 129, no. 1: 61–103.

Krueger, Dirk, and Felix Kubler. 2006. Pareto-Improving Social Security Reform When Financial Markets Are Incomplete!? *American Economic Review* 96, no. 3: 737–55.

Laubach, Thomas, and John C. Williams. 2016. Measuring the Natural Rate of Interest Redux. *Business Economics* 51, no. 2: 57–67.

Mehrotra, Neil R. 2017. Debt Sustainability in a Low Interest Rate World. Unpublished manuscript. Brookings Institution, Washington.

Rios-Rull, José-Victor. 1996. Life-Cycle Economies and Aggregate Fluctuations. *Review of Economic Studies* 63, no. 3: 465–89.

Schmitt-Grohe, Stephanie, and Martin Uribe. 2003. Closing Small Open Economy Models. *Journal of International Economics* 61: 163–85.

Summers, Lawrence. 2013. Why Stagnation Might Prove to be the New Normal. *Financial Times*, December 13.

Woodford, Michael. 1990. Public Debt as Private Liquidity. *American Economic Review* 80, no. 2: 382–88.

2

Slow Productivity Growth Will Pressure Sovereign Debt Sustainability

ELENA DUGGAR

A growing body of research documents a global and persistent collapse in productivity growth (see Moody's 2017c and IMF 2017 for overviews). Globally, annual labor productivity growth averaged 1.5 percent in 2011–17, down from 2.7 percent in 1995–2007, a decline of almost half. Labor productivity growth after the global financial crisis was lower than in the precrisis period for 85 of the 122 countries for which data are available (figure 2.1).

A collapse in total factor productivity (TFP) growth is evident in almost all economies. The fall in capital intensity has played a large role in the decline in labor productivity in the United States and other advanced economies (figure 2.2). Global TFP growth dropped from an annual average rate of 1.3 percent before the crisis to 0.1 percent in 2011–15. Baily and Montalbano (2016) show that the decline in productivity growth is also broad-based across industries. It is evident even in the high-tech sectors and does not reflect a rising share of slow-growing industries.

In Moody's view, the productivity growth slowdown presents significant risks to GDP growth recovery (Moody's 2017a). Global growth since the global financial crisis has remained about 1.3 percentage points lower than before the crisis. Moody's estimates that about one-third of this decline reflected the drop in employment growth and about two-thirds the drop in labor productivity growth. Given the cyclical economic recovery, Moody's

Elena Duggar is the chair of Moody's Macroeconomic Board and also manages the Research team in the Credit Strategy and Research group. She is grateful to Richard Cantor, Karen Dynan, Neil Mehrotra, Adam Posen, Louise Sheiner, and Jeromin Zettelmeyer for helpful comments and discussion and Claire Li for excellent research assistance.

Figure 2.1 The collapse of productivity growth is global and persistent

Difference between precrisis and postcrisis labor productivity growth rate

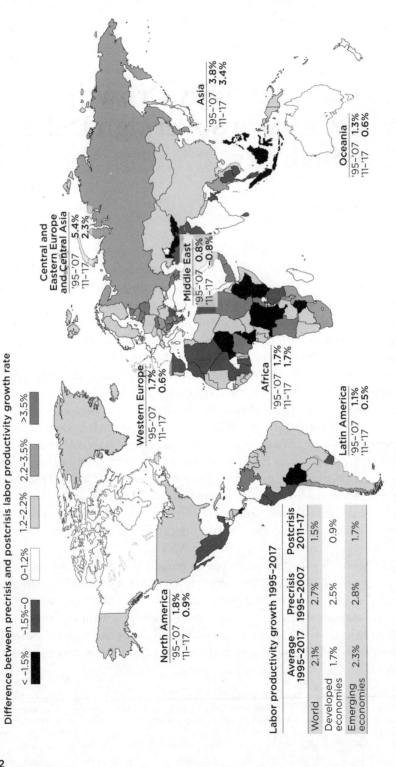

< −1.5%	−1.5%−0	0−1.2%	1.2−2.2%	2.2−3.5%	>3.5%

North America
'95–'07 1.8%
'11–'17 0.9%

Western Europe
'95–'07 1.7%
'11–'17 0.6%

Central and Eastern Europe and Central Asia
'95–'07 5.4%
'11–'17 2.3%

Middle East
'95–'07 0.8%
'11–'17 −0.8%

Asia
'95–'07 3.8%
'11–'17 3.4%

Oceania
'95–'07 1.3%
'11–'17 0.6%

Africa
'95–'07 1.7%
'11–'17 1.7%

Latin America
'95–'07 1.1%
'11–'17 0.5%

Labor productivity growth 1995–2017

	Average 1995–2017	Precrisis 1995–2007	Postcrisis 2011–17
World	2.1%	2.7%	1.5%
Developed economies	1.7%	2.5%	0.9%
Emerging economies	2.3%	2.8%	1.7%

Note: For country coverage, see appendix 2A. Unweighted averages across regions.

Source: Moody's Investors Service; The Conference Board® Total Economy Database™ (adjusted version), November 2017.

Figure 2.2 Pre- and postcrisis drivers of labor productivity growth: The role of capital intensity has varied, but a collapse in total factor productivity growth is evident in almost all economies

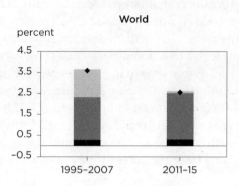

World
percent

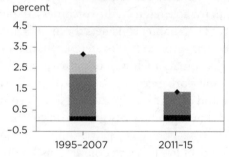

Developed economies
percent

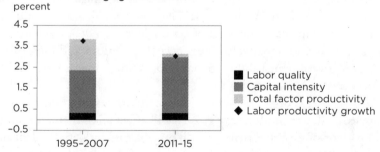

Emerging economies
percent

■ Labor quality
■ Capital intensity
■ Total factor productivity
◆ Labor productivity growth

Note: Unweighted averages across 36 developed economies and 86 emerging economies. Labor productivity growth decomposition is based on model estimates assuming a Cobb-Douglas production function, which differs from measured labor productivity growth in other figures.

Sources: Moody's Investors Service; The Conference Board Total Economy Database™ (adjusted version), November 2017.

expects productivity growth to recover somewhat in 2018–19, driven by a rebound in aggregate demand and investment, consistent with better credit conditions and business expectations. Productivity growth over the medium term will remain lower than before the crisis, however, because many of the causes of the productivity growth slowdown are secular trends, which will not reverse easily over the short term.[1] Lower-than-expected productivity growth is a key source of downside risk to economic growth, as population aging will exert negative pressures on labor growth in most countries (figure 2.3 and Moody's 2014). For example, should labor productivity growth remain at its low 2016 pace (1.0 percent a year) or at its average 2011–17 pace (1.5 percent a year), global growth in 2019 could be as low as 2.2 percent or 2.7 percent, respectively—much lower than Moody's current baseline expectation of 3.6 percent (implying labor productivity growth of about 2.4 percent).[2]

Given the significant risks it presents for economic recovery, what would slower productivity growth mean for sovereign creditworthiness, in particular sovereign debt sustainability? This chapter considers the implications of a sustained period of low productivity growth for sovereign debt dynamics. It draws on the literature on the impact of low productivity growth on interest rates, as well as on emerging work on the impact of low productivity growth on government revenue and expenditure presented in this volume. The focus is the overall impact of slower productivity growth on government debt dynamics.

In a world of historically high debt levels, aging populations, and rising interest rates, slow productivity growth poses a significant risk for sovereign debt sustainability (Moody's 2017c). All else equal, lower productivity growth is likely to have a negative effect on sovereign debt dynamics. The impact on sovereign creditworthiness over the medium and long run will depend on governments' ability to make policy adjustments that moderate the pressures on budget deficits.

This chapter is organized around the main drivers of government debt dynamics, as slower productivity growth will affect all of them. It examines the impact of slow productivity growth on government deficits, debt flows arising from the materialization of contingent liabilities, the interest rate–growth differential, and debt flows arising from potential exchange rate movements. It concludes by summarizing the implications for sovereign debt sustainability of a slowdown in productivity growth.

---

1. For a review of the causes of the global productivity slowdown, see Moody's (2017a).

2. Because this chapter focuses on cross-country trends, global growth is cited as an unweighted average across countries. For details, see Moody's (2018).

Figure 2.3 Lower labor productivity growth presents a risk to global growth (global GDP growth under three scenarios)

percent

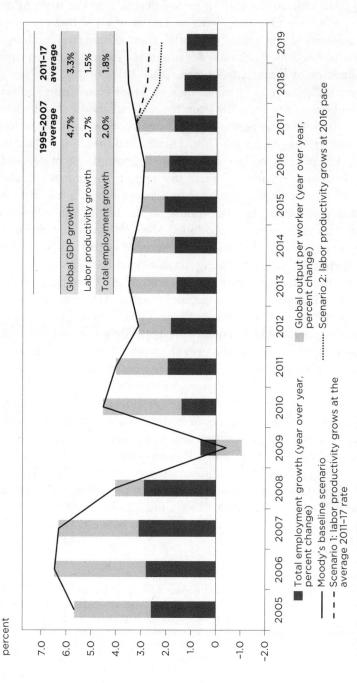

	1995–2007 average	2011–17 average
Global GDP growth	4.7%	3.3%
Labor productivity growth	2.7%	1.5%
Total employment growth	2.0%	1.8%

■ Total employment growth (year over year, percent change)

▨ Global output per worker (year over year, percent change)

— Moody's baseline scenario

- - - Scenario 1: labor productivity grows at the average 2011–17 rate

········· Scenario 2: labor productivity grows at 2016 pace

Note: Real unadjusted GDP growth rate, unweighted average across countries.

Sources: Moody's Investors Service; International Labor Organization (ILO); The Conference Board Total Economy Database™ (adjusted version), November 2017.

Effect of Low Productivity Growth on Government Deficits, Especially in an Aging World

Conceptually, the debt dynamics can be represented as in figure 2.4. The debt-to-GDP ratio in the current period depends on the stock of debt in the last period, the primary balance as a share of GDP, flows arising from the interest rate–growth rate differential, flows arising from exchange rate movements, and any stock-flow adjustments capturing, for example, the materialization of contingent liabilities (IMF 2013).

Historically, large debt buildups have often come from the primary deficit and fiscal costs resulting from the materialization of contingent liabilities, as well as exchange rate depreciations in emerging markets. In many countries, including Japan, the United States, and the United Kingdom, for example, the primary budget deficit was the main driver of debt-creating flows over the last decade and a half (figure 2.5). The primary balance was a key determinant of government debt dynamics in countries that experienced a large debt buildup. Depending on the way in which government support is provided (e.g., bank bailouts), the fiscal costs from the materialization of contingent liabilities may be recorded as part of the fiscal deficit or as a cashflow adjustment raising the stock of debt.

Lower productivity growth and lower economic growth are expected to lead to lower income and consumption growth and lower tax revenues relative to the counterfactual scenario of higher productivity growth. In theory, if labor income and tax revenues were perfectly correlated with productivity growth, the decline in the growth of tax revenue would be the same as the decline in the growth of GDP, leaving tax revenue as a share of GDP unchanged. In practice, tax revenue in progressive tax systems is likely to fall somewhat as a share of GDP, as a result of less "real bracket creep" (the phenomenon in which increases in nominal income because of inflation push taxpayers into higher tax brackets) in the tax code.

Tax systems are often indexed to inflation, which prevents bracket creep. Over time, however, real growth in incomes will still push taxpayers into higher tax brackets. Slower productivity growth would likely reduce the extent of real bracket creep, which would lead to a somewhat lower tax revenue-to-GDP ratio.[3] For payroll taxes (such as Social Security taxes), for

---

3. Dynan (chapter 3 of this volume) and Sheiner (chapter 4) present qualitative and quantitative analyses, respectively, of the impact of lower productivity growth on tax revenue in the United States. Sheiner finds that a 0.6 percentage point lower productivity growth rate would be associated with about a 0.6 percentage point lower tax revenue-to-GDP ratio in the United States over the next 25 years, as a result of the smaller real bracket creep effect. This estimate is equivalent to a reduction in average annual tax revenue of 0.25 percent of GDP.

Figure 2.4   Contributions to changes in government debt (percent of GDP)

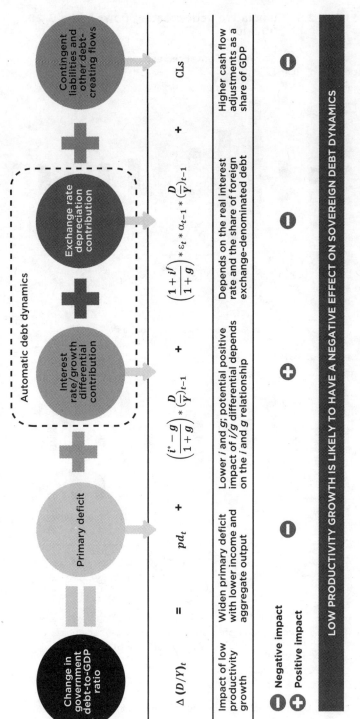

$$\Delta (D/Y)_t \quad = \quad pd_t \quad + \quad \left(\frac{i^* - g}{1 + g}\right) * \left(\frac{D}{Y}\right)_{t-1} \quad + \quad \left(\frac{1 + i^f}{1 + g}\right) * \varepsilon_t * \alpha_{t-1} * \left(\frac{D}{Y}\right)_{t-1} \quad + \quad CLs$$

| Impact of low productivity growth | Widen primary deficit with lower income and aggregate output | Lower i and g; potential positive impact of i/g differential depends on the i and g relationship | Depends on the real interest rate and the share of foreign exchange-denominated debt | Higher cash flow adjustments as a share of GDP |

LOW PRODUCTIVITY GROWTH IS LIKELY TO HAVE A NEGATIVE EFFECT ON SOVEREIGN DEBT DYNAMICS

D = debt; Y = GDP; pd = primary deficit as a share of GDP; i = average nominal interest rate; g = nominal GDP growth rate; α = share of foreign currency-denominated debt; i^f = interest rate on foreign currency-denominated debt; ε = nominal exchange rate depreciation; and CLs = cash flow adjustments from the materialization of contingent liabilities and other debt-creating flows as a share of GDP.

Source: Moody's Investors Service.

Figure 2.5   Cumulative debt-creating flows in the G-20, 2002–16

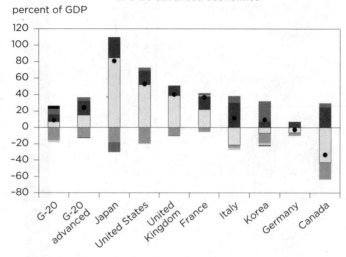

a. G-20 advanced economies

percent of GDP

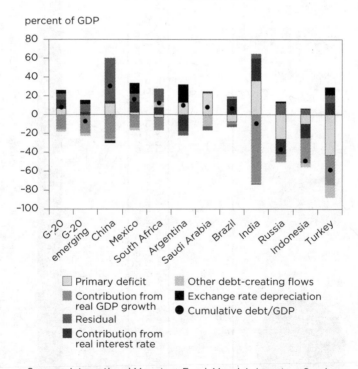

b. G-20 emerging economies

percent of GDP

Primary deficit

Contribution from real GDP growth

Residual

Contribution from real interest rate

Other debt-creating flows

Exchange rate depreciation

● Cumulative debt/GDP

Sources: International Monetary Fund; Moody's Investors Service.

which the tax rate is mostly flat, tax collection would likely move close to one-to-one with wages and hence productivity.

In chapter 4 of this volume, Louise Sheiner shows that lower productivity growth is likely to increase government expenditures as a share of GDP. Assuming discretionary expenditure remains unchanged, a slowdown in productivity would mean that discretionary expenditure as a share of GDP would rise as GDP grew more slowly. Similarly, as many benefits programs, such as Social Security, are not indexed to wages but to inflation for existing beneficiaries, their share of GDP would rise as productivity growth slowed. Slower productivity growth and the corresponding slower income growth would likely mean that the number of people eligible for government programs would rise.[4]

Together, lower government revenue and higher expenditures in the event of lower productivity growth would likely lead to wider primary budget deficits. The magnitude of the effect depends on the structure of the tax and expenditure system of each country.[5] If lower productivity growth also leads to lower labor participation rates, fiscal pressures would increase further.

The effect of lower productivity growth on government budget deficits is likely to be especially challenging given the unprecedented pace of population aging over the next two to three decades. The demographic transition will create an additional negative feedback loop that will exacerbate the decline in productivity growth and put additional pressure on primary budget deficits.

Population aging will likely lead to a slower rate of growth in the productivity of the workforce (see figure 2.6). Liu and Westelius (2016) estimate that an aging workforce may have reduced annual TFP growth in Japan by as much as 0.7–0.9 percentage point between 1990 and 2005. Aiyar, Ebeke, and Shao (2016) estimate that the growing number of workers 55 and older reduced TFP growth in Europe by about 0.1 percentage point a year over the past two decades. They project that workforce aging may reduce TFP growth by 0.2 percentage point a year between 2014 and 2045.

Population aging will also likely have a profound impact on government finances, pension systems, and health care over the next two decades.

---

4. The literature estimating the impact of lower productivity growth on fiscal metrics is nascent, but Sheiner's work suggests that the effect could be large. In a detailed program-by-program analysis for the United States, based on analysis by the Congressional Budget Office, the Social Security Trustee report, and the Medicare Trustee report, she finds that government spending would increase by about 0.8 percent of GDP on average over the next 25 years if productivity growth slowed by 0.6 percentage points (see chapter 4).

5. For example, Sheiner finds that 0.6 percentage point lower productivity growth in the United States would lead to a 1 percent wider primary deficit as a share of GDP on average over the next 25 years.

Figure 2.6 Correlation between old-age dependency ratio and labor productivity growth in developed economies

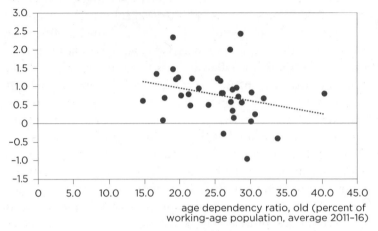

labor productivity (year over year, percent change, average 2011–16)

Sources: Moody's Investors Service; World Bank; The Conference Board Total Economy Database™ (adjusted version), November 2017.

Projecting government expenditures under different scenarios for France, Germany, the United Kingdom, and the United States, Moody's (2011) projects that, assuming unchanged program benefits and costs, aging alone would require governments to spend an additional 1–2 percent of GDP every year on health care and 1–4 percent of GDP on pensions over the next 40 years. The associated cumulative increases in government debt-to-GDP levels of up to 280 percent on top of current levels of debt are clearly not realistic, but they illustrate the magnitude of the challenge reforms will face.

Effect of Low Productivity Growth on Contingent Liabilities

The realization of contingent liabilities has often led to a large buildup in public debt and, in extreme cases, triggered sovereign debt crises (see, for example, Moody's 2017b). Bova et al. (2016) show that over 1990–2014 the materialization of contingent liabilities in 80 countries resulted in an average fiscal cost of 6 percent of GDP per episode, with peak costs of up to 57 percent of GDP (in Indonesia during the Asian financial crisis). The most common cause was financial sector crises, followed by natural disasters, support for public enterprises, and support for subnational governments. These fiscal costs represent a 0.6 percentage point annual increase in debt-

Figure 2.7 Fiscal cost of realization of contingent liabilities in developed and emerging economies, 1990–2014

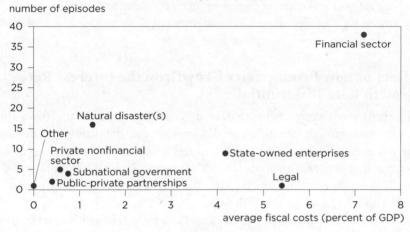

a. Developed economies

number of episodes

b. Emerging economies

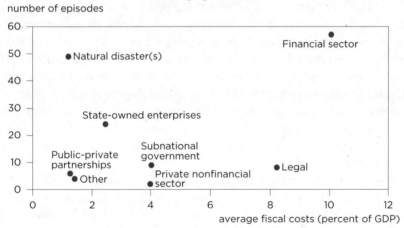

number of episodes

Source: Bova et al. (2016).

to-GDP levels on average across countries (0.7 percentage point for G-20 economies).

Financial sector crises have represented the biggest risk to sovereign balance sheets (figure 2.7). Episodes of bank restructuring or recapitalization during such crises led to an average 0.5 percentage point annual increase in debt-to-GDP levels across countries (about 0.6 percentage point for G-20 economies). In South Korea during the Asian financial crisis (the most extreme case), fiscal costs related to contingent liabilities arising from financial distress amounted to 31.2 percent of GDP.

In general, lower GDP growth—associated with lower productivity growth—would mean that cashflow adjustments would represent a larger share of GDP over time. Additional risks may arise from the fact that lower interest rates—more often at the lower interest rate bound—would serve as a constraint on the effectiveness of monetary policy to support the economy in the event of a crisis.

Effect of Low Productivity Growth on the Interest Rate–Growth Rate Differential

The third main component of debt dynamics is flows arising from the interest rate–growth rate differential. Conceptually, stabilizing or reducing the government debt-to-GDP ratio requires a sufficient primary surplus to be generated in the future if the interest rate–growth rate differential is positive. If the differential is negative, the debt trajectory can generally be stabilized with a larger government deficit.

Over the past decade, interest rates have remained at historically low levels, reducing debt servicing costs across countries. As of end-2017, the differential was positive (e.g., the real interest rate was higher than real GDP growth) in Brazil and Russia among the G-20 economies but negative in many advanced economies and fast-growing emerging markets (figure 2.8). As interest rates in the United States and the euro area start normalizing, debt servicing costs will rise over the medium term. At the same time, inflation in emerging markets is falling toward developed economy levels, even as emerging markets' growth stabilizes at more than twice the growth rate of developed economies. As a result, real interest rates have been rising in a number of emerging markets, including Brazil, Russia, India, and South Africa.

Even where the interest rate–growth rate differential is negative, there is a significant risk of reversion to a positive differential—as the result, for example, of an external shock. For a sample of 17 advanced economies, Mehrotra estimates the likelihood of the differential changing from negative to positive in the next five years at about 40 percent (see chapter 1 of this volume). A near-term G-20 example is Russia, where the average negative differential over 2002–16 will turn positive over the next five years.

Lower productivity growth would affect both the growth rate and the real interest rate. The impact on the interest rate–growth rate differential will depend on consumer preferences, specifically consumers' intertemporal elasticity of substitution. If people are very willing to substitute consumption over time, economic theory would predict small declines in real interest rates; if people are not willing to substitute consumption over time, economic theory would predict larger declines in real interest rates.

Figure 2.8 Differential between real interest rate and real growth rate in the G-20

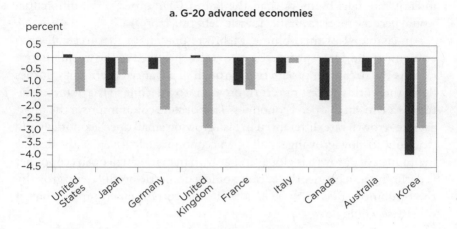

a. G-20 advanced economies

percent

b. G-20 emerging economies

percent

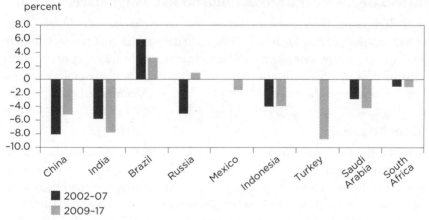

■ 2002–07
▨ 2009–17

Note: Real interest rates are proxied by the policy rate adjusted for inflation, as measured by the consumer price index. 2002–07 data for Mexico and Turkey are not available.

Sources: Moody's Investors Service, national central banks, and national statistics offices.

The academic literature suggests that changes in the real interest rate may have a one-for-one to two-for-one relationship with changes in the growth rate of the economy, but the relationship is somewhat uncertain and varies across time and across samples—and in some periods the relationship is negative or zero.[6]

---

6. For details, see the chapters in this volume by Mehrotra (chapter 1), Dynan (chapter 3), and Sheiner (chapter 4).

If lower productivity growth affects GDP growth and the interest rate by the same amount, the differential would remain unchanged. If the interest rate falls by more than the fall in GDP growth, the differential would become more favorable for the debt trajectory.[7]

In chapter 1 of this volume, Mehrotra points out that in small open economies, the domestic interest rate is closely linked to the world interest rate. As the decline in productivity growth in advanced economies pushes down the world interest rate, it translates into a decline in the domestic interest rate in small open economies. This decline could improve the interest rate–growth rate differential in fast-growing small open economies and worsen it in slow-growing small open economies. However, as the decline in productivity growth is global and growth in many small open economies is declining independently (because of low domestic productivity growth), the combined effect may be smaller in the current environment than it otherwise would be.[8]

Effect of Interest Rate Decline on Exchange Rates

The decline in the interest rate may lead to exchange rate depreciation, which would lead to additional increases in debt as a share of domestic GDP in countries with foreign currency–denominated debt. The size of the effect depends on the differential between the domestic and the global interest rate, as well as on the share of foreign currency–denominated debt.

Conclusion

Low productivity growth will likely have a negative effect on sovereign debt dynamics. In a scenario of lower productivity growth, the debt accumulation flows arising from higher primary deficits, the materialization of contingent liabilities, and exchange rate depreciation could easily offset the benefit of a more favorable interest rate–growth rate differential. The quantitative effects will depend on the structure of the tax and expenditure system of each country as well as the current level of debt. But without any other policy adjustment, lower productivity growth by itself could result in a rising debt path and create headwinds for sovereign creditworthiness.

The economic literature suggests that the relationship between the change in the real interest rate and the change in growth (given lower pro-

---

7. Lower productivity growth could also reduce inflation, which would somewhat diminish the improvement in the flows coming from the interest rate–growth rate differential, given that inflation helps lower the real burden of nominal debt over time.

8. Between the precrisis 1995–2007 period and the postcrisis 2011–17 period, productivity growth declined in 85 of the 122 countries for which data are available (figure 2.1).

ductivity growth) is likely to be between one-for-one and one-for-two (i.e., a 1 percentage point drop in real GDP growth is likely to be correlated with 1–2 percentage point decline in the real interest rate). Abstracting from exchange rate effects and potential cashflow adjustments, if lower productivity growth affects GDP growth and the interest rate by the same amount, the change in flows from the interest rate–growth rate differential will be zero and increases in the primary deficit will lead to corresponding increases in the debt-to-GDP ratio. If lower productivity growth lowers the interest rate by twice as much as GDP growth, the flows from the differential will somewhat offset the increase in the primary deficit. The impact on the debt-to-GDP ratio will depend on the relative magnitude of the two effects.

Additional negative fiscal pressures will likely arise if lower productivity growth reduces the inflation rate or affects labor participation rates. Still more pressures on government finances will come from the rise in age-related expenditures as the unprecedented demographic transition will likely exacerbate both the decline in productivity growth and the pressure on government primary budget deficits.[9]

Ultimately, the impact on sovereign creditworthiness over the medium and long run will depend on governments' ability to make policy adjustments and to restructure eligibility for government programs and program benefits—or alternatively, to increase tax revenues—in a way that moderates the pressure on budget deficits. Prospects for economic and fiscal reform are uneven across countries (Moody's 2017c). The current economic backdrop broadens the window for sovereigns to pursue unpopular or costly economic and fiscal reforms. The longer-term credit impact of the supportive growth environment will depend on how well they manage to do so. Many governments will focus on addressing short-term vulnerabilities rather than fundamental weaknesses, leaving countries with high debt and lower growth susceptible to weakening credit profiles in the event of a downturn.

References

Aiyar, S., C. Ebeke, and X. Shao. 2016. *The Impact of Workforce Aging on European Productivity.* IMF Working Paper 16/238. Washington: International Monetary Fund.

Baily, M.N., and N. Montalbano. 2016. *Why Is U.S. Productivity Growth So Slow? Possible Explanations and Policy Responses.* Hutchins Center Working Paper 22. Washington: Brookings Institution.

---

9. The analysis in this chapter assumes no changes in income distribution. In chapter 9 of this volume, Furman and Orszag argue that lower productivity growth may be associated with higher income inequality.

Bova, E., M. Ruiz-Arranz, F. Toscani, and H. Elif Ture. 2016. *The Fiscal Costs of Contingent Liabilities: A New Dataset.* IMF Working Paper 16/14. Washington: International Monetary Fund.

IMF (International Monetary Fund). 2013. *Staff Guidance Note for Public Debt Sustainability Analysis in Market-Access Countries* (May). Washington.

IMF (International Monetary Fund). 2017. *Gone with the Headwinds: Global Productivity.* IMF Staff Discussion Note 17/04. Washington.

Liu, Y., and N. Westelius. 2016. *The Impact of Demographics on Productivity and Inflation in Japan.* IMF Working Paper 16/237. Washington: International Monetary Fund.

Moody's Investors Service. 2011. *Assessing Future Health- and Age-Related Government Expenditures in France, Germany, the UK and the US* (December). New York.

Moody's Investors Service. 2014. *Population Aging Will Dampen Economic Growth over the Next Two Decades* (August). New York.

Moody's Investors Service. 2017a. *Global Macro Risks: Collapse of Global Productivity Growth Remains Sizeable Risk to Credit Conditions* (May). New York.

Moody's Investors Service. 2017b. *Sovereign Contingent Liabilities: Public Enterprises Represent a Material Source of Fiscal Risk to Some Sovereigns* (January). New York.

Moody's Investors Service. 2017c. *Sovereigns: Global 2018 Outlook Stable as Healthy Growth Tempers High Debt, Geopolitical Tensions* (November). Singapore.

Moody's Investors Service. 2018. *Global Macro Outlook: 2018–2019 (February 2018 Update): Growth Will Hit a High-Water Mark in 2018 as Inflation and Interest Rates Gently Rise* (February). New York.

Appendix 2A   Country coverage in figure 2.1

Developed Economies

Asia: Hong Kong, Japan, Singapore, Korea, and Taiwan

Central and Eastern Europe and Central Asia: Czech Republic, Estonia, Latvia, Lithuania, Slovak Republic, and Slovenia

Middle East: Israel

North America: Canada and the United States

Oceania: Australia and New Zealand

Western Europe: Austria, Belgium, Cyprus, Denmark, Finland, France, Germany, Greece, Iceland, Ireland, Italy, Luxembourg, Malta, Netherlands, Norway, Portugal, Spain, Sweden, Switzerland, and the United Kingdom

Emerging Economies

Africa: Algeria, Angola, Burkina Faso, Cameroon, Côte d'Ivoire, Democratic Republic of the Congo, Egypt, Ethiopia, Ghana, Kenya, Madagascar, Malawi, Mali, Morocco, Mozambique, Niger, Nigeria, Senegal, South Africa, Sudan, Tanzania, Tunisia, Uganda, Zambia, and Zimbabwe

Asia: Bangladesh, Cambodia, China, India, Indonesia, Malaysia, Myanmar, Pakistan, Philippines, Sri Lanka, Thailand, and Vietnam

Central and Eastern Europe and Central Asia: Albania, Armenia, Azerbaijan, Belarus, Bosnia and Herzegovina, Bulgaria, Croatia, Georgia, Hungary, Kazakhstan, Kyrgyz Republic, Macedonia, Moldova, Poland, Romania, Russia, Serbia and Montenegro, Tajikistan, Turkey, Turkmenistan, Ukraine, and Uzbekistan

Latin America: Argentina, Barbados, Bolivia, Brazil, Chile, Colombia, Costa Rica, Dominican Republic, Ecuador, Guatemala, Jamaica, Mexico, Peru, St. Lucia, Trinidad and Tobago, Uruguay, and Venezuela

Middle East: Bahrain, Iran, Iraq, Jordan, Kuwait, Oman, Qatar, Saudi Arabia, the United Arab Emirates, and Yemen

3

Implications of Lower Trend Productivity Growth for Tax Policy

KAREN DYNAN

The slow observed rate of productivity growth in recent years has been a source of disappointment, concern, and—to some extent—surprise in both the academic and policymaking communities. In the United States, annual labor productivity growth in the nonfarm business sector averaged just 0.8 percent between 2012 and 2017 (figure 3.1).

Low rates of capital investment in the wake of the Great Recession may be contributing to recent sluggishness, but the disappointing performance of productivity growth appears to have roots that predate the downturn. A growing body of research documents a downshift in the rate of US labor productivity growth and total factor productivity growth in the early 2000s (Fernald 2015; Fernald et al. 2017). Other studies demonstrate that the slowdown in productivity growth extends well beyond the United States (Adler et al. 2017). Many advanced economies have seen low productivity growth in recent years. In the OECD countries, for example, productivity growth averaged 0.8 percent a year from 2011 to 2016.[1]

Because part of the slowdown in productivity growth appears to be a hangover from the Great Recession, many analysts are optimistic that the extremely low productivity growth rates of recent years will not persist. But most forecasters do not foresee productivity growth returning to long-run

Karen Dynan is a professor of the practice in Harvard University's Economics Department and nonresident senior fellow at the Peterson Institute for International Economics. She thanks Elena Duggar, Doug Elmendorf, Adam Posen, Louise Sheiner, and Jeromin Zettelmeyer for helpful comments and discussion.

1. This estimate is based on data on real GDP per hour worked from OECD.Stat.

Figure 3.1 Labor productivity growth in the US nonfarm business sector, 1949–2018

8-quarter moving average in percent

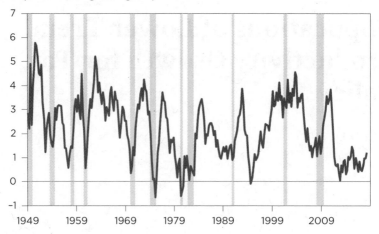

Note: Shaded bars correspond to recessions.
Source: US Bureau of Labor Statistics, www.bls.gov/lpc/data.htm.

historical averages. For example, in August 2018, the Congressional Budget Office (CBO) projected that under current fiscal policy, labor productivity growth in the US nonfarm business sector will pick up to 1.8 percent a year by the end of the coming decade, down from an average pace of 2.2 percent in the second half of the last century.[2] Results from the Survey of Professional Forecasters (SPF) suggest that many other forecasters foresee a similar shortfall in productivity growth relative to historical averages. The SPF results also suggest considerable downside risk to what forecasters expect on average. For example, about a quarter of SPF participants believe that productivity growth over the coming decade will be 35 basis points below the mean forecast and about one tenth expect productivity growth to be more than 1 percentage point below the mean.[3]

This chapter considers the implications of a sustained period of low productivity growth for the design of tax systems. To some extent, it draws on the large body of related literature on how to reform tax systems to boost

---

2. CBO forecasts for productivity growth are available under the heading "Potential GDP and Underlying Inputs" at www.cbo.gov/about/products/budget-economic-data.

3. As of January 2018, the mean SPF forecast for average labor productivity growth over the following decade was 1.6 percent, the 25th percentile of forecasts was 1.2 percent, and the 10th percentile was 0.5 percent. The SPF data are available at www.philadelphiafed.org/research-and-data/real-time-center/survey-of-professional-forecasters/data-files/prod10.

productivity growth (see, for example, IMF 2017). The central issue of interest in this chapter is different from that explored in those studies, however. The reforms to tax systems examined elsewhere emphasize reforms that are always desirable from an efficiency point of view. In contrast, this chapter explores changes that should be made in response to a decline in productivity growth relative to historical norms.

The chapter is organized as follows. It begins by stipulating lower trend productivity growth and discussing the key relevant economic implications. It then turns to the question of how to adapt tax policy to these changes. The discussion is organized around the major objectives of tax policy: collecting revenue, incentivizing work and saving, redistributing income, mitigating business cycle fluctuations, and improving resource allocation in other ways, such as minimizing tax-based distortions and correcting for externalities. Slower productivity growth and related changes in the economy have consequences for each of these objectives that suggest that some change in policy will be needed. The chapter concludes by summarizing the implications of a slowdown in productivity growth for tax policy.

Slower Productivity Growth and Key Economic Implications

All of the chapters in this volume are conditioned on the assumption that both labor productivity and total factor productivity growth rates settle at paces that are a few tenths of a percentage point below historical norms in the baseline and 0.5 percentage point lower than the baseline in the downside-risk scenario. The downside risk scenario is not implausible. Many forecasts of long-term productivity have been marked down by a similar amount over the last half-decade.[4] (Much of the discussion is qualitative, so the precise assumptions about productivity growth are not crucial.)

A sustained period of lower productivity growth would lead to changes in other factors that are relevant for tax policy. In particular, lower productivity growth would lead to lower interest rates, somewhat lower inflation, lower wage growth, and less "real bracket creep" in the tax code, each of which is addressed below. Although much of the discussion that follows cites evidence from the United States, most of the changes are expected in other countries as well (with the exception of the result for real bracket creep, which depends on the nature of each country's tax code).

---

4. For example, in its August 2012 forecast, CBO assumed that annual US labor productivity growth would settle at 2.1 percent over the longer run.

Figure 3.2 Congressional Budget Office projections of real interest rate on 10-year Treasury notes and potential output growth, 2012 and 2018

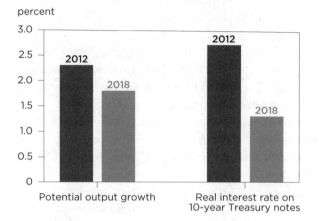

Note: Figure compares August 2012 forecasts with August 2018 forecasts.
Source: Congressional Budget Office.

Interest Rates

Economic theory predicts that the real interest rate will be lower when productivity growth is lower. Consistent with theory, forecasts of long-term real interest rates have been revised downward in recent years along with forecasts of economic growth over the longer run. Between 2012 and 2018, CBO reduced its projection of the real interest rate on 10-year Treasury notes as well as its projection of potential output growth (figure 3.2)

CBO's 1.4 percentage point downward revision to the real interest rate is a good deal larger than its 0.5 percentage point downward revision to the growth rate of potential output. The larger revision to the real interest rate is perhaps not surprising given that the low real interest rates of recent years have drawn attention to other factors that may be weighing on rates. These factors include the aging of the population, changes in global preferences for safe assets, and higher income inequality.

Theory can offer some guidance on how much interest rates decline when productivity growth falls. The Ramsey model of optimal consumption and saving over time implies that the amount by which interest rates decline with the growth rate of the economy depends on preferences. A simple version of the model yields the following relationship:

$$r_{t+1} = \rho + \sigma\, g_{t+1},$$

where r_{t+1} equals the real interest rate on saving between periods t and $t + 1$, ρ is inversely related to the rate of time discount, σ is inversely related to the intertemporal elasticity of substitution, and g_{t+1} is the growth rate of consumption between periods t and $t + 1$. In the steady state, g will be equal to the per capita growth rate of the economy, which is determined by productivity growth.

Reasonable parameter choices for ρ and σ imply that changes in real interest rates may have a roughly one-for-one relationship with changes in the growth rate of the economy, as a report by the Council of Economic Advisers (CEA 2015) shows. This result suggests that real interest rates might be between a few tenths (in the baseline scenario) and 0.75 percentage point (in the downside-risk scenario) lower than they would be if productivity growth were closer to its long-term historical average.

Of course, this calibration is sensitive to the underlying assumptions. If people are not very willing to substitute consumption over time, the model would imply even larger declines in real interest rates. Moreover, although other models of consumption and saving, such as the overlapping generations model, also suggest a link between productivity growth and the interest rate, the implied quantitative relationship could be different.

Inflation

The decline in interest rates that accompanies slower productivity will tend to make the effective lower bound on the federal funds rate more binding more of the time. This constraint on the ability of monetary policy to spur economic activity when aggregate demand is weak has a number of implications for macroeconomic performance (Kiley and Roberts 2017). It implies that inflation will be somewhat lower on average unless the Federal Reserve significantly alters its approach to policymaking or fiscal policy becomes significantly more countercyclical (a topic examined below).

Wage Growth

In the first three decades after World War II, wage growth in the United States closely tracked productivity growth. Since then the gap between aggregate productivity and various measures of average compensation has widened, even though the link between average productivity growth and average pay growth remained strong. The gap grew as a result of other factors that put downward pressure on workers' compensation (as Stansbury and Summers show in chapter 8 of this volume). A sustained productivity slowdown would be expected to further reduce wage growth.

A prolonged period of slow productivity growth could be particularly painful for workers at the lower end of the income distribution. The limited growth in the earnings of low- and middle-skill workers over the last several decades may partly reflect skill-biased technical change, which has reduced these workers' relative productivity (Violante 2008). Low productivity growth in the aggregate might therefore be associated with even lower productivity growth—and even lower wage growth—for some types of workers.

Slower wage growth has implications in and of itself for tax policy; it may also affect lifetime income paths. Wages tend to rise with age for many workers, for a number of reasons, one of which is rising economywide productivity. A reduction in productivity growth would therefore be expected to result in some flattening of the path of income over a worker's lifetime.

Real Bracket Creep

Tax systems are often largely indexed for inflation (in the United States, e.g., the federal tax code has been largely indexed for inflation since 1986). Such indexing takes away the traditional form of bracket creep, by which increases in nominal incomes that occur as a result of inflation push taxpayers into higher tax brackets. However, over time real growth in incomes will still push taxpayers into higher tax brackets through what might be called "real bracket creep." It subjects an ever-larger portion of income to higher tax rates and pushes more taxpayers above the eligibility threshold limits for various tax credits.

Slower productivity growth reduces the extent of real bracket creep. Because real bracket creep is quantitatively significant, a reduction in its magnitude may be an important consideration in tax policy. For the United States, CBO estimates that tax revenues as a share of GDP will rise by 1.1 percentage points over the next 30 years as a result of structural factors, particularly real bracket creep (CBO 2016). Real bracket creep also explains a significant part of the projected rise in the marginal tax rate on labor income in coming years.

The effects of real bracket creep are larger for lower- and middle-income households, because they lose eligibility for targeted tax credits such as the Earned Income Tax Credit and the Child Tax Credit. Therefore, a reduction in the magnitude of real bracket creep helps those households more than others. Louise Sheiner reports the results of a quantitative analysis of the effects on tax revenues of the changes in real bracket creep implied by the assumptions about productivity growth used in this volume (see chapter 4).

Objectives of Tax Policy

A straightforward way to think about the implications for tax policy of lower productivity growth and related changes in the economy is to consider each of the major objectives of tax policy:

- collect revenues,
- minimize disincentives for work,
- reduce disincentives for saving,
- redistribute income,
- mitigate business cycle fluctuations, and
- minimize tax-based distortions and correct for externalities.

Collecting Revenues

A tax system needs to collect enough revenues to sustain government benefits and purchases of goods and services. In the United States and many other countries, population aging is putting significant pressure on government spending, because a significant share of government benefits goes to older people.

Old-age dependency ratios—which measure the size of the population over the age of 65 relative to the size of the working-age population—are rising around the world (figure 3.3). In most countries, government social insurance programs provide both income support and health care for older people. Even if productivity growth were to remain close to its historical average, these spending needs would be expected to strain government budgets.

In a recent effort to quantify the uncertainty surrounding projections for the US Social Security program, CBO reported the results of simulations based on different assumptions for productivity growth and other key economic and demographic variables. In nearly all of these simulations, the program (as currently financed) would not be able to pay all scheduled benefits beyond the mid-2030s (CBO 2015). A sustained period of productivity growth that is substantially below historical norms would sharply increase these budget challenges, because under the current structures of taxes and benefits, lower productivity growth reduces the incomes of the working-age population (and thus tax revenue) by more than it reduces government benefits and services.

In 2016 CBO projected the federal debt as a percentage of GDP under current fiscal policy for both a baseline scenario for productivity growth and an alternative scenario in which average annual productivity growth is

Figure 3.3 Population 65 and older as share of working-age population in selected countries

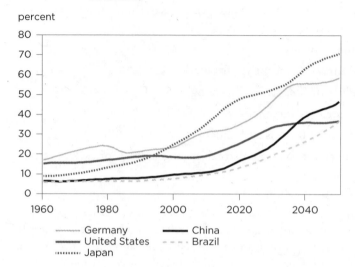

percent

Legend:
- Germany
- United States
- Japan
- China
- Brazil

Source: World Bank, http://databank.worldbank.org/data/source/health-nutrition-and-population-statistics.

0.5 percentage point lower.[5] Even under the baseline scenario, federal debt is projected to rise on an unsustainable path; the problem is more severe if productivity growth is lower than in the baseline (figure 3.4). With lower productivity growth, federal debt would be roughly 30 percent of GDP larger 30 years from now. This projection incorporates the reduction in interest rates that CBO expects would result from lower productivity growth (which should offset some of the direct effects of lower productivity growth).[6]

The CBO analysis embeds particular assumptions for a single country. Similar results (at least in terms of the degree to which the budget projec-

---

5. CBO published an updated but less detailed analysis in June 2018. Using that projection would have not have changed the discussion in the text, although the levels of projected debt in both the baseline and alternative scenarios would be somewhat higher because of the 2017 tax cuts.

6. A natural question would be whether the greater fiscal imbalances in the downside risk scenario reflect a smaller markdown in projected real interest rates than in assumed productivity growth, so that the projected unit cost of servicing the public debt is higher (see chapter 1 in this volume for a discussion of the relationship between debt servicing costs and fiscal sustainability). CBO did not publish its projections for interest rates in this scenario, so the question cannot be answered directly. However, footnote 9 in chapter 7 of the CBO document suggests that it may have changed its interest rate by slightly more than one for one with the change in assumed growth, suggesting that projected unit debt servicing costs are lower in this scenario.

Figure 3.4 Projected federal debt under baseline and downside risk productivity growth scenarios, 2000–46

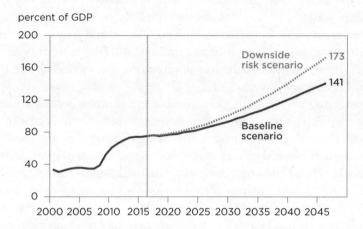

percent of GDP

Note: Figure assumes fiscal policy as of March 2016.
Source: CBO (2016).

tions worsen under the downside risk scenario) would be expected in other situations for the United States and for other countries.

The CBO analysis implies that a sustained period of slower productivity growth would require a larger increase in taxes (or a larger cut in government spending) to keep government debt on a sustainable course. In the United States, if spending is not changed, taxes will need to be increased relative to their current level to make fiscal policy sustainable; they will need to increase by almost 1 percent of GDP more (or roughly 5 percent of the current level more) if productivity growth is 0.5 percentage point lower than expected.

Reducing Disincentives for Work

The reduction in wage growth that would likely accompany a sustained period of low productivity growth would be expected to reduce the incentive of people to work, although this "substitution effect" would likely be offset in part by the "income effect" arising from people having lower total lifetime income. Labor force participation by prime-age men has been falling for years in many countries, with the United States experiencing one of the largest declines (CEA 2016). Indeed, over the last 60 years, the prime-age male labor force participation rate has fallen by roughly 10 percentage points. Studies suggest that many factors are contributing to the decline. The lack of robust wage growth for less-skilled workers appears to be one of the primary drivers (Black and Powell 2017). Female labor force participation has risen in many countries. In contrast, like male participation, it has been on the decline in the United States since the turn of the 21st century.

Lower labor force participation because of lower productivity growth would increase the fiscal pressures described above. It would be associated with less tax revenue from the working population and greater spending for programs that support low-income families. Both factors would exacerbate the budget imbalances created as populations age, increasing the importance of encouraging work.

Increasing labor force participation is also important because it increases engagement with society and the assessment of self-worth. Recent research suggests that not participating in the labor force appears to be associated with undesirable social consequences, such as "deaths of despair" (Case and Deaton 2017) and addiction to opioid pain medication (Krueger 2017).

The implication of these considerations is that tax systems should be modified to reduce disincentives for work. Doing so is especially important for the groups whose labor supply appears to be most responsive to changes in after-tax earnings—second earners—and groups for which the social consequences of being out of the workforce appear to be greatest—less-skilled men. For the former group, increasing childcare subsidies might increase labor supply. For the latter group, expanding the Earned Income Tax Credit could be effective.

The slowdown in real bracket creep that would result from lower productivity growth means that people's incomes rise above the ranges in which those tax provisions apply more slowly than they otherwise would. As a result, these changes can be less aggressive than they would otherwise have to be.

Reducing Disincentives for Saving

In considering the implications of slower productivity growth for tax disincentives to save, one should start by considering the implications of slower productivity growth for optimal national saving. In a Ramsey model, a reduction in trend productivity growth has an ambiguous effect on desired saving. The substitution effect (based on a lower return to saving) implies that less national saving would be desirable. The income effect (which arises from the fact that future generations are likely to be poorer) implies that more national saving would be desirable. Elmendorf and Sheiner (2016) report that, for their choices of parameter values for the Ramsey model, lower productivity growth in the United States today argues for slightly more national saving.[7]

---

7. Their Solow model approach is implicitly predicated on the view that the economy will be at full employment. Under the "secular stagnation" view of low productivity growth, the

One should also consider how lower productivity growth would affect optimal saving by individual households. If governments respond to the increased fiscal pressures in a low-productivity-growth world partly by cutting benefits for older people, people should save more while working. The flattening of lifetime income profiles that might arise from lower productivity growth would also argue for households saving more for retirement earlier in their working lives than they otherwise would.

The implications for tax policy are twofold. First, for the United States at least, given the desirability of slightly greater national saving, taxes should be raised (or spending reduced) by at least enough to fully offset the negative implications of lower productivity growth for the fiscal balance. Second, tax policy should be adjusted to provide further encouragement for household saving.

Why and how tax policy should be changed to encourage more household saving are complicated issues. Tax policy has an important role to play both because it can distort behavior and because even absent any tax-related distortions to behavior, many households appear to find it much more difficult to accumulate assets than traditional economic theory assumes (Dynan 2017). In principle, taxes on capital income can reduce saving. Empirical studies yield little evidence that reducing the marginal tax rate on investment and saving would materially raise saving, however, and doing so would have undesirable consequences on revenue collection and the distribution of after-tax income (see pages 8–9 of CBO 2014 for a discussion of this issue). The evidence suggests that defaults, nudges, and other aspects of behavioral design have much greater effects on the saving behavior of many households than do rates of return (Chetty et al. 2014). Therefore, encouraging saving through the tax code might best be done by offering tax breaks to offset the costs of firms establishing well-designed retirement saving plans for their employees.

Lower productivity growth is associated with less real bracket creep. One manifestation would be that households lose their eligibility more slowly for tax provisions that increase the return on saving for the lower part of the income distribution, such as the Saver's Credit in the United States. Economic theory would predict that less loss of eligibility might increase the

---

economy will not consistently be at full employment, because of a persistent shortfall of aggregate demand. This view might argue for policies that reduce national saving (at least relative to the demand for loanable funds). With GDP now close to potential GDP in the United States, and with the recent tax cuts likely to stimulate aggregate demand further, it is not clear that the United States will suffer from secular stagnation—and there are other ways to address it (such as a revenue-neutral policy that raises public or private investment) if it does arise. Other countries may suffer from secular stagnation, but there are multiple approaches to solving the problem.

saving of this group, implying less need for tax changes that would encourage saving. However, the empirical evidence suggests that these programs have limited success at encouraging saving (Duflo et al. 2006). As a result, lower real bracket creep probably would not make much of a difference in this context.

Redistributing Income

Lower trend productivity growth implies that the distribution of changes in compensation would be shifted in a direction that increases inequality. Even with no change in the degree of dispersion around the mean, lower mean compensation growth means that more people would experience no growth in or lower compensation.[8] Such outcomes are especially harmful in countries where nominal financial commitments are common (as in the United States, given the prevalence of fixed-rate mortgages). If lower productivity growth resulted in lower inflation, the problem could be even worse, given that inflation erodes the real burden of fixed nominal financial commitments over time.

Perhaps more important than this consideration, many people may be frustrated by a persistent lack of improvement in their standard of living because they expect that standards of living should improve over time. In the United States, about close to 60 percent of people expect today's children to be worse off financially than their parents (Pew Research Center 2017); findings for other advanced economies are similar. One would expect this share to grow if wage growth were to decline further, creating yet more frustration and anger about the economic and political system. Such sentiments can be politically destabilizing and hinder countries' ability to adopt policies that would be good for overall economic growth, such as reducing restrictions on international trade.

These considerations argue for using tax systems to increase the level of income redistribution in a world with slower trend productivity growth. Doing so could take two broad forms: providing more insurance against bad outcomes and creating more widespread opportunity. To provide more insurance against bad outcomes, governments could make their tax systems more progressive or strengthen the insurance features of their tax codes (e.g., by adopting a tax-based wage insurance program such as the one Kling 2006 describes). To create more widespread opportunity, governments could pro-

---

8. Furman and Orszag argue that lower productivity growth may be associated with higher inequality (see chapter 9 of this volume). They note that the relationship is not causal (in either direction); rather, reduced dynamism and competition cause both. If inequality is higher in a low productivity growth world, one might expect even more people to experience no or negative income growth.

vide more tax incentives for firms that provide training for their workers or more tax subsidies to finance higher education for low-income families.

The real bracket creep considerations in this context are mixed. On the one hand, people move into higher tax brackets more slowly with slower wage growth. As a result, the progressivity of the tax code rises more slowly absent explicit changes in the tax code, suggesting the need to increase its progressivity. On the other hand, lower-income people's incomes rise above eligibility thresholds for certain tax credits more slowly than they otherwise would, reducing the need to expand those credits.

Mitigating Business Cycle Fluctuations

Tax policy has long been used to help stabilize the economy in the face of a negative shock to aggregate demand. For example, countries sometimes legislate explicit changes to tax policy such as an income tax rebate to spur consumer demand or larger deductions for the depreciation of new investment to encourage business spending. In addition, some regular features of tax systems provide automatic countercyclical stimulus without deliberate policy changes. For example, the progressive income tax system in the United States automatically reduces taxes more than proportionately to income when the country enters a downturn.

Many countries used monetary policy as their primary macroeconomic stabilization tool in the decades leading up to the financial crisis. The perceived dominance of monetary policy in this context partly reflected the lags associated with developing, legislating, and implementing fiscal policy. Disagreement in the empirical literature about how effective fiscal policy is for countercyclical purposes may also have helped push policymakers to opt for monetary policy (see Ramey 2011 and Auerbach 2012).

Lower productivity growth has reduced real interest rates. As a result, central banks reach the effective lower bound on their policy rates more quickly when they reduce rates in the face of negative shocks to aggregate demand. The Federal Reserve cut the federal funds rate by more than 5 percentage points in each of the past three recessions. Its projections of future federal funds rates imply that it will have much less room to cut rates in the next downturn.[9]

Central banks have other tools for easing credit conditions when policy rates near zero, such as making large-scale asset purchases (sometimes known as quantitative easing [QE]), changing forward guidance about policy rates, and pushing policy rates into negative territory. A growing body of literature

---

9. As of June 2018, the median Federal Open Market Committee projection for the federal funds rate over the "longer run" was 2.9 percent.

is skeptical that these alternative tools are sufficient to offset the inability to lower policy rates substantially, however (Blanchard and Summers 2017).

With the countercyclical power of monetary policy blunted, countercyclical fiscal policy will be substantially more important in stabilizing macroeconomic conditions going forward, increasing the need to strengthen the automatic stabilizers in tax systems. Specific approaches deserve further study. In the United States, one possibility would be to legislate automatic reductions in payroll taxes when unemployment rates hit certain thresholds and coupling the measure with automatic general revenue contributions to Social Security to make up for the forgone revenue.[10] Policymakers should also be prepared to take discretionary fiscal policy actions to counter economic downturns.

Minimizing Other Distortions in Resource Allocation

Tax policy should aim to minimize tax-based distortions in resource allocation and correct for externalities that distort the allocation of resources apart from taxes. A large body of literature documents ways in which current tax systems lead to misallocations of resources, including distorting investment across industries and asset types, the choice of financing for investment, and how businesses are organized and where they are located (IMF 2017). In addition, current tax systems often do not do enough to correct for both negative and positive spillovers of certain kinds of economic activity, such as the harmful effects of carbon emissions and other kinds of pollution and the beneficial effects of much research and technological development.

Improving tax systems to address these problems is important regardless of underlying productivity growth; it is especially important when productivity growth is weak. Making tax systems more efficient should be a high priority for policymakers if productivity growth falls 0.5 percentage point below the already modest baseline projections.

Conclusion

A sustained period of very low productivity growth—together with various accompanying changes in the economic environment—would justify a number of changes in tax policy. Given aging populations, many countries could face significant fiscal shortfalls in coming years even if productivity growth were to rebound to historical averages. Lower productivity growth would reduce the income of the working population, exacerbating these challenges, because tax revenues would fall. Even assuming that lower pro-

---

10. Blinder (2016) discusses other options along these lines.

ductivity growth results in lower interest rates, tax systems will need to collect more revenue per dollar of GDP to support their aging populations.

Lower incomes are also likely to put downward pressure on labor force participation rates, increasing budget pressures (because tax revenues from the working population would be even lower and spending on social insurance programs might need to rise). This consideration suggests a need to increase tax incentives for working, particularly for groups that are very responsive to such incentives and groups for which the social consequences of dropping out of the labor force are most harmful.

Although the optimal level of national saving appears to be little changed by the assumption of lower productivity growth (at least in the United States), there would arguably be a need for lower- and middle-income households to start saving for retirement earlier given the possibilities of flatter lifetime income profiles. The potential for future cuts in government benefits also argues for more retirement saving incentives for such households. Research suggests that changing the after-tax return on savings would not have a large effect on the saving of this group and that changes in tax law that encouraged more well-designed workplace retirement saving plans are likely to have a larger effect.

The lower real interest rates that would result from sustained low productivity growth reinforce concerns about the future efficacy of monetary policy as a macroeconomic stabilization tool, lending support to the view that the tax system should build in more automatic stabilizers. The fiscal and social consequences of the lower income growth that would result from lower productivity growth raise the urgency of moving toward a tax system that minimizes distortions to resource allocation.

Even if future productivity growth were to follow the baseline assumption (only slightly below the historical average), it would probably be worthwhile for tax systems to move in many of the directions suggested in this chapter. Many countries are already on track to experience fiscal imbalances, low income growth has already had many negative social consequences, concerns about the limits of future monetary policy are already widespread, and countries should always be seeking to minimize distortions from their tax systems.

The specific tax system changes needed will vary by country and depend on how much a reduction in productivity growth would reduce interest rates and change income growth at different points in the distribution. One lesson of the last few decades is that changes in aggregate productivity growth may have very different impacts on incomes at different points in the distribution; such variation has social and fiscal consequences.

Political feasibility is another important issue. If the optimal policies cannot be achieved, policymakers should consider second-best alternatives.

References

Adler, Gustavo, Romain Duval, Davide Furceri, Sinem Kiliç Çelik, Ksenia Koloskova, and Marcos Poplawski-Ribeiro. 2017. *Gone with the Headwinds: Global Productivity*. IMF Staff Discussion Note 17/04. Washington: International Monetary Fund.

Auerbach, Alan J. 2012. The Fall and Rise of Keynesian Fiscal Policy. *Asian Economic Policy Review* (December): 157–75.

Black, Sandra, and Wilson Powell. 2017. Where Have All the (Male) Workers Gone? Econofact (July 10).

Blanchard, Olivier, and Lawrence Summers. 2017. *Rethinking Stabilization Policy. Back to the Future* (October). Washington: Peterson Institute for International Economics.

Blinder, Alan S. 2016. *Fiscal Policy Reconsidered*. Policy Proposal 2016-05. Washington: Brookings Hamilton Project.

Case, Anne, and Angus Deaton. 2017. Mortality and Morbidity in the 21st Century. *Brookings Papers on Economic Activity* (Spring). Washington: Brookings Institution.

CBO (Congressional Budget Office). 2014. *How CBO Analyzes the Effects of Changes in Federal Fiscal Policies on the Economy* (November). Washington.

CBO (Congressional Budget Office). 2015. *CBO's 2015 Long-Term Projections for Social Security: Additional Information* (December). Washington.

CBO (Congressional Budget Office). 2016. *The 2016 Long-Term Budget Outlook* (July). Washington.

CBO (Congressional Budget Office). 2018. *The 2018 Long-Term Budget Outlook* (June). Washington.

CEA (Council of Economic Advisers). 2015. *Long-Term Interest Rates: A Survey* (July). Washington.

CEA (Council of Economic Advisers). 2016. *The Long-Term Decline in Prime-Age Male Labor Force Participation* (June). Washington.

Chetty, Raj, John N. Friedman, Søren Leth-Petersen, Torben Heien Nielsen, and Tore Olsen. 2014. Active vs. Passive Decisions and Crowd-Out in Retirement Savings Accounts: Evidence from Denmark. *Quarterly Journal of Economics* 129, no. 3: 1141–219.

Duflo, Esther, William Gale, Jeffrey Liebman, Peter Orszag, and Emmanuel Saez. 2006. Saving Incentives for Low- and Middle-Income Families: Evidence from a Field Experiment with H&R Block. *Quarterly Journal of Economics* 121, no. 4: 1311–46.

Dynan, Karen. 2017. Many American Households Are Still Struggling to Build Wealth. Econofact (October 7).

Elmendorf, Douglas, and Louise Sheiner. 2016. *Federal Budget Policy with an Aging Population and Persistently Low Interest Rates*. Working Paper 18. Washington: Brookings Hutchins Center.

Fernald, John G. 2015. Productivity and Potential Output before, during, and after the Great Recession. *NBER Macroeconomics Annual* 29, no. 1. Cambridge, MA: National Bureau of Economic Research.

Fernald, John G., Robert E. Hall, James H. Stock, and Mark W. Watson. 2017. The Disappointing Recovery of Output after 2009. *Brookings Papers on Economic Activity* (Spring). Washington: Brookings Institution.

IMF (International Monetary Fund). 2017. Upgrading the Tax System to Boost Productivity. *IMF Fiscal Monitor* (April). Washington.

Kiley, Michael T., and John M. Roberts. 2017. Monetary Policy in a Low Interest Rate World *Brookings Papers on Economic Activity* (Spring). Washington: Brookings Institution.

Kling, Jeff. 2006. *Fundamental Restructuring of Unemployment Insurance: Wage-Loss Insurance and Temporary Earnings Replacement Accounts.* Policy Brief 2006-05. Washington: Brookings Hamilton Project.

Krueger, Alan. 2017. Where Have All the Workers Gone? An Inquiry into the Decline of the U.S. Labor Force Participation Rate. *Brookings Papers on Economic Activity* (Fall). Washington: Brookings Institution.

Pew Research Center. 2017. Children's Financial Future. *Global Indicators Database*. Washington. Available at www.pewglobal.org/database/indicator/74/survey/all/response/Worse+off/.

Ramey, Valerie A. 2011. Can Government Purchases Stimulate the Economy? *Journal of Economic Literature* 49, no. 3: 673–85.

Violante, Giovanni L. 2008. Skill-Biased Technical Change. In *The New Palgrave Dictionary of Economics*, 2nd. ed., ed. Steven N. Durlauf and Lawrence E. Blume. London: Palgrave Macmillan.

4

Effects of Low Productivity Growth on Fiscal Sustainability in the United States

LOUISE SHEINER

Productivity growth in the United States slowed in the past decade. After rising 2.2 percent a year between 1996 and 2004, growth in labor productivity slowed to an average rate of just 1.0 percent between 2004 and 2015.[1]

Analysts disagree about the prospects for productivity growth. Some, like Robert Gordon, see growth continuing to be relatively muted. Others, like Erik Brynjolffson, expect productivity growth to pick up rapidly as the economy learns to make better use of recent advances in computing and robotics.[2]

Productivity growth is the key determinant of changes in future living standards, because with slower productivity growth, consumption grows more slowly. Productivity growth is also an important conditioning assumption for projections of government revenues and expenditures, which tend to move with GDP. Although the Congressional Budget Office (CBO) sometimes presents the sensitivity of its projections to its assumptions about productivity growth, it does not release the details of its analysis or examine the channels through which productivity might affect the fiscal

Louise Sheiner is the Robert S. Kerr Senior Fellow at the Hutchins Center on Fiscal and Monetary Policy at the Brookings Institution. She is grateful to Vivien Lee for excellent research assistance and to Jeromin Zettelmeyer, Karen Dynan, Axel Börsch-Supan, and Adam Posen for helpful comments.

1. Based on CBO data supplementing information in CBO (2017), www.cbo.gov/publication/52480.

2. "The Future of Work and Innovation: Robert Gordon and Erik Brynjolfsson Debate at TED2013," https://blog.ted.com/the-future-of-work-and-innovation-robert-gordon-and-erik-brynjolfsson-debate-at-ted2013/.

outlook. In addition, because of the complexities of modeling policies across 50 states, there are few analyses of the effects of productivity growth on the budgets of state and local government.

This chapter explores the implications of productivity growth for the long-term outlook for government budgets. It is organized as follows. The first section examines the low-productivity scenario and the relationship between productivity growth and interest rates. The second section assesses the direct effect of changes in productivity growth on federal, state, and local government revenues and noninterest spending. The third section explores the impact of a productivity slowdown on interest costs and debt dynamics. Because of the lack of CBO-like projections for state and local governments, the analysis of them is less comprehensive, although it does shed some light on the channels through which productivity might affect the state and local sector. The last section summarizes the chapter's main findings.

Low Productivity and the Relationship between Productivity Growth and Interest Rates

Debt and Deficit Projections

Under current law, CBO regularly publishes 10- and 30-year projections of federal budget deficits and federal debt. The most recent 10-year projection—which incorporates the effects of the legislation enacted in late 2017 and early 2018—shows that the deficit rises from 3.5 percent of GDP in 2017 to 5.0 percent in 2028, and the federal debt climbs from 78 percent to 96 percent of GDP (CBO 2018b).[3] The most recent 30-year projection preceded the recent legislation. Incorporating the legislation would mean that the projected federal debt would climb from 77 percent of GDP in 2017 to about 134 percent of GDP by 2043.[4,5] The projected increases in

---

3. The legislation consists of the Tax Cuts and Jobs Act of 2017, the Bipartisan Budget Act of 2018, and the Consolidated Appropriations Act 2018.

4. The basic methodology behind these calculations is to take each part of the budget—Social Security, Medicare, individual income tax revenues, and so forth—and extend it past 2028 (the last year of the most recent CBO 10-year projection) using the growth rates for those components in the *March 2017 Long-Term Budget Outlook* (CBO 2017). I made two exceptions to this procedure for parts of recent legislation that are likely to change growth rates after 2028. First, I estimated the effects of switching from the Consumer Price Index for All Urban Consumers (CPI-U) to the chained CPI for individual income taxes. Second, I made a rough estimate of the effects of the repeal of the individual mandate under the Affordable Care Act on tax revenues. Both modifications were modest and had the effect of lowering future deficits.

5. Although the recent legislation increases deficits in the near term, it reduces them further out. Thus the debt-to-GDP ratio in 2028 is higher than it was in CBO's *March 2017 Long-Term Budget Outlook* (CBO 2017) but about the same by 2043. The budgetary effects of the recently enacted legislation were muted by the fact that many of the provisions that raised deficits are

deficits and debt can be attributed to population aging, as the other forces on the budget—rising revenues, falling nonentitlement spending, and steep increases in medical costs—are essentially offsetting (Sheiner 2018).

Projected Changes in Productivity

Productivity growth—the efficiency with which inputs are turned into outputs—is a key assumption underlying these projections. To some extent, the slowdown in productivity may reflect temporary factors associated with the aftermath of the Great Recession. CBO expects labor productivity to average 1.6 percent a year over the next 25 years, about the same as the average over the past 30 years but well below the rates observed during the high-productivity years of the late 1990s and early 2000s.[6]

Productivity growth is extremely difficult to predict, but many commentators believe that it is likely to remain subdued. To measure a reasonable downside risk, I analyze the effects of a 0.6 percentage point decline in economywide labor productivity growth, so that it rises about 1.0 percent a year instead of the 1.6 percent assumed by CBO in its baseline projections (figure 4.1).

I assume that the decline in productivity growth relative to CBO's baseline affects income growth uniformly across the board rather than having differential effects by skill or income level. This assumption is important, because the distribution of income has important implications for government revenues and expenditures. Whether this assumption is reasonable is hard to know. Many observers believe that the widening disparity in income observed in the United States over recent decades is attributable to the fact that technological advancements have improved the productivity of the highly skilled but not people at the bottom of the skill distribution. If productivity growth is slowing, it could be slowing across the board or at the top of the earnings distribution.[7]

---

temporary. For example, the individual income tax cuts expire in 2025, and the discretionary spending caps are lifted for only two years. Auerbach, Gale, and Krupkin (2018) estimate that given a baseline in which today's policies are assumed to continue (a current policy baseline instead of a current law baseline), the deficit would reach 7 percent of GDP by 2028.

6. I use CBO's *March 2017 Long-Term Budget Outlook* (CBO 2017) measure for labor productivity (the ratio of real output to hours worked). Productivity growth is often measured for the nonfarm business sector, omitting the household, nonprofit, and government sectors. Here I use the figures for the whole economy, because they are more relevant for projecting government revenues and expenditures. CBO's 10-year reports use a different measure—potential labor productivity—which is the ratio of potential output to the potential labor force size.

7. It is also possible to imagine scenarios in which a slowdown in productivity growth goes hand in hand with widening income inequality. Such a scenario might occur, for example, if the productivity slowdown were coupled with an increasing productivity divergence between

Figure 4.1 Labor productivity in the United States, 1991–2042

output per hour overall economy (five-year moving average, percent)

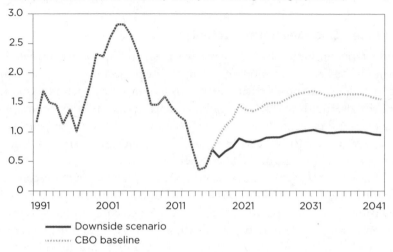

Downside scenario
CBO baseline

CBO = Congressional Budget Office
Source: Based on CBO data supplementing information in CBO (2017),
www.cbo.gov/publication/52480.

Productivity Growth and Interest Rates

Assumptions about interest rates are important in projecting the fiscal outlook. They likely depend on productivity growth. There is a strong theoretical link between interest rates and productivity growth. In both the Ramsey model and the baseline New Keynesian model, two common models of economic growth, interest rates move with productivity growth, as Hamilton et al. (2015) note.[8] The exact relationship depends on the intertemporal elasticity of consumption, which measures how willing people are to forgo consumption today in order to consume more tomorrow. A decline in productivity growth means that people will be poorer in the future. When consumption is not very substitutable across time, people respond to perceptions of a less rosy future by increasing saving now, in order to mitigate the impact on future consumption, pushing down interest rates. However, when

highly productive and less productive firms (as documented by Andrews, Criscuolo, and Gal 2016 for firms in the OECD since the early 2000s), or if the slowdown in productivity were caused by a reduction in competition and economic dynamism (as suggested by Furman and Orszag 2018).

8. These growth models relate the safe real rate to a representative consumer's discount factor and expected consumption growth; they tie the equilibrium rate to the trend rate of growth in consumption (and thus the economy).

consumption is very substitutable over time, people do not increase saving much in response to lower future income, and interest rates do not decline as much.

Empirically, there is some evidence that interest rates do move with productivity growth. Laubach and Williams (2015) estimate that a 1 percentage point reduction in the growth rate of the economy lowers interest rates by 1.3 percentage points. Pointing to empirical estimates of the intertemporal elasticity of consumption, Lukasz and Smith (2015) and Mehrotra (chapter 1 of this volume) suggest that a 1 percentage point reduction in productivity growth could lower interest rates by as much as 2 percentage points.

However, Hamilton et al. (2015) note that the relationship between interest rates and productivity growth is "much more tenuous than widely believed." They show that the correlation of average US GDP growth with average interest rates from peak to peak varies across time and across samples and is often negative or zero. They argue that "if, indeed, we are headed for stagnation for supply-side reasons, any such slowdown should not be counted on to translate to a lower equilibrium rate over periods as short as a cycle or two or a decade."

Because of this uncertainty, I analyze the effects of a productivity slowdown under three different assumptions about interest rates: interest rates move one for one with productivity growth, interest rates move two for one with productivity growth, and interest rates are invariant to productivity growth.

Effect of Changes in Productivity on Government Revenues, Noninterest Spending, and Poverty

The effect of productivity growth on government deficits and fiscal sustainability depends on the extent to which government spending and revenues are implicitly "indexed" to GDP growth. If spending and revenues moved one for one with GDP and the government had no debt, changes in productivity growth would not affect fiscal sustainability; deficits relative to GDP and ratios of debt to GDP would be unaffected. Of course, even in this case, lower productivity growth would have real effects on taxpayers. Government spending and tax payments would both be lower, but no new legislation would be required to restore fiscal sustainability.

If, however, government outlays and revenues do not move one for one with productivity growth, changes in productivity growth can affect the fiscal outlook and require policy changes to restore fiscal sustainability. If, for example, tax collections move with GDP but government spending does not, a decline in productivity will increase the deficit.

**Figure 4.2 Composition of federal, state, and local
tax revenues in the United States, 2017**

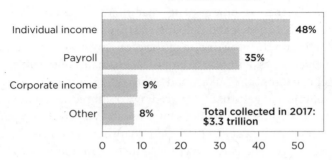

a. Federal revenues

Individual income — 48%
Payroll — 35%
Corporate income — 9%
Other — 8%

Total collected in 2017: $3.3 trillion

Source: CBO (2018a).

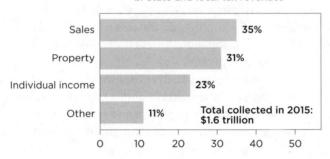

b. State and local tax revenues

Sales — 35%
Property — 31%
Individual income — 23%
Other — 11%

Total collected in 2015: $1.6 trillion

Source: Author's calculations based on US Census Bureau, State and Local Government Finances, Table 1.

In addition, when the government holds debt, a slowdown in GDP growth boosts the debt-to-GDP ratio and makes fiscal sustainability more difficult. If interest rates also decline, this effect will be muted or even reversed, depending on how much interest rates fall. If interest rates fall one for one with productivity growth, holding the primary deficit constant as a share of GDP, the debt-to-GDP ratio will not change very much with a productivity slowdown.

In the rest of this chapter, I examine the implications of the downside productivity scenario on the federal and state and local outlooks.

Effect on Federal Revenues

Individual income taxes and payroll taxes are by far the most important components of federal revenues (figure 4.2a). How do they move with productivity?

Federal Individual Income Taxes

The individual income tax system in the United States is progressive and almost fully indexed to inflation, so that increases in inflation do not push people into higher tax brackets. However, the tax system is not indexed for real income growth. As productivity gains increase national income, more and more income is pushed into higher tax brackets, and tax collections increase. This phenomenon is known as "real bracket creep," because real growth causes average tax rates to creep up over time. In the *June 2018 Long-Term Budget Outlook*, CBO estimated that real bracket creep would increase federal individual income taxes by 1.4 percent of GDP over the next 30 years (CBO 2018b).[9]

A slowdown in productivity growth would reduce real bracket creep. Given average annual growth of real labor productivity of 1.6 percent in the baseline and 1.0 percent in the low-productivity scenario, real income is 60 percent higher in the baseline and 35 percent higher in the low-productivity scenario after 30 years.[10] Assuming that the effects of real bracket creep rise linearly with income growth, rather than boosting tax revenues by 1.4 percent of GDP as in the baseline, real bracket creep under a low-productivity scenario would increase tax revenues by only about 0.8 percent of GDP.[11] By the 30th year of the low-productivity scenario, federal individual income tax revenues as a share of GDP would be about 0.6 percentage point lower than in the baseline. Assuming that individual income taxes decline linearly over time, the share of individual income taxes in GDP would rise 0.02 percentage point less a year under the low-productivity scenario than in the baseline, with the difference averaging 0.25 percent of GDP over 25 years.

Payroll Taxes

For payroll taxes, tax collections move close to one for one with wages (and hence productivity), because the tax rate is mostly flat. Social Security taxes (half levied on employers and half levied on employees) are equal to 12.4 percent of wages up to a cap ($128,400 in 2018). The cap is adjusted annually, so that it rises with economywide average wages. Lower productivity

---

9. The average productivity growth assumed over the next 30 years is just slightly lower than in the 2017 projection.

10. CBO uses the GDP deflator to calculate real productivity growth and the chained-CPI to calculate real bracket creep. Both are projected to rise at roughly the same rate. The reduction in real productivity growth thus translates into about a one-for-one reduction in real taxable income.

11. This estimate is a rough one, because the effects of productivity growth on real bracket creep are unlikely to be linear. Once all income is in the highest tax bracket, the system is no longer progressive, and real bracket creep ends.

Table 4.1 Effect of slower productivity growth on federal revenues in the United States (percent)

Item	GDP share, 2018	Average share of GDP, 2018–42	Estimated change relative to GDP over 25 years
Taxes			
Individual income	8.2	9.6	–0.25
Payroll	5.9	6.1	0
Corporate	1.2	1.5	0
Other	1.4	1.2	0
Total revenues	16.6	18.4	–0.25

Source: Author's calculations based on CBO (2017, 2018a).

growth that lowers wages equally across the board reduces Social Security taxes proportionately.[12]

For most workers, the Medicare tax is 2.9 percent of all wages (paid half by employers and half by employees). However, two types of Medicare taxes are levied only on high-income taxpayers, adding a progressive component to the Medicare tax. First, individual taxpayers with earnings of more than $200,000 and couples with earnings of more than $250,000 face an additional 0.9 percent tax on their earnings above those amounts. Second, taxpayers with income above these amounts face a 3.8 percent tax on net investment income. Although these taxes represent only a small share of payroll taxes (on the order of 2 percent in 2018), the thresholds are not indexed, so that over time they will affect a larger share of earners. The tax rate is low and the share small, however, so real bracket creep will have negligible effects on payroll tax collections.

Federal Tax Summary

Table 4.1 summarizes the effects of the downside productivity scenario on federal revenues. Only individual income taxes are likely to fall as a share of GDP from a slowdown in productivity growth, and the effect is not large, averaging less than 0.25 percent of GDP over 25 years.

Effect on State and Local Revenues

State and local governments collected revenues of $1.6 trillion in 2015 (figure 4.2b). Sales tax (35 percent) and property tax (31 percent) together accounted for about two-thirds of these revenues.

---

12. The earned income tax credit, which can offset payroll taxes paid by lower-income workers, is treated as part of the income tax scheme.

Table 4.2 Average federal and state income tax rates in the United States by expanded cash income percentile (percent)

Income level	Federal	State
Quintile		
Bottom	-4.8	0
Second	-1.9	0.7
Middle	2.9	1.3
Fourth	6.1	1.8
Top	13.1	3
All	8.1	2.2
Bracket		
80–90 percent	8	2.2
90–95 percent	10	2.5
95–99 percent	13.9	3
Top 1 percent	20.2	4.3

Source: Sammartino and Francis (2016).

State Individual Income Taxes

The degree of progressivity in income taxes varies widely across states. According to Sammartino and Francis (2016), 41 states have a broad-based income tax; 33 of these states have a graduated rate structure with multiple tax brackets. In many states, the top tax bracket begins at a very low income level, however, so that most income is taxed at the highest tax bracket, leaving very little room for real bracket creep. In other states, tax rates rise measurably with income.

Table 4.2 reproduces the table on the variation in tax rates by income in Sammartino and Francis (2016). It shows that state tax rates are much lower than federal tax rates and vary much less. Thus although state tax collections as a share of GDP may decline with lower productivity growth, the effect is likely to be very small.

State and Local Property Taxes

Property taxes account for about a third of state and local tax revenue. Changes in the property tax base therefore have important implications for the health of state and local finances.

A simple model of the value of residential property would suggest that a change in productivity growth could affect the ratio of property values to GDP. If one assumes that the value of real property is the discounted present value of housing rent, the value of real property is

$$V = R \int_0^\infty e^{-(r-g)t}$$ (4.1)

which solves to

$$V = \frac{R}{(r-g)}$$ (4.2)

where R is housing rent, r is the interest rate, g is GDP growth, and t is time. If, as the data appear to indicate, rents move with GDP,[13] so that $R = b * GDP$,

$$V = \frac{b * GDP}{(r-g)}$$ (4.3)

and

$$\frac{V}{GDP} = \frac{b}{(r-g)}$$ (4.4)

In steady state, when r and g are fixed, the property tax base is a constant proportion of GDP.

What happens when productivity growth falls? If interest rates move one for one with productivity growth, $r - g$ will be unchanged, and a slow-down in productivity will not change the share of property taxes in GDP. However, if interest rates decline more than productivity growth, so that the denominator in equation (4.4) declines, a reduction in productivity growth can raise the share of property taxes in GDP, holding tax rates constant. If interest rates do not fall when productivity growth falls, a decline in productivity growth will lower the ratio of property taxes to GDP, putting pressure on state and local governments.

Sales Taxes

General sales taxes move one for one with consumption, which moves with productivity and GDP. Sales tax collections that are administered as a percent of sales are thus likely to be a constant share of GDP.

State and Local Tax Summary

State and local revenues will remain about constant as a share of GDP if interest rates move one for one with labor productivity growth, which seems like a reasonable base case. If interest rates do not move with productivity growth, states may see higher tax revenues relative to GDP.

---

13. The share of housing and utility services in consumption has been about 18 percent since 1980 (Bureau of Economic Analysis, 2018, Table 2.3.5 Personal Consumption Expenditures by Major Type of Product, https://bea.gov/iTable/iTable.cfm?reqid=19&step=3&isuri=1&1910=x&0=-9&1921=survey&1903=6&1904=2015&1905=2017&1906=a&1911=0#reqid=19&step=3&isuri=1&1921=survey&1903=65).

Figure 4.3 Federal, state, and local government outlays in the United States, 2017

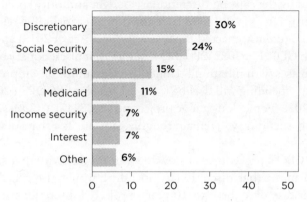

a. Federal outlays (21 percent of GDP)

Source: CBO (2018a).

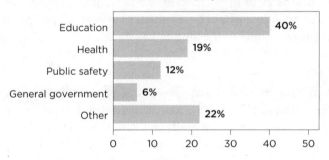

b. State and local spending out of own funds (10 percent of GDP)

Note: Includes all spending less charges, utilities, liquor store revenue, and federal grants.

Sources: Author's calculations based on data from US Census Bureau, State and Local Government Finances, 2015, Table 1; Office of Management and Budget, Historical Table 12.2.

Effect on Federal Noninterest Spending and Poverty

The effect of a productivity slowdown on spending will depend on several factors, including program rules and the effects of productivity on relative prices, healthcare demand, and interest rates. To gauge the effects, it is necessary to examine each major element of government spending (figure 4.3a).

Discretionary Spending

It is hard to know how to project discretionary spending on a "current law" basis, because discretionary spending is subject to annual appropriations by legislators rather than controlled by program rules. CBO makes different assumptions about discretionary spending for the first 10 years of its projection than for its last 20 years. Over the first 10 years, CBO projects that discretionary spending will fall as a share of GDP. Through 2021, spending is controlled by the caps on discretionary budget authority specified in the Budget Control Act of 2011 (and later amendments, including relevant provisions of the recently enacted Bipartisan Budget Act of 2018) and will not change with GDP. For 2022–28, CBO assumes that discretionary budget authority increases with inflation.[14] Under those assumptions, it projects that discretionary spending will decline from 6.3 percent of GDP in 2017 to 5.4 percent in 2028. For its long-range projection (2028–47), CBO assumes that discretionary spending will remain roughly constant as a share of GDP at its 2028 level.

Under CBO's procedures, a slowdown in productivity that starts next year would mean that discretionary spending would rise a little relative to GDP, because over the next 10 years, projected discretionary spending would be unchanged while GDP growth slowed. A slowdown in productivity growth of 0.6 percentage point would increase the share of discretionary spending in 2028 to 5.7 percent, 0.3 percentage point higher than in the baseline. Spending would be assumed to stay at 5.7 percent of GDP throughout the remainder of the long-term forecast.

Social Security

Social security benefits are indexed to wages, so benefits decline when productivity falls. However, benefits for retirees are indexed to the CPI, not real wages, so they are unaffected by a productivity slowdown (put another way, retirees do not get the benefits of real wage growth once they retire and are unaffected when wage growth slows). When productivity growth falls, government spending on Social Security benefits falls, too, albeit by less than GDP, thereby raising the share of Social Security in GDP.

The 2017 Social Security Trustees report contains information on the effects of productivity growth on benefits (Board of Trustees 2017). It shows that a decline in real wage growth from 1.2 to 0.6 percent (using the CPI deflator to define real wages) increases the share of Social Security spending in GDP by 0.3 percentage point on average over the next 25 years.[15] Because inflation using the CPI deflator is about 0.4 percentage point higher than inflation using the GDP deflator, this sensitivity analysis indicates what

---

14. Budget authority allows agencies to contract to spend certain amounts; some of that spending may actually occur in later years.

15. Board of Trustees (2017, Table VI.D4) shows the effect on taxable payroll. Table VI.G5 shows the relationship between taxable payroll and GDP. I assume this relationship is invariant to productivity changes.

would happen to Social Security spending were annual labor productivity growth to fall from 1.6 to 1.0 percent.

This calculation ignores a number of potential effects, including the possibility that changes in productivity will affect life expectancy, fertility, labor force participation and hours, immigration, and the share of compensation that is taxable (which also affects benefits, which are based on taxable wages). These effects are not likely to have large effects on spending, however, particularly over the next 25 years.

More important is the assumption that a slowdown in productivity growth affects wages across the board. The wage base that determines Social Security taxes and benefits is capped. If productivity growth mostly affects wages at the top of the wage distribution, Social Security benefits would not decline as much with productivity growth, and the increase in Social Security outlays as a share of GDP would be larger than estimated here.

Medicare

Medicare spending increased from 1.2 percent of GDP in 1980 to 3.8 percent in 2015.[16] The forces driving the increase are largely the same as those driving up health spending in general. They include the effects of higher income on healthcare demand, improvements in technology, and relative price pressures. Analysts disagree about the importance of each of these factors (see, e.g., Technical Review Panel Report 2012, p. 47), mostly because they disagree about whether the observed increase in measured health prices represents true relative price increases or mismeasurement related to the lack of quality adjustments in healthcare services.

Regardless of why health spending has increased in the past, forecasting health spending is extremely difficult. It has tended to increase faster than GDP, but it cannot continue to do so forever (lest it take up all of GDP) and is therefore likely to eventually decelerate.

Both CBO and the Medicare Trustees develop detailed year-by-year forecasts for the first 10 years of the projection. Because of the way Medicare payments are set, both agencies would lower their projections of Medicare spending over the next 10 years if productivity growth were to slow.[17] The reduction would probably be roughly in line with GDP, although it is possible that Medicare spending would not slow quite as much.

---

16. Medicare Spending Net of Beneficiary Premiums, CBO Historical Budget Data, June 2017, www.cbo.gov/about/products/budget-economic-data#2.

17. In particular, the payment rates for many parts of Medicare are set as equal to the growth in prices less the 10-year average of economywide multifactor productivity growth. The 10-year average would mean that Medicare payments would slow more slowly than GDP. But lower productivity growth would also lower demand for health spending, which would likely lead to some reduction as well.

The agencies take different approaches after the first 10 years. Acknowledging the inherent difficulty in making long-range projections of health spending, CBO has taken a formulaic approach. It assumes that the rate of excess cost growth in Medicare—defined as the difference between per beneficiary health spending and per capita GDP—will decline linearly from year 10 (2027) to year 30 of its forecast, and end at 1 (i.e., in 30 years per beneficiary spending is projected to rise 1 percentage point faster than per capita GDP).[18] Because of this one-for-one relationship between Medicare spending and GDP growth, a slowdown in productivity would have little effect on CBO's projection of Medicare spending as a share of GDP.

The Medicare Trustees take a slightly different approach, decomposing changes in health spending into its various factors. Doing so requires specifying and projecting the income elasticity of health spending, relative price inflation, and price elasticities. To slow spending over the projection future, the Trustees assume a falling income elasticity of demand and a rising price elasticity. Because they start their projection with an income elasticity of demand greater than 1, however, they would likely project that a fall in productivity would lead to a reduction in Medicare spending as a share of the economy. Over the first 25 years of their projection, this effect would likely be quite small. Assuming that Medicare spending grows in line with GDP is thus reasonable.

One question is whether the reduction in Medicare spending would mean a real reduction in health services. If medical prices increase because the health sector is labor intensive—and thus has slower labor productivity growth than the economy as a whole (i.e., is subject to Baumol's cost disease; Baumol and Bowen 1966)—a reduction in economywide productivity would lower the price of medical care, allowing spending to drop without a reduction in real benefits. If labor intensity is not an important explanation for the rise in medical spending, a drop in productivity would lower Medicare spending by reducing real healthcare benefits.[19]

Other Mandatory Programs

Productivity growth can affect spending on means-tested programs (table 4.3) in two ways. First, reductions in productivity growth might increase the number of people whose income is low enough to make them eligible for

---

18. CBO (2017, supplemental data, Table 8, Projected Excess Cost Growth, www.cbo.gov/about/products/budget-economic-data#1).

19. Furthermore, to the extent certain industries do not contribute to productivity growth, a drop in economywide productivity of 0.6 percentage point would mean a larger drop in the industries that do contribute to productivity growth—and hence a larger drop in other types of consumption.

Table 4.3   Mandatory federal spending in the United States, 2017

Program	Spending (billions of dollars)	Share of total outlays (percent)
Social Security	939	24
Medicare	591	15
Medicaid, State Children's Health Insurance Program, and Affordable Care Act exchange subsidies	439	11
Refundable earned income and child tax credits	83	2
Supplemental Nutrition Assistance Program (SNAP)	70	2
Supplemental Social Security (SSI)	55	1
Federal employee retirement	92	2
Veterans programs	105	3
Other	145	4
Total	2,519	63

Source: CBO (2017).

Figure 4.4   Poverty rate in the United States, 1960–2015

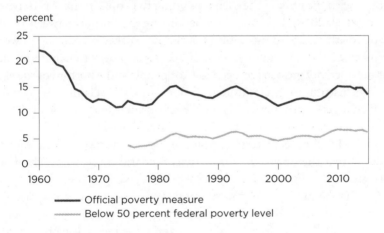

Source: US Census Bureau (2017).

the programs. Second, a change in productivity can affect the dollar value of the program benefits themselves.

Poverty

The official poverty rate—which is based on pretax cash income (including Social Security but excluding the benefits of tax credits like the earned income tax credit and in-kind benefits, such as Medicaid)—has remained flat since the late 1960s (figure 4.4). As the threshold that determines whether a family is poor is linked to inflation, not productivity, all else equal one might have expected poverty to decline.

Poverty rates might not move with productivity growth for several reasons. First, many poor people do not work very much. According to Semega, Fontenot, and Kollar (2017), only 11 percent of poor 18- to 64-year-olds worked full time in 2016, and only 38 percent had worked at all during the year. If people do not work, they will not benefit from real wage increases. Other sources of income that are counted as money income for the definition of the official poverty measure, such as Supplemental Security Income, are indexed only to inflation and thus will not increase with productivity growth. Furthermore, many poor people have income well below the poverty threshold. In 2016 about half of poor households had income less than 50 percent of the poverty threshold, meaning that even substantial increases in income would not have pushed them out of poverty.

Over the past few decades, changes in the distribution of wages have hurt people at the bottom of the distribution. Between 1979 and 2012, workers in the bottom 90 percent of the wage distribution saw increases in real annual wages of only 17 percent, while average wages increased about 35 percent, with the bulk of the increases going to people in the top 10 percent (Bivens et al. 2014). It is unclear whether the disconnect between productivity growth and earnings reflects declining worker bargaining power, as Bivens et al. (2014) argue, or skill-biased technological change (meaning that productivity growth has been low for people at the bottom of the skills/earnings distribution), as Autor and Salomons (2017) claim.

If changes in productivity growth occur primarily at the top of the wage distribution, a slowdown in productivity may have little effect on poverty and eligibility for means-tested programs. For the purposes of this exercise, I assume that the downside productivity scenario is one in which productivity growth declines uniformly across the board. To gauge the impact of such a change in wage on poverty rates, I use results from Hoynes, Page, and Huff Stevens (2006), who estimate a regression model that examines the impact of changes in median wages and wage inequality on nonelderly poverty rates (they use the ratio of wages at the 50th percentile and the 20th percentile as a measure of wage inequality). Holding wage inequality (and the fraction of women working, which also has an important effect on poverty) constant, they find that a 10 percent increase in the real median weekly wage lowered the poverty rate by 1.1 percentage points between 1980 and 2003.

A decline in the annual growth of real wages from 1.2 to 0.6 percent would lower real wages by 14 percent after 25 years. Using the Hoynes, Page, and Huff Stevens (2006) results, this decline would lead to a 1.5 percentage point increase in the nonelderly poverty rate after 25 years, an increase of about 11 percent. I assume that eligibility for programs tied to federal poverty guidelines (even if tied to 125 percent of poverty) would also increase by this amount after 25 years. On average over 25 years, then, I assume that eligibility for poverty-based programs would increase by about 5 percent.

Means-Tested Government Programs

With this estimate, I can gauge the likely impacts of a productivity slow-down on means-tested government programs.

Medicaid, Children's Health Insurance Program, and Affordable Care Act Exchange Subsidies

Medicaid, the Children's Health Insurance Program (CHIP), and Affordable Care Act exchange subsidies tie eligibility to federal poverty guidelines, which are indexed only to inflation. Hence a slowdown in productivity growth would likely increase spending on these means-tested health programs as a share of GDP because of the increase in poverty.

A similar reasoning to that used for Medicare suggests that a slowdown in productivity would not affect per person health spending for Medicaid, CHIP, or the tax subsidies provided under the Affordable Care Act rela-tive to GDP. However, changes in family income can affect the number of people eligible for these programs and the benefit amount they receive.

Refundable Part of Earned Income and Child Tax Credits

Most of the earned income credit that is received is through a tax refund. For most recipients, their benefit makes their income tax liability negative.

About half of the child tax credit is refundable. In 2017 the refundable parts of these two tax credits amounted to $90 billion, or about 2 percent of federal outlays (Maag 2017). Refundable tax credits are technically clas-sified as spending. CBO's estimates of the effects of productivity growth on tax revenues (real bracket creep) do not include the effects of real growth on the refundable part of the earned income tax credit.

The earned income tax credit is a tax credit for low-income working families. The credit amount is equal to a fixed percentage of earnings (until the credit reaches its maximum, at which point it begins to phase out). The credit thresholds are indexed for inflation, not real wage growth, so reduc-tions in productivity raise the number of people receiving the credit and the share of the credit that is refundable.

In general, the benefit amount is tied to earnings, so a decline in earnings reduces benefit amounts about one for one with earnings. The maximum credit is indexed to inflation, however, so for people receiving the maximum benefit, the amount increases relative to earnings when productivity slows. On the whole, earned income tax credit outlays would likely increase by a very small amount relative to GDP if productivity growth were to decline.

Supplemental Nutrition Assistance Program (SNAP)

To be eligible for SNAP, households generally have to meet income tests that require that their gross income be less than 130 percent of the poverty threshold.[20] Because poverty guidelines are indexed to the CPI, increases in productivity growth that raise family income can reduce the number of families eligible for the program.

The benefit amount is calculated as the monthly allotment less 30 percent of household income (because households are expected to spend 30 percent of their income on food). The monthly allotment is tied to the cost of the Department of Agriculture's Thrifty Food Plan and is therefore effectively indexed by food prices. A reduction in productivity growth would not affect the monthly allotment, but it could lower household income and so raise benefit amounts slightly for families.

Supplemental Security Income (SSI)

SSI is based on poverty or disability. Few SSI recipients have wage income, so eligibility is unlikely to be affected by changes in productivity growth. SSI is indexed to inflation, so that benefits rise as a share of GDP if productivity growth declines.

Federal Noninterest Outlays and Poverty Summary

Table 4.4 summarizes the effects of a slowdown in productivity growth on federal government outlays. To calculate the effect on Medicaid, I use the Hoynes, Page, and Huff Stevens (2006) poverty estimate as a measure of the effect on eligibility. Because I do not have detailed breakdowns of CBO's projections of other mandatory spending (mandatory spending excluding Social Security and major health programs by category), I do not know what CBO assumes in the baseline, making it difficult to make a detailed estimate of the effects of the downside productivity scenario. But CBO's projections show that other mandatory spending is declining as a share of GDP (an average of 0.2 percent less over the next 25 years; table 4.4). Instead of separately estimating benefit and eligibility effects category by category, I

---

20. In addition, there is a requirement that net monthly income (income less a number of deductions) be less than 100 percent of the poverty threshold and that families not have assets exceeding certain amounts. Families receiving Temporary Assistance for Needy Families, Supplemental Security Income, or, in some places, general assistance do not have to meet income tests. See www.fns.usda.gov/snap/eligibility#Income.

Table 4.4 Effect of slower productivity growth in the United States on federal outlays and primary deficits

Item	GDP share, 2018 (percent)	Average share of GDP, 2018–42 (percent)	Change in nominal benefit relative to GDP as a result of slower productivity growth	Change in eligibility as a result of slower productivity growth	Change relative to GDP over 25 years as a result of slower productivity growth (percent)
Noninterest outlays					
Discretionary	6.4	5.6	Higher	n.a.	0.24
Social Security	4.9	5.8	Higher	Unchanged	0.3
Medicare	2.9	4.4	Lower/unchanged	Unchanged	0
Medicaid, Children's Health Insurance Program (CHIP), Affordable Care Act exchange subsidies	2.3	2.6	Lower/unchanged	Higher	0.13
Other mandatory programs (Supplemental Nutrition Assistance Program, Earned Income Tax Credit, Child Tax Credit, other)	2.6	2.4	Higher	Higher	0.1
Total noninterest outlays	19	20.8			0.77
Revenues	16.6	18.4			−0.25
Primary deficit (outlays less revenues)	2.4	2.4			1.02

n.a. = not available

Source: Author's calculations based on CBO (2017, 2018a).

assume that the decline in CBO's projection of other mandatory spending is attributable to the effects of real GDP growth; because productivity growth in the downside scenario is about half that in the baseline, I assume that other mandatory spending declines by half as much. Adding the effects, I find that when productivity slows, outlays increase by about 0.8 percent of GDP on average over the next 25 years.

Effect on State and Local Noninterest Spending

Figure 4.3b reports the composition of state and local spending out of own funds. This spending is net of charges (e.g., higher education is net of student-paid tuition) not financed by federal grants (e.g., only the state share of Medicaid, rather than the part paid for by the federal government that flows through to states as federal grants, is included).

Most state and local spending is discretionary and appropriated annually. In addition, most states have balanced budget requirements. As a result, in some sense, "current law" spending automatically declines when the tax base shrinks. A key question is how difficult it will be for states and localities to continue to balance their budgets in the face of slower productivity growth.

The big ticket items for state and local governments are education (about 40 percent of total spending out of own revenues), Medicaid and other health spending (19 percent), and public safety (12 percent). Because much of this spending represents compensation for state and local workers, state and local government expenditures will likely decline with GDP, as competition between state and local governments and the private sector for employees should equilibrate wages. If private sector wage growth declines in response to lower productivity growth, the growth in government compensation should decline as well.

As in the case of health care, an important policy question is the extent to which this decline in spending will represent a price decrease, because of a less intense Baumol effect or a decrease in real services. Even with some quality adjustments, measured productivity in the K–12 education sector has generally been negative (figure 4.5). If these quality adjustments are adequate, education spending increases, because of the need to maintain comparability in wages with other more productive sectors. In this case, government spending on education will decline with lower productivity growth without any loss in the real quantity/quality of education. If this low measured productivity growth reflects mismeasurement, a slowdown in productivity growth may result in slower productivity growth in education as well. In this case, the reduction in spending would also be accompanied by a cutback in real education services.

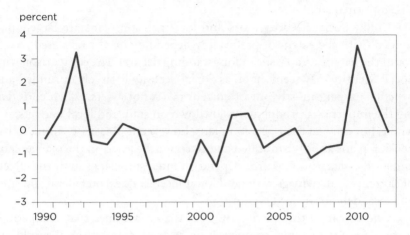

Figure 4.5 Productivity growth of public K–12 educational services in the United States, 1990–2012

percent

Source: US Bureau of Labor Statistics (BLS 2016).

Medicaid

The largest mandatory state program (in the sense that states can change spending only by changing program rules) is Medicaid, which in 2015 represented about 15 percent of state own-spending (other health spending includes spending on hospitals and public health, which is discretionary). The Medicaid program is a joint federal/state program, in which the federal government pays at least half (more in lower-income states). On average, in 2016 the federal government paid 63 percent of Medicaid costs (CMS 2016).

Medicaid spending as a share of GDP is likely to increase a little if productivity growth declines, because eligibility should increase somewhat faster than in the baseline. States will have to cut other programs in order to maintain their balanced budget requirements. Using the methodology adopted for determining the change in federal Medicaid spending, I estimate that a slowdown in productivity growth that increases poverty and hence Medicaid eligibility will increase state Medicaid spending by about 2.5 percent on average over 25 years, equal to 0.4 percent of own-spending. As a share of GDP, the increase represents about 0.1 percent.

Defined Benefit Pensions

Most state and local governments offer their employees a defined-benefit pension plan. These plans operate much like Social Security, in the sense that the initial benefit depends on final wages and thus moves one for one with productivity growth. As with Social Security, once employees retire, their benefits move with inflation (in general) but almost never with wage growth. A slowdown in productivity growth will thus increase the share of GDP accounted for by state and local expenditures on the pensions of already retired employees.

Unlike Social Security, state and local pension plans are largely prefunded (with the extent of prefunding depending on the rate used to discount the liabilities, an issue of longstanding debate). The comparison with Social Security may seem inapt, as Social Security is largely unfunded and benefits are paid mostly out of current taxes, not assets. When considering the impact of a productivity slowdown on state and local budgets as a whole, not only on their pension plans, however, it is easier to think of the pension plans as fully unfunded and to count the assets in the plan as state and local assets whose returns depend on interest rates.[21] I show the effects of slower productivity growth (and lower interest rates) on federal and state and local debt in the next section.

One caveat to this methodology is that it assumes that competitive forces determine the real compensation costs of state and local employees (including the costs of providing their pensions). A decline in interest rates raises the costs of providing defined-benefit pensions. This analysis (implicitly) assumes that this increase is offset by reductions in other compensation or by a paring back of pension benefits. If it is not, a reduction in the interest rate would raise employee compensation costs, having much larger negative effects on state and local budgets.

I use the Social Security Trustees' estimate of the effects of lower productivity to gauge the likely effects of lower productivity on state and local pension obligations. In 2016 state and local pension benefit payments amounted to $304 billion, or about 1.6 percent of GDP and 20 percent of state and local tax revenue. If, like Social Security, state and local pension benefits climb with population aging, these benefits will be about 20 percent higher on average over the next 25 years than they are today, or about 1.9 percent of GDP.[22] For Social Security, a 0.6 percentage point reduction in labor productivity increases the average spending on Social Security benefits by 5 percent, on average, over 25 years, implying that slower produc-

---

21. Social Security also has a trust fund, but budget analysts, including CBO, prefer to analyze the unified budget rather than distinguishing between on-budget (excluding Social Security) and off-budget (Social Security) surpluses and deficits.

22. There are no annual projections of state and local pension payments, making it hard to know whether or when payments will rise. On the one hand, the share of employment in the state and local sector has been fairly constant since 1970, suggesting that the pattern of demographic change in that workforce should mirror that of the workforce overall. On the other hand, state and local governments have made more changes to the generosity of pension benefits than has Social Security, and the age of retirement is often much lower for state and local workers than it is for Social Security.

tivity growth will increase state and local pension spending by about 0.1 percent of GDP, or about 1 percent of state and local revenues.

State and Local Noninterest Outlays Summary

State and local noninterest outlays should move almost one for one with productivity, so that a slowdown in productivity should not create substantial fiscal stresses. Some small increases in Medicaid and pension expenditures as a share of GDP will require some offsets, but they appear minor.

Effect of Changes in Productivity on Spending on Interest and Debt

Federal Level

The federal debt has increased sharply in recent years. In 2018 it stood at about 78 percent of GDP and is projected to increase sharply, surpassing 130 percent of GDP by 2043 (CBO 2018b). Increases in primary deficits arising from slower productivity would lead to further acceleration in the ratio of debt to GDP. If interest rates fall along with productivity, however, these effects will be muted and possibly even reversed.

To gauge these effects, I calculate the deficit- and debt-to-GDP ratios under a number of scenarios. In all of them, I assume that productivity growth is 0.6 percentage point lower than in the CBO baseline. I estimate that this slowdown in productivity growth will lower federal revenue by about 0.25 percent of GDP and increase spending by about 0.8 percent of GDP, increasing the primary deficit by 1.0 percent of GDP, on average, over the next 25 years (see tables 4.1 and 4.4). Figure 4.6 compares the primary deficits in CBO's baseline and the low-productivity simulation.

To see the effects of lower interest rates, I run these simulations under the three interest rate assumptions described above: no effect, a one-for-one reduction in interest rates, and a two-for-one reduction in interest rates. Not all the US debt is rolled over each year, so some of the interest rate effects take time to materialize. The average maturity of marketable US debt is five years.[23] As a rough adjustment for the interest rate delays, I start lowering interest rates only in 2023.

Without an interest rate adjustment, the slowdown in productivity growth increases the debt-to-GDP ratio at the end of 25 years from 130 percent in the baseline to 173 percent (figure 4.7 and table 4.5). If interest rates fall one for one with GDP, the debt-to-GDP ratio climbs less dramati-

---

23. Treasury Presentation to TBAC, Office of Budget Management, Fiscal Year 2015 Q3 Report, www.treasury.gov/resource-center/data-chart-center/quarterly-refunding/Documents/August2015TreasuryPresentationToTBAC.pdf.

Figure 4.6   Projected primary deficits in the United States under baseline and low productivity scenarios, 2018–42

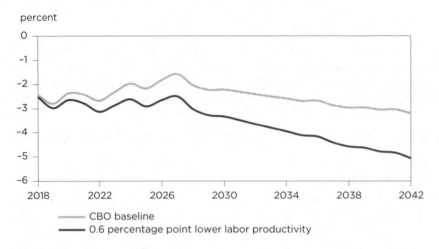

percent

CBO = Congressional Budget Office

Note: For the CBO baseline, data for 2018–28 are from CBO (2018a). Out-years were calculated by extending revenues and spending by their respective growth rates in CBO (2017) (see footnote 5).

Source: Author's calculations based on CBO (2017, 2018a).

cally, reaching 159 percent by 2042.[24] Even if interest rates fall two for one, the slowdown in productivity still worsens the fiscal outlook. In this case, however, the effect is not large. Instead of reaching 130 percent of GDP, as in the baseline, debt reaches 146 percent of GDP.

This exercise includes both the effects of lower productivity on primary deficits and the effects of lower interest rates and GDP on debt dynamics. If I assume no changes in primary deficits as a share of GDP from lower productivity growth, a reduction in productivity growth that lowers interest rates one for one has almost no effect on the ratio of debt to GDP. In contrast, a two-for-one interest rate reduction lowers the debt-to-GDP ratio to about 120 percent of GDP after 25 years (Mehrotra finds a similar result in chapter 1 of this volume).

State and Local Level

In contrast to the federal government, the state and local sector is a net lender once pension assets are included and unfunded pension liabilities are

---

24. This estimate is a bit higher than the effects of lower productivity growth that CBO reports. CBO shows a decline in productivity growth of about the same magnitude as the one studied here, increasing the debt-to-GDP ratio in 2042 to 149 percent of GDP. Because CBO gives few details about its methodology, it is hard to know the sources of the difference.

Figure 4.7 Projected debt-to-GDP ratios in the United States under baseline and downside low productivity scenarios, 2018–42

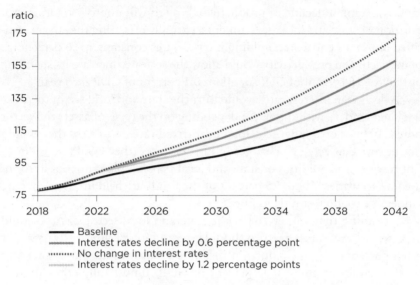

ratio

Source: Author's calculations based on CBO (2017, 2018a).

Table 4.5 Projected debt-to-GDP ratios in the United States under baseline and low productivity scenarios

Item	Baseline scenario	Low productivity scenario		
		No interest rate adjustment	Interest rate adjustment is one for one	Interest rate adjustment is two for one
Average annual productivity growth (percent)	1.2	0.6	0.6	0.6
2042 primary deficit as share of GDP (percent)	3.2	5.1	5.1	5.1
Interest rates	Baseline	Baseline	Baseline minus 0.6 percentage point	Baseline minus 1.2 percentage points
2042 debt-to-GDP ratio (percent)	130	173	159	146

Source: Author's calculations based on CBO (2017, 2018a).

omitted.[25] According to the most recent Financial Accounts of the United States, ignoring the unfunded liabilities of state and local pension plans, the net assets of the state and local sector totaled $2.9 trillion in 2016, about 15

---

25. Increases in pension payments will likely make the sector less of a net saver.

percent of GDP.[26] A decline in productivity growth that does not lower the return to capital will increase the asset-to-GDP ratio, because the value of assets will be unaffected but GDP growth will be slower.[27] Holding interest rates constant, a decline in productivity growth will improve the financial position of state and local governments, partially offsetting the effects identified above. In particular, holding interest rates constant, a 0.6 percentage point decline in productivity would allow the sector to increase its spending by 0.006 * 15 percent of GDP, or about 0.1 percent of GDP each year.[28]

A decline in interest rates would hurt the state and local sector (because it is a net lender), with the extent depending on the types of assets the sector holds. If pension plans held long-term fixed-rate securities, they would not be much affected by changes in interest rates (they would be hedged). But most of the holdings of state and local pension plans are not in fixed-income securities: About 75 percent of the funds are held in assets that are vulnerable to interest rate declines.[29]

Assuming that 75 percent of the state and local sector's assets would experience lower rates of return should interest rates decline, I estimate that a 0.6 percentage point reduction in interest rates would lower state and local revenues by about 0.07 percent of GDP, almost fully offsetting the benefits received from the slower productivity growth. If interest rates fell by twice as much as productivity growth, the net effect would be to increase the stress on state and local governments, as the interest rate effects (0.14 percent of GDP) would be larger than the benefits of slower productivity

---

26. Board of Governors of the Federal Reserve System, Federal Reserve Statistical Release, Z.1 Financial Accounts of the United States, Flow of Funds, Balance Sheets, and Integrated Macroeconomic Accounts, June 7, 2018, www.federalreserve.gov/releases/z1/20180607/z1.pdf.

27. For a change in productivity not to affect interest rates and the marginal return to capital, capital intensity must fall. If it does, even though the physical product of existing capital falls when productivity falls, wages will fall as well. The drop may be enough to fully offset the decline in the physical product of capital.

28. To maintain a stock of assets relative to GDP, the sector can consume $(i - g) * A$, where A is the assets-to-GDP ratio, i is the interest rate, and g is the rate of growth. When g declines, consumption can decrease. To see this another way, think about how much one would have to save for retirement if the amount of income one wanted in retirement was dependent on final wages. With slower productivity growth, the amount of savings relative to current wages would decline, because retirement needs would decline much more than current income (because the decline in productivity growth compounds over time).

29. According to the Financial Accounts, 65 percent of the assets of state and local pension plans in 2016 were corporate equities and 6 percent were mutual funds. Plans held about 25 percent of their assets in Treasuries, government-sponsored enterprises, and corporate and foreign bonds. The accounts do not report on the average maturity of those holdings.

growth. In this case, property values would likely increase, leaving the sector relatively immune to productivity changes.

Concluding Remarks

A slowdown in productivity growth will lower living standards, increase poverty, and worsen the fiscal outlook for federal, state, and local governments. A reduction in labor productivity growth of 0.6 percentage point a year (from 1.6 to 1.0 percent) would increase primary deficits relative to GDP, because some outlays are invariant to changes in productivity growth and revenues are tied more than one for one with productivity growth, so that a productivity slowdown lowers revenues more than it lowers GDP. These increased deficits imply that the federal debt will reach 146–173 percent of GDP by 2042, compared with the baseline estimate of 130 percent of GDP. The range is attributable to differences in assumptions about the relationship between productivity growth and interest rates, which is subject to a great deal of uncertainty.

It is much harder to project the long-term fiscal outlook of the state and local sector, as it is more complicated and studied far less. Still, it is possible to get some idea of the effects slower productivity might have on the sector. In general, state and local tax revenues are less tied to productivity growth than are federal revenues, because the state and local income tax system is less progressive than the federal system and sales taxes and property taxes make up a much larger fraction of tax collections. The relationship between interest rates and productivity is important as well, because the value of the property tax base should depend on how much interest rates change in response to a productivity slowdown. Assuming a one-for-one relationship, changes in productivity should have little effect on state and local revenues. There is also likely to be some upward pressure on state and local spending relative to GDP, stemming from the somewhat heavier burden of pension spending and increased eligibility for Medicaid and other poverty-related programs, but these increases are likely to be small.

Interest and debt dynamics move in opposite directions for the state and local sector and the federal sector. Because the state and local sector is a net lender, reductions in productivity increase the stock of assets relative to GDP and reductions in interest rates lower asset returns relative to GDP. If interest rates move one for one with productivity growth, there is little effect on the fiscal outlook of the state and local sector.

References

Andrews, D., C. Criscuolo, and P.N. Gal. 2016. *The Best versus the Rest: The Global Productivity Slowdown, Divergence across Firms and the Role of Public Policy*. OECD Productivity Working Paper 2016-05. Paris: OECD Publishing.

Auerbach, Alan, William Gale, and Aaron Krupkin. 2018. *The Federal Budget Outlook: Even Crazier after All These Years.* Tax Policy Center (April). Washington: Urban Institute and Brookings Institution. Available at www.brookings.edu/wp-content/uploads/2018/04/es_20180423_budgetoutlook.pdf.

Autor, David, and Anna Salomons. 2017. Robocalypse Now: Does Productivity Growth Threaten Employment? In *Investment and Growth in Advanced Economies.* Proceedings of the European Central Bank Forum on Central Banking, Sintra, Portugal, June 2–28. Available at www.ecb.europa.eu/pub/pdf/other/ecb.ecbforumcentralbanking2017.en.pdf.

Baumol, William, and William Bowen. 1966. *Performing Arts, the Economic Dilemma: A Study of Problems Common to Theater, Opera, Music, and Dance.* New York: Twentieth Century Fund.

Bivens, Josh, Elise Gould, Lawrence Mishel, and Heidi Shierholz. 2014. *Raising America's Pay: Why It's Our Central Economy Policy Challenge.* Briefing Paper 378 (June 4). Washington: Economic Policy Institute.

BLS (Bureau of Labor Statistics). 2016. *Labor Productivity Growth in Elementary and Secondary School Services: 1989-2012.* Washington. Available at www.bls.gov/opub/mlr/2016/article/labor-productivity-growth-in-elementary-and-secondary-school-services.htm.

Board of Trustees, Federal Old-Age and Survivors Insurance and Federal Disability Insurance Trust Funds. 2017. *The 2017 Annual Report of the Board of Trustees of the Federal Old-Age and Survivors Insurance and Federal Disability Insurance Trust Funds.* Washington.

CBO (Congressional Budget Office). 2017. *The 2017 Long-Term Budget Outlook* (March). Washington.

CBO (Congressional Budget Office). 2018a. *The Budget and Economic Outlook: An Update* (April). Washington.

CBO (Congressional Budget Office). 2018b. *The 2018 Long-Term Budget Outlook* (June). Washington.

CMS (Centers for Medicare and Medicaid Services). 2016. *2016 Actuarial Report on the Financial Outlook for Medicaid.* Baltimore, MD. Available at www.cms.gov/Research-Statistics-Data-and-Systems/Research/ActuarialStudies/Downloads/MedicaidReport2016.pdf.

Furman, Jason, and Peter Orszag. 2018. *Slower Productivity and Higher Inequality: Are They Related?* PIIE Working Paper 18-4. Washington: Peterson Institute for International Economics.

Hamilton, James D., Ethan S. Harris, Jan Hatzius, and Kenneth D. West. 2015. *The Equilibrium Real Funds Rate: Past, Present, and Future.* Hutchins Center Working Paper 16. Washington: Brookings Institution.

Hoynes, Hilary W., Marianne E. Page, and Ann Huff Stevens. 2006. Poverty in America: Trends and Explanations. *Journal of Economic Perspectives* 20, no. 1: 47–68.

Laubach, Thomas, and John Williams. 2015. *Measuring the Natural Rate of Interest Redux.* Hutchins Center Working Paper 15. Washington: Brookings Institution.

Lukasz, Rachel, and Thomas D. Smith. 2015. *Secular Drivers of the Global Real Interest Rate.* Staff Working Paper 571. London: Bank of England.

Maag, Elaine. 2017. *Refundable Credits: The Earned Income Tax Credit and the Child Tax Credit* (March 23). Washington: Tax Policy Center. Available at www.taxpolicycenter.org/sites/default/files/publication/139841/2001197-refundable-credits-the-earned-income-tax-credit-and-the-child-tax-credit_0.pdf.

Sammartino, Frank, and Norton Francis. 2016. *Federal-State Income Tax Progressivity*. Tax Policy Center (June). Washington: Urban Institute and Brookings Institution. Available at www.taxpolicycenter.org/sites/default/files/publication/131621/2000847-federal-state-income-tax-progressivity.pdf.

Semega, Jessica L., Kayla R. Fontenot, and Melissa A. Kollar. 2017. Income and Poverty in the United States: 2016. *Current Population Report P60-25* (September). Washington: US Census Bureau.

Sheiner, Louise. 2018. *The Long-Term Impact of Aging on the Federal Budget*. Hutchins Center Working Paper 40. Washington: Brookings Institution.

Technical Review Panel on the Medicare Trustees Report. 2012. *Review of Assumptions and Methods of the Medicare Trustees*. Financial Projections (December). Baltimore, MD: Centers for Medicare and Medicaid Services.

US Census Bureau. 2017. *Historical Poverty Tables: People and Families—1959 to 2016*. Tables 13 and 22. Suitland, MD. Available at www.census.gov/data/tables/time-series/demo/income-poverty/historical-poverty-people.html.

5

Impact of a Productivity Slowdown on Pension Systems in Europe

AXEL BÖRSCH-SUPAN

Pensions—including public pensions, occupational pensions, and individual saving plans for old age—are an important social program. They account for a large and increasing part of GDP and are the main source of income for a large and increasing share of the population.[1] Pensions are also a political hotspot, often called the "third rail," in reference to their potentially electrocuting impact during elections (Lynch and Myrskyl 2009).[2]

Pension systems have to maintain a delicate balance between providing adequate benefits and maintaining financial sustainability. In the pay-as-you-go (PAYG) pension systems used in almost all advanced economies, this balance reflects the intergenerational distribution between old and young. Generous pension benefits are good for the older generation but have to be financed from taxes on and contributions by the young. If population aging

Axel Börsch-Supan is director of the Munich Center for the Economics of Aging (MEA) at the Max Planck Institute for Social Law and Social Policy, professor at the Technical University of Munich, and research associate at the National Bureau of Economic Research. He thanks Jeromin Zettelmeyer for his helpful comments and editorial advice, participants at the Peterson Institute conference on which this volume is based for their lively discussion, and Johannes Rausch for conducting the simulations.

1. In 2014 public and private spending on pensions was 10.7 percent of GDP in the United States, 10.8 percent in the United Kingdom, 12.1 percent in Germany, 14.1 percent in France, and 17.0 percent in Italy (OECD 2015).

2. William Safire, "The Third Rail," *New York Times Magazine*, February 18, 2007, www.nytimes.com/2007/02/18/magazine/18wwlnsafire.t.html.

reduces the number of younger workers relative to the number of pension recipients, PAYG systems may become financially unsustainable.[3]

This delicate balance is easier to handle if the underlying economy is growing. In Germany long-term annual labor productivity growth has been around 1.5 percent in real terms (Buchheim 1997). Population aging will reduce the number of contributing workers divided by the number of pension beneficiaries by about 0.5 percent a year. Thus even if pension benefits are cut by 0.5 percent a year to keep the pension system's financial balance unchanged, the system can still afford a benefit increase of 1.0 percent a year in real terms.

This chapter examines the effect of a slowdown in productivity growth, which may endanger this balance. It is part of a project on the consequences of a productivity slowdown and hence takes the projected productivity slowdown and its direct effects on wages and interest rates as given. From this somewhat pessimistic perspective, the chapter analyzes how the slowdown will affect pension systems. The key question is whether declining wage growth and capital returns in the wake of declining productivity growth will undermine the financial sustainability of pension systems and/or the adequacy of pensions as important social programs. The answers depend very much on the type of pension system and whether one is concerned about the relative or the absolute level of pension benefits (i.e., relative to past and present wages or with respect to some politically defined poverty line).

The chapter is organized as follows. The first section describes six prototypical pension systems. Most real-world pension systems can be interpreted as combinations of these stylized pension systems. Section 2 uses a simulation model to compute the quantitative impacts of the stylized productivity slowdown on the level of pension benefit income for retirees and the balanced-budget contribution rates for workers. These trajectories serve as indicators of the financial situation of a pension system and the adequacy of pension benefits. Section 3 presents the simulation results. Section 4 analyzes five types of adaptation based on increasing the quantity of labor and capital in order to offset the lower than previously expected value of labor and capital that has been precipitated by the productivity slowdown. The last section summarizes the chapter's main conclusions.

---

3. The dependency ratio is expected to increase most in Italy (from 36.5 in 2015 to 68.3 in 2050) and Germany (from 35.5 to 65.1). Increases are expected to be much more moderate in the United Kingdom (from 30.8 to 46.4) and France (from 30.0 to 49.0) and even smaller in the United States (from 24.7 to 39.5) (OECD 2015).

Figure 5.1 Prototypical pension systems

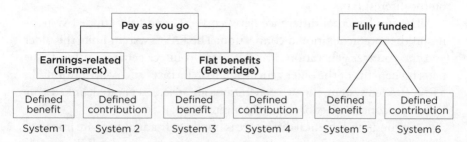

Types of Pension Systems

The effects of a productivity slowdown on pension benefit levels and contribution rates depend strongly on the type of system. Six prototypical pension systems can be distinguished, characterized by three dimensions (figure 5.1). Two real-world variants are also examined.

The first fundamental difference is between PAYG and fully funded systems.[4] PAYG systems carry this name because benefits are paid to older pension beneficiaries as contributions from younger workers come in. The sum of the benefits paid to current retirees is equal to the sum of the contributions received from current workers. There is no capital stock. Hence the younger generation pays the benefits for the older generation, hoping that this implicit contract will also hold for them.

Members of the younger generation not only hope that their children will finance their retirement, as they financed the parents'; they also hope for a real return on the notional investment that they made when paying contributions. In a PAYG system, population and productivity growth determine this rate of return. If the next generation has more members, the burden of financing the pensions of the older generation is spread over more shoulders; if the next generation is more productive, the pie to be redistributed to the older generation is larger. More formally, the rate of return from a PAYG system is $n + g$, where n denotes the growth rate of the labor force and g the annual increase in labor productivity. There is thus a direct channel through which a productivity slowdown can potentially affect pensions.

Unlike PAYG systems, fully funded systems have a capital stock. A generation accumulates funds as part of this capital stock; it later receives benefits from the accumulated stock. The rate of return of a fully funded system is simply the market interest rate in real terms, r. The effects of a

---

4. Börsch-Supan, Härtl, and Leite (2016) provide a formal survey of pension systems in times of population aging.

productivity slowdown work indirectly, through the effect of the slowdown on the interest rate.

The fundamental difference between PAYG and fully funded systems lies in the intergenerational connection. The PAYG system links the older and the younger generation directly, as the younger generation funds the pension benefits of the older generation with its taxes and contributions. In a fully funded system, the two generations are strictly separated, linked only by macroeconomic feedback via the interest rate.

A second fundamental difference is how benefits at old age are linked to contributions at younger ages. In a prototypical earnings-related (Bismarckian) system, benefits are proportional to contributions, which are in turn proportional to earnings. The other extreme is occupied by Beveridgean pension systems, which provide flat benefits (benefits that are independent of earnings and contributions).

Most pension systems are some mixture of these two extremes. Many systems provide a minimum, or base, pension (the Beveridgean part of the pension system) in addition to an earnings-related scheme (the Bismarckian part of the pension system). In Germany, for example, in 2001 the Bismarckian system was augmented by flat social assistance for the very poor (*Grundsicherung im Alter*). The US Social Security system provides benefits that are linked to earnings but in a nonlinear fashion, in which workers with low earnings receive a higher replacement rate than workers with higher earnings. In principle, fully funded systems could provide flat benefits. However, all actual fully funded systems relate benefits in old age to contributions when young. The intragenerational distribution of the effects of a productivity slowdown depends heavily on the link between contributions and benefits.

Both PAYG and fully funded systems can be of the defined-benefit or defined-contribution type. This distinction determines who bears the risk of macroeconomic or demographic changes that may affect pension benefits. In its prototypical version, a defined-benefit system promises an earnings-related replacement rate (in a Bismarckian system) or a flat benefit (in a Beveridgean system) at a young age, independent of economic and demographic circumstances that develop in the life course. Potential risks—lower than expected rates of return in the capital market for fully funded systems, greater than expected population aging in a PAYG system—have to be compensated by the sponsors of the system while the retirees are protected. The opposite holds for a defined-contribution system. In a PAYG defined-benefit system, the government as sponsor promises a replacement rate (if Bismarckian) or a flat benefit (if Beveridgean), which it has to finance with higher contributions imposed on the young if economic or demographic circumstances turn out worse than expected (e.g., as a result of a productivity slowdown). In a fully funded system, the sponsor (e.g., a company in an occupational pension system) has to make up for a lower than expected return on the capital market (e.g., lower interest rates as a result of a productivity slowdown). In contrast, a defined-contribution system keeps the contribution rate to the system constant, independent of economic and demographic circumstances. If economic or demographic conditions turn out worse than expected, pension benefits for the older generation will be lower than expected. Retirees thus bear all of the economic and demographic risks.

Traditionally, PAYG pension systems have been of the defined-benefit type (an example is the US Social Security system). The Swedish PAYG system broke with this tradition by introducing a "notional defined-contribution system," in which benefits are linked to economic and demographic circumstances (see Palmer 2002).[5] In the Anglo-Saxon countries, fully funded occupational pensions have experienced a secular shift from defined benefit to defined contribution.

Defined benefit and defined contribution are extreme cases, however; in practice, any degree of risk sharing is possible. An example of a hybrid system is the current German PAYG system, which includes elements of defined benefits in its pension formula but has a link to demography through its "sustainability factor" (Börsch-Supan and Wilke 2005). The intergenerational distribution of the effects of a productivity slowdown depends heavily on whether the system is a defined-benefit or defined-contribution system.

Real-world pension systems are much more complex. They often add layers ("pillars") of subsystems and mix the three fundamental dimensions by redistributing between young and old and between rich and poor. Sometimes government subsidies financed by general taxes or debt are used to support the pension system, making the system nontransparent.

One aim of this chapter is to delineate the effects of a productivity slowdown in a transparent fashion, with the help of these stylized/prototypical pension systems. Actual effects for real-world pension systems can then be computed as the weighted sum of the effects on each subsystem.

The chapter examines six prototypical and two real-world examples of pension systems:

- **System 1: Prototypical earnings-related, PAYG, defined-benefit system with a constant net replacement rate** (similar to the US Social Security system and many European and the Japanese public pension systems). Population aging will increase the contribution rate and unilaterally burden the young. The effect of a productivity slowdown is dif-

---

5. Italy adopted a similar system (see Franco and Sartor 2005).

ferent. The absolute level of benefits will grow less if productivity slows, but a productivity slowdown is neutral to both the contribution and the replacement rates, because both rates are defined relative to wages.

- **System 2: Prototypical earnings-related, PAYG, defined-contribution system with a constant contribution rate** (similar to the Swedish pension system). Population aging will unilaterally burden the older generation by decreasing the replacement rate. As in System 1, the absolute level of benefits will grow less if productivity slows, but a productivity slowdown is neutral to both the replacement and the contribution rate.

- **System 3: Flat pension (€1,000 a month in 2015) indexed to the average gross wage** (similar to the Swiss pension system). This system is akin to a defined-benefit system, as the replacement rate is independent of economic and demographic developments. The absolute level of benefits is not protected and will grow less if productivity slows.

- **System 4: Flat pension (€1,000 a month in 2015) indexed to inflation** (similar to basic pension in the United Kingdom). This system is akin to a defined-contribution system in the sense that the replacement rate of the system depends on economic and demographic developments that change the real wage.

- **System 5: Fully funded defined-benefit system with a constant net replacement rate** (similar to occupational defined-benefit pensions [e.g., in the Netherlands]). Population aging will unilaterally increase the contribution rate.

- **System 6: Fully funded defined-contribution system with a constant contribution rate** (similar to individual retirement accounts and most new occupational pensions in the United States). Population aging will unilaterally decrease the replacement rate.

- **System 7: Additional spillover effects if pension system's budget and government's budget are interlinked.**

- **System 8: Actual German pension system (earnings-related, mixed defined-benefit/defined-contribution system).** Population aging and/or productivity slowdown will result in equiproportional adaptations of contribution and replacement rates through a "sustainability factor."

The Model

A productivity slowdown poses two central threats to a pension system, which can be compared with the well-known threats to pension systems that population aging exerts. First, a pension system may become financially unsustainable if economic or demographic circumstances push the contribution rate up beyond a threshold at which the negative incentive effects on labor supply outweigh the revenue effect of increased contributions. The second threat is lack of adequacy, which occurs if economic or demographic circumstances drive benefits down below a certain normative level (e.g., the poverty line or a certain percentage of median income).

I use a simulation model to compute two trajectories of pension systems, which represent how these two threats are handled: the replacement rate (i.e., average pension benefits to retirees as a percentage of average wages) and the contribution rate (i.e., average taxes and contributions paid by workers as a percentage of average wages). Whether the replacement rate is a good indicator of pension adequacy is debatable and subject to the long-standing controversy about absolute or relative poverty. As pension issues are very long term, I argue that a relative measure is more appropriate. The one used here is based on the historical observation that social standards have adapted to societies' economic development.

The drivers of these trajectories are economic development, especially the development of labor productivity, and demography, especially population aging. I assume that higher/lower labor productivity is translated one-to-one into higher/lower wages. I also assume that inflation is 1.5 percent in 2020 and declines in line with labor productivity. In the following section, I do not consider other macroeconomic feedback effects, such as the indirect effects of population aging on wages and interest rates. I discuss such feedback effects in section 4 based on an overlapping generations framework.

Based on these basic assumptions, I model three scenarios:

- **Baseline:** This scenario adopts the German population forecast of strong population aging generated by baby-boom/baby-bust transition, constant low fertility, and continuing increases in life expectancy; constant productivity growth of 1.5 percent a year in real terms; and 1.5 percent annual inflation.

- **Productivity slowdown:** In this scenario, productivity growth per se is not a parameter for pension systems; their performance depends on wage growth. The scenario assumes that wage growth follows productivity growth, which in turn follows the common assumptions in this project. Real wages grow by 1.5 percent a year in 2020; the rate decreases linearly to 0.9 percent in 2030 and then remains at this level. Inflation is 1.5 percent in 2020 and declines proportionally to real wages. Nominal wage growth thus declines from 3.0 percent a year in 2020 to 1.8 percent in the long run.[6]

- **Constant life expectancy:** In order to compare the magnitude of the effects of the productivity slowdown with another secular trend, I compute a third scenario, which assumes no further increases in life expectancy. This assumption may be interpreted as a slowdown in medical/societal progress in increasing life expectancy. Ironically, given a fixed retirement age, this change will reduce population aging and therefore stabilize pension systems. The other assumptions are the same as in the baseline.

The projections use the pension simulation model MEA-PENSIM, originally designed to map the German pension system in all relevant parameters in a way that permits implementing various reform suggestions (Wilke 2004; Holthausen, Rausch, and Wilke 2012; Rausch and Gasche 2016). MEA-PENSIM was extended to also model the stylized pension systems depicted in figure 5.1. I stick, however, with the German demography, which represents a particularly rapidly aging European economy.[7]

The projections are based on detailed calculations of receipt and payment accounts. The calculation of these accounts as well as the projection of the contribution rate and pension level requires assumptions about the development of the population, the labor market, and wages. As a consequence, MEA-PENSIM includes modules for generating demographic and labor market projections.

Demography is described by the initial size of each cohort and the survival of that cohort. Let $N_{t,j}$ denote the number of individuals of age j at time t. Individuals were either born in year $c = t - j$ and are the survivors of the original birth cohort $N_{c,0}$ or migrated at age j in time t.

$$N_{t,j} = \sigma_{t,j} \cdot N_{c,0} + M_{t,j}, \tag{5.1}$$

where $\sigma_{t,j}$ denotes the unconditional probability to survive until age j, which will be in year t. The original cohort size for cohort c depends on the fertility of women aged k at time $c = t - j$:

---

6. In 2016 German labor productivity was growing by about 0.9 percent a year. The baseline scenario of 1.5 percent thus assumes a fairly vigorous recovery. The downside scenario assumes that labor productivity growth does not recover.

7. Germany and Italy have the oldest populations in Europe, as measured by the level of the old-age dependency ratio. More important for the subsequent analysis is the change in the old-age dependency ratio given today's level. This change is similar for most European countries except France, the Scandinavian countries, and the United Kingdom, where the aging process is considerably slower.

$$N_{c,0} = \sum_{k=0}^{\infty} f_{c,k} \cdot N_{c,k}.^{8} \tag{5.2}$$

Population aging therefore has three demographic components: (a) past and future increases in longevity, expressed by $\sigma_{t,j}$, and (b) fertility below replacement in many countries, expressed by past, current, and future low levels of $f_{t,k}$. Population aging is only partially offset by the stream of migrants $M_{t,j}$.

I treat all three demographic forces as exogenous. The starting point of the projection is the German population in 2015. I use the same assumptions as the high-immigration version of the official population projection (the 13th coordinated population forecast of the German Federal Statistical Office, variant "continuity under stronger immigration"). This projection includes the following assumptions through 2060:

- a constant fertility rate of 1.4,

- a constant net influx of 200,000 migrants year starting in 2021 (between 2015 and 2021 net immigration is assumed to decrease linearly from 500,000 to this value), and

- life expectancy at birth of 84.8 years for men and 88.2 years for women in the baseline and productivity slowdown scenarios and otherwise constant.

Labor supply is determined by multiplying population numbers with age- and gender-specific labor force participation rates $l_{t,j}$:

$$NW_t = \sum_{j=1}^{70} l_{t,j} N_{t,j}. \tag{5.3}$$

Labor force participation rates of the simulation's base year (2015) are taken from the German Mikrozensus, which provides differentiated labor force participation rates. Projections of the development of the labor market follow the short-term assumptions of the medium variant of the 2015 *Pension Report* (German Federal Ministry of Labor and Social Affairs 2015). I reflect the gradual increase in the statutory retirement age by two years (a consequence of a pension reform enacted in 2007) by assuming that individuals over 62 postpone their retirement accordingly, which I model by adjusting the labor force participation rate in the respective cohorts.

The number of pensioners is computed indirectly. MEA-PENSIM considers a retirement window from 51 to 70 (i.e., the first workers retire at age 51 and the last individuals claim their pensions at 70). I assume that the

---

8. I use an infinite summation to avoid the assumption of a fixed time of death. The notation does not imply that households have infinite lifespans. Because $\sigma_{t,j}$ and $f_{c,k}$ become very small for $j > 100$ and $k > 50$, respectively, $N_{t,j}$ is zero for large j, and all sums in this chapter are finite.

labor market exit age and pension-claiming age are identical. MEA-PENSIM then computes the number of pensioners at time t, denoted by NP_t, as the decrease in the number of workers from age 50 onward, correcting for mortality. In addition, I assume that nonmandatorily insured individuals (among them the self-employed, civil servants, and homemakers) claim their public pension at the statutory eligibility age.

MEA-PENSIM models a PAYG pension system with three key equations. At the macro level, the first equation is the PAYG identity of revenues and expenditures:

$$\tau_t \cdot w_t \cdot NW_t = p_t \cdot NP_t, \tag{5.4}$$

assuming that the pension budget is balanced every year.[9] Revenues are the contribution rate (τ_t) times the wage rate (w_t) times the number of workers (NW_t). Expenditures are pension benefits (p_t) times the number of pensioners (NP_t).

The second equation at the macro level determines either the replacement rate (in a defined-benefit system) or the contribution rate (in a defined-contribution system). If the PAYG system is of the defined-benefit type, a cohort of retirees is promised a pension benefit p_t, which is typically defined by a replacement rate q_0, $p_t = q_0 \cdot w_t$.[10] The contribution rate must be adjusted up or down to keep the PAYG defined-benefit system balanced, such that current workers cover the demographic risk for the benefit of the retirees:

$$\tau_t = q_0 \cdot NP_t / NW_t. \tag{5.5}$$

If the PAYG system is of the defined-contribution type, the pension system fixes the contribution rate τ_0 for a cohort of workers. Their replacement rate then follows the path

$$q_t = \tau_0 \cdot NW_t / NP_t, \tag{5.6}$$

which reacts passively to developments in demography and employment.

---

9. Many PAYG systems have a reserve and/or other multiyear balancing mechanisms (e.g., Settergren 2001 for Sweden). Other PAYG systems have budgets that are effectively part of the general government's budget and may increase or decrease the government's debt (see Kotlikoff 2002 for the United States).

10. Alternatively, the replacement rate relates to the net wage $w_t \cdot (1 - \tau_t)$. Defining benefits as a percentage of earnings is typical for Bismarckian pension systems, such as those in Germany and the United States. A defined-benefit scheme may also provide a fixed pension benefit, real or nominal, independent of earnings, which is typical of Beveridgean pension systems, such as the systems in the Netherlands and the United Kingdom.

Pure defined-benefit and pure defined-contribution systems are extreme points in the intergenerational risk distribution. The two pension benefit determination rules can be combined as

$$p_t / p_{t-1} = w_t / w_{t-1} \cdot (DR_{t-1} / DR_t)^{\alpha}, \tag{5.7}$$

where $DR_t = NP_t / NW_t$ is the dependency ratio and the weight $0 \leq \alpha \leq 1$ represents all compromises between a pure defined benefit and a pure defined contribution system. Such a hybrid defined PAYG pension system is modeled as System 8 and corresponds to the actual German PAYG system. The term DR_{t-1} / DR_t is called the "sustainability factor." The system's internal rate of return is[11]

$$irr = g + (\alpha \cdot n). \tag{5.8}$$

The parameter α can be set as a political compromise between current voters' preferences and financial sustainability. It determines the intergenerational distribution of the demographic risk generated by population aging. Setting $\alpha = 0$ stabilizes the replacement rate of pension benefits to the older generation; setting $\alpha = 1$ stabilizes the contribution rate of the younger generation. In MEA-PENSIM, α is set to 0.25, the value according to current German law.

At the micro level, the key equation of MEA-PENSIM defines pension benefits $p_{i,R}$ for an individual i claiming benefits at age R by three multiplicative components:

$$p_{i,R} = \bar{q} \, s_i \, \omega_R, \tag{5.9}$$

where $\bar{q}$ is the basic replacement rate for an average worker retiring at the statutory retirement age. It is either q_0 or q_t, depending on the type of pension system (defined benefit or defined contribution). s_i is an individual component linking the pension benefit to this individual's earnings. ω_R is an adjustment factor that links pension benefits to the actual claiming age R of individual i.

For pension systems with flat benefits, I set $s_i = 1$. In an earnings-related pension system, I model the relation between earnings and benefits in the form of earnings points. In each working year, earnings points reflect the labor income position of a worker at age i relative to the average earnings $\overline{wh}$. Earnings points are accumulated during the entire working life:

$$s_i = \sum_{i=0}^{R-1} \frac{w_i h_i}{\overline{wh}} / R. \tag{5.10}$$

---

11. Equation (5.8) is derived from equation (5.7) by taking the total differential and assuming that there is no cross-effect between wage growth and labor force shrinkage.

Life-time earnings points depend on the claiming age, the hours of work supplied (intensive and extensive margin), and their valuation (hourly wage).

I model the adjustments of pension benefits to the retirement age in a linear fashion, where the steepness of the adjustment is driven by a single adjustment rate (ω). If the household claims its pension at the statutory eligibility age $\overline{R}$, there is no deduction or premium ($\omega_R = 1$). For one year of earlier retirement, benefits are reduced by ω percent; for one year of later retirement, benefits are increased by ω percent:[12]

$$\omega_R = 1 + (R - \overline{R})\omega. \tag{5.11}$$

Many countries feature adjustment factors ω that are lower than actuarially neutral.[13]

I model a fully funded pension system following its fundamental assumptions: A generation pays into a fund during its working life and receives interest on the accumulated capital, which is then used to finance the consumption of the same generation during retirement. In its most abstract two-period form, workers receive wage income w in period 1, from which they pay a percentage (τ) into the pension fund. Pension income (p) is then

$$p = (1 + r) \cdot \tau \cdot w, \tag{5.12}$$

where r is defined in units that are commensurable with the period length. At this level of abstraction, a funded system is equivalent to voluntary private saving and the internal rate of return is the interest rate on the capital market (r). In a fully funded defined-contribution system, r is the realized capital market ex post; in a fully funded defined-benefit system, r is the ex ante rate of return that the sponsor of the fully funded pension system has guaranteed.

Results: How Large Is the Impact?

I display the results as trajectories of the three scenarios described in the preceding section. The trajectories show either the contribution rate (for

---

12. Some countries have two adjustment rates: ω_{ER} for retirement before the statutory "normal retirement age" and ω_{LR} for retirement thereafter. Adjustment factors are only one way to link pension benefits to the claiming age. They fit well with earnings point, notional defined contribution, and similar pension systems. Other mechanisms include age-varying benefit accrual rates.

13. The actuarial neutral adjustment rate at age 65 is about 6.3 percent for the average of France, Germany, and Italy underlying the calibration described in this section (see Queisser and Whitehouse 2006).

defined-benefit systems) or the replacement rate (for defined-contribution systems); for hybrid PAYG pension systems, I show both trajectories.

Population aging is the main driver of the trajectories. It increases the contribution rates of defined-benefit systems and reduces the replacement rates of defined-contribution systems. The difference between the baseline and the productivity slowdown scenarios shows the effect of declining real wage growth on the contribution (or replacement) rate precipitated by the productivity slowdown. The magnitude of this difference can be compared with the difference between the baseline scenario and the constant life expectancy scenario.

System 1 (Pay-as-You-Go, Earnings-Related, Defined-Benefit System)

In a prototypical Bismarckian PAYG defined-benefit pension system, the replacement rate is set by the political process independent of demography and productivity. Hence a productivity slowdown decreases pension benefits in absolute terms but keeps them constant relative to wages. As long as the system is fully wage indexed, financial sustainability is not affected. If adequacy is defined relative to wages (e.g., by a relative poverty line), it is also not affected.

Figure 5.2 shows this line of thinking using the MEA-PENSIM model applied to the German population, representing the aging Europe (see the qualifications in section 2). Population aging puts the pension system under pressure for two reasons: low fertility and increasing life expectancy. Low fertility has two components: the historical baby-boom/baby-bust transition, which produced a sudden decline from a relatively high to a much lower fertility rate mainly in the 1970s, and the continuing low fertility since then, which causes one generation to be about a third smaller than its predecessor (assuming a generation encompasses about 30 birth cohorts). As the replacement rate is constant by assumption, the contribution rate is steeply increasing until about 2035, when the size of the baby-boom generation decreases. After about 2035, the change in the old-age dependency ratio is driven by the steady increase of life expectancy, as the pressure from the "age boom" ends. Hence the increase in the baseline scenario flattens, and (by assumption) the contribution rate in the constant life expectancy scenario stabilizes.

The contribution rate is virtually identical in the two productivity scenarios (baseline and productivity slowdown). As by assumption the replacement rate in a PAYG defined-benefit pension system is constant, the productivity slowdown has no effect on the budget balance of the PAYG defined-benefit system in terms of the wage bill. In absolute terms, the pension system's budget shrinks proportionally with the wage bill.

This argument assumes that the productivity slowdown has no effects

Figure 5.2 Contribution rate in earnings-related, defined-benefit system with replacement rate fixed at 48 percent, 2014–60

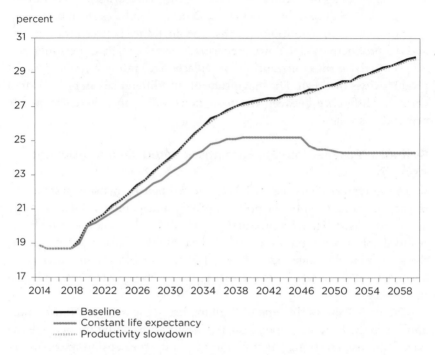

percent

Baseline
Constant life expectancy
Productivity slowdown

Source: Author's calculations.

on employment; the wage bill thus declines in proportion to the wage level. There may be more subtle effects if wages do not decline with productivity, as a result of staggered wage contracts or similar frictions, and employers react with lower labor demand, which decreases the tax and contribution base for the pension system.

As PAYG defined-benefit pension benefits that are strictly earnings related are fully wage indexed, neither financial sustainability nor adequacy defined relative to wages is affected.

This is not the case if adequacy (and thus also old-age poverty) is defined in absolute terms. In this situation, the case for policy intervention depends on two opposing trends. Even under the productivity slowdown scenario, labor productivity and hence wages and pension benefits grow, albeit at a slower than historical rate. This development is overlaid, however, by the pressures of population aging, which increases contributions and thus decreases net wages, to which pension benefits are indexed. Which of these forces is dominant depends on the speed of the productivity decline versus the speed of population aging.

In Germany the dependency ratio is expected to increase by about 0.5 percent a year. This figure corresponds to a similar loss in workers per capita and a corresponding increase in contributions to the pension system and declining real wages net of contributions. Productivity adds new resources, at the rate of 1.5 or 0.9 percent (depending on the scenario). In the baseline scenario, real wages grow by 1.5 percent a year, so absolute pension benefits could still increase by 1.0 percent a year without creating financial sustainability problems. This degree of political freedom is substantially reduced in the productivity slowdown scenario, in which real wages grow by only 0.9 percent a year. The balance still remains positive, at 0.4 percent a year.

The assumed productivity slowdown and associated decline in real wage growth would thus still imply increasing pension payments, even in a strongly aging economy such as Germany. Population aging is a slow process that takes fewer resources away than the new resources that are created by increasing productivity. The balance can be used to increase benefits, reduce contributions, or achieve a mixture of both.

There are many real-world complications to this fundamental argument. First, some countries have laws that limit the decrease in nominal pension payments. If inflation is low and productivity not only slows but decreases, the replacement rate would rise, which would require higher contributions or government subsidies, which could lead to a financially unsustainable situation.

Second, earnings-related schemes are often not as strict as modeled here. Contributory earnings may be capped from below and above, for reasons of intragenerational redistribution. Third, population aging may increase other taxes and contributions (e.g., because of higher healthcare costs and/or long-term care, as described in chapter 4 of this volume). All of these issues complicate country-specific projections of pension benefits and finances, but the fundamental argument remains.

System 2 (Pay-as-You-Go, Earnings-Related, Defined-Contribution System)

An earnings-related, PAYG, defined-contribution pension system is the mirror image of System 1. In the idealized PAYG defined benefit system, pensioners are protected in relative terms, and workers have to pay the increasing bill of population aging. In the PAYG defined-contribution system, workers are protected from contribution increases, but pension benefits will fall in both absolute and relative terms. The replacement rate in figure 5.3 is therefore the mirror image of the contribution rate in figure 5.2. Following the logic of the previous exercise, the effect of population aging is virtually identical in the baseline and productivity slowdown scenarios.

Figure 5.3 Replacement rate in earnings-related, defined-contribution system with contribution rate fixed at 19 percent, 2014–60

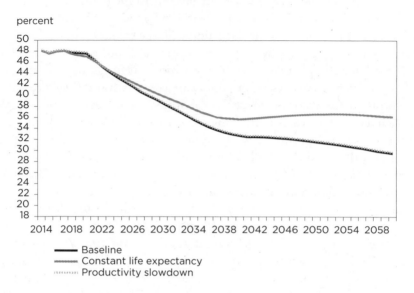

percent

Source: Author's calculations.

Stagnation of the historical increase in life expectancy has a large effect on stabilizing the replacement rate in the constant life expectancy scenario.[14]

As long as the system is fully wage indexed, employment is fixed, and there are no nominal minimum benefits rules, the financial sustainability of the system is not affected. Moreover, the productivity slowdown per se should not raise concerns about adequacy, as the replacement rates are identical in the baseline and productivity slowdown scenarios, and productivity growth outpaces the rise of the dependency ratio even in the low-growth scenario, implying that pensions would continue to rise in real terms.

System 3 (Pay-as-You-Go, Wage-Indexed, Flat-Benefits System)

If pension benefits are independent of individual earnings but indexed to wages (as social assistance is) and the system is financed by taxes on labor income, we are back to System 1. The replacement rate remains constant by definition. The contribution rate increases as a result of population aging, rising identically in the baseline and productivity slowdown scenarios (figure 5.4).

---

14. The slight deviations in figure 5.3 reflect the technicalities of pension benefit indexation.

Figure 5.4 Contribution rate in wage-indexed, flat-benefits system, 2014–60

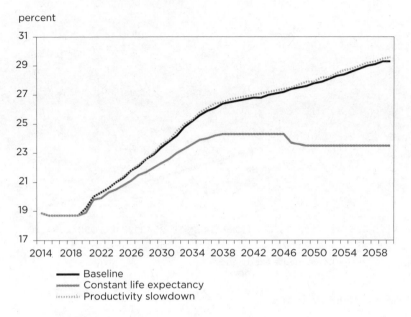

percent

Baseline
Constant life expectancy
Productivity slowdown

Source: Author's calculations.

As both the contribution rate and the replacement rate are identical in the two productivity scenarios, the productivity slowdown has no effect on the budget balance of the wage-indexed Beveridge system in terms of the wage bill. In absolute terms, the pension system's budget shrinks in proportion to the wage bill. As long as the system is fully wage indexed, employment is fixed, and there are no nominal minimum benefits rules, the financial sustainability of the system is not affected. Adequacy is also unaffected relative to wages.

If adequacy is defined in absolute terms, public policy action may be warranted, but only if the force of aging dominates the remaining wage increase after a productivity slowdown. As argued earlier, this is not the case for the assumed productivity slowdown and demographic projections.

System 4 (Pay-as-You-Go, Inflation-Indexed, Flat-Benefits System)

If the system provides flat pension benefits that are indexed only to inflation, not to wages, the replacement rate will fall over time, because retirees will not profit from productivity increases. Hence, relative to wage earners, pensioners grow increasingly worse off. This eroding effect is smaller if productivity rises more slowly, as the difference between the baseline and

Figure 5.5 Replacement rate in inflation-adjusted, flat-benefits system, 2014–60

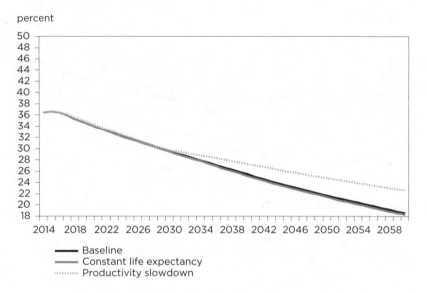

percent

Source: Author's calculations.

productivity slowdown scenarios shows (figure 5.5). In relative terms, the productivity slowdown thus strengthens adequacy. This seemingly ironic finding is the implication of a smaller gap between wage and pension benefit development. Productivity affects only the denominator, not the numerator of the replacement rate.

As the pension benefit amount is fixed in terms of purchasing power, demography has no effect on the replacement rate. The baseline and constant life expectancy scenarios thus show identical trajectories.

The effect of a productivity slowdown in the presence of population aging is more complex, as the two forces have opposite signs. The contribution rate to this system first increases and then declines (figure 5.6). Between 2020 and about 2037, population aging is strong and dominates the erosion effect. After about 2040, when mortality hits the baby-boom generation, the erosion effect will begin to dominate, reducing the contribution rate that is necessary to balance the pension system's budget. Relative to the baseline case, the contribution rate is higher in the productivity slowdown scenario, as the benefits increase relative to wages. If productivity growth slows and productivity declines in absolute terms, the situation may become financially unsustainable relative to the baseline.

Figure 5.6 Contribution rate in inflation-adjusted, flat-benefits system, 2014–60

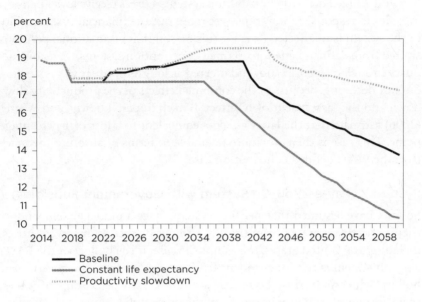

percent

Source: Author's calculations.

System 5 (Fully Funded Defined-Benefit System)

When productivity declines, fully funded pension systems suffer from lower interest rates. Whether this effect is larger or smaller than the decline in real wage growth assumed in the analysis of PAYG systems depends on the reaction of interest rates to productivity growth. If higher/lower labor productivity is translated one to one into higher/lower interest rates, the relative effects are numerically equal to the PAYG case.

If the decline in interest rates is larger than the decline of productivity (and thus the wage decline), retirees are shielded from benefit reductions despite declining capital returns. The sponsors of the system, however, have to increase their contributions. If the sponsors are enterprises, the increase will cut into their profits, reducing the financial sustainability of the system. This effect may trigger increases in output price and/or reduce gross wages during a wage-bargaining process. The final incidence for workers and retirees depends on many parameters, such as the price elasticity of demand and the bargaining powers of employers and workers.

At first sight, fully funded systems appear to be independent of population aging, as each generation pays into a fund and then receives benefits from that fund. Demography, however, does reduce interest rates, an effect sometimes referred to as the "asset meltdown." This term reflects a massively exaggerated choice of words (see Poterba 2004 and below).

System 6 (Fully Funded Defined-Contribution System)

In a fully funded defined-contribution system, retirees receive lower pension incomes in response to lower interest rates, but the financial sustainability of the system is unaffected (it is for this reason that occupational pensions shifted from defined-benefit to defined-contribution systems). Pension adequacy in a relative sense is not endangered as long as productivity is slowing but not declining, because of the combined effects of the productivity slowdown and the "asset meltdown" effect. Börsch-Supan, Ludwig, and Winter (2006) estimate that the latter effect is equivalent to a loss of 1 percentage point. This case is therefore more favorable in terms of absolute adequacy than the PAYG defined-contribution case.

System 7 (Pay-as-You-Go System with Government Subsidies)

So far I have assumed that pension systems have an independent budget that is strictly separated from the government budget. In many countries, including the United States, this is not the case. If the budget of the PAYG pension system is not independent from, or even part of, the government budget, which is paid by taxes that are not a fixed percentage of wages, there are various spillover effects from the mismatch between the (implicit) indexation mechanisms of revenues and the (implicit) indexation mechanisms of expenditures (e.g., the rate of inflation, the rate of wage growth, and the interest rate; see chapter 4 of this volume). These spillover mechanisms can be negative (via declining tax income from earnings) or positive (via declining debt service costs because of lower interest rates). Analysis needs to be tailored to the public finance system of a country.

System 8 (German Hybrid Pay-as-You-Go System)

Most European countries have mixed and hybrid systems. A "mixed" system consists of several parallel "pillars" (e.g., public PAYG, occupational defined benefit, private defined contribution). "Hybrid" systems emerge when the system combines defined-contribution and defined-benefit elements according to equation 5.7. Examples are the Swedish and Italian notional defined-contribution systems and the German "sustainability" system. The impact on pension income and financial sustainability can then be derived as a combination of the prototypical systems.

The German public PAYG pillar represents a hybrid between a defined-benefit and a defined-contribution system. The results are a combination of Systems 1 and 2 (figures 5.7 and 5.8).

As the budget balance of the PAYG system in terms of the wage bill is unaffected by the productivity slowdown, both contribution rate and

Figure 5.7 Contribution rate in earnings-related hybrid system, 2014–60

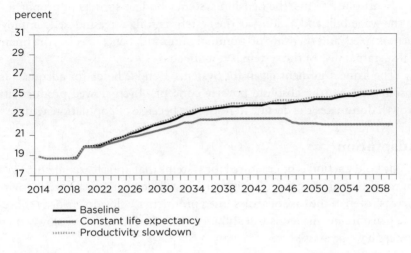

percent

Source: Author's calculations.

Figure 5.8 Replacement rate in earnings-related hybrid system, 2015–60

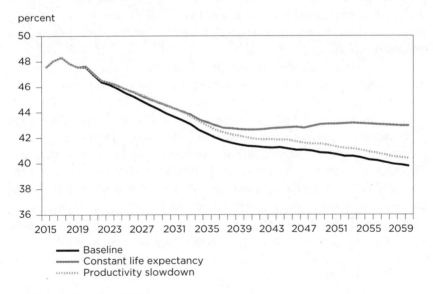

percent

Source: Author's calculations.

replacement rate are (almost) identical for the baseline and the productivity slowdown scenarios. Relative adequacy is not affected.

In absolute terms, the pension system's budget shrinks in proportion to the wage bill, and as long as the system is fully wage indexed, employment is fixed, and there are no nominal minimum benefits rules, the financial sustainability of the system is not affected.

The same argument given for Systems 1 and 2 holds for adequacy in absolute terms (the absolute poverty concept). Even slowed productivity growth dominates the decline in resources because of population aging.

Adaptation

Public policy action is not required for systems that are self-stabilizing. Even for those that are not, population aging is still slower than the productivity increase even in the case of an assumed productivity slowdown, hence absolute pension income levels will still increase, albeit much more slowly than retirees have been used to.

If this slower increase appears politically unacceptable, public policy actions should be used to increase the quantity of labor and capital in order to offset the lower than previously expected value of labor (because of lower productivity) and capital (because of lower interest rates) precipitated by the productivity slowdown. I analyze five types of adaptation: working longer, working more, attracting well-trained migrants, saving more, and improving education.

I first use a back-of-the-envelope calculation to assess the orders of magnitude necessary to increase quantity in order to compensate for the loss in value. A reduction in the annual increase in labor productivity from 1.5 percent to 0.9 percent corresponds to a loss of about 20 percent in productive capacity between 2020 and 2050. Quantity therefore has to increase by about 20 percent over this period to compensate for that loss. This large increase may have negative feedback effects on wages and/or the interest rate. I therefore also briefly discuss how large these feedback effects are, based on results from published macroeconomic studies that use overlapping generation models that are calibrated to European data and simulate the key parameters of pension systems in aging populations.[15]

Working Longer

Changing the average exit age from the labor force increases the size of the workforce that contributes to the pension system. If the claiming age also

---

15. Auerbach and Kotlikoff (1987) introduced the basic methodology.

changes at the same time, the system gains from a double bonus: more contributors and fewer beneficiaries.

Using the figures cited above and assuming that exit and claiming age are in sync, the length of a working life has to increase from roughly 40 years in 2020 to about 48 years in 2050. Assuming the same start of the working life and a current "retirement age" of 62, the "retirement age" would have to rise to 70 in 2050. Given current political preferences, such a change would hardly be a trivial policy action (see Boeri, Börsch-Supan, and Tabellini 2001, 2002; Galasso 2007).

I put "retirement age" in quotation marks because labor force exit age and pension claiming age increasingly tend to differ. So-called flexibility reforms try to disentangle these two dates even farther. If people work longer but keep claiming their pensions early, not much is gained, particularly if people working past their claiming age do not contribute to the pension system. The effect may even be negative, because theory and evidence suggest that more hours are lost before the typical retirement age when partial retirement is introduced than gained after the typical retirement age when the adjustment of benefits to the chosen claiming age are less than actuarial (Börsch-Supan et al. 2018).[16] In these systems, "soft" flexibility reforms are thus no alternatives to a "tough" policy of increasing the claiming age.

Increasing the claiming age may not work as well as intended. One also has to be sure that there will be no misuse of disability pensions and special preretirement arrangements as escape routes for workers who do not qualify for these pathways to retirement. Before the 1992–2005 pension reform sequence in Germany, the rule of thumb was that a one-year increase in the statutory claiming age increased the average claiming age by only four months because of such slippage in the system. After many pathways were closed, this slippage is probably considerably smaller, as the recent increase in the claiming age appears to show.[17]

If the pension system is fully actuarial—which none of the European systems is and the US system is only between ages 60 and 65—by definition a change in the claiming age does not change the financial balance of the system. The macroeconomic feedback effects of this gradual increase in the labor force on wages are small, as Börsch-Supan et al. (2014) show.

Increasing the average exit age and thus labor force participation at older ages may be of little effect if labor productivity declines with age, as is commonly assumed. The evidence, however, is inconclusive. The more

---

16. Börsch-Supan et al. (2018) provide both theory and international evidence. Graf, Hofer, and Winter-Ebmer (2011) provide supporting detailed evidence for the flexibility reform in Austria.

17. See the econometric estimates in Börsch-Supan et al. (2004).

sophisticated the econometric analyses used to measure the age-productivity profile and purge the results from selection effects, the flatter the age-productivity profile (Göbel and Zwick 2009, Börsch-Supan and Weiss 2016).

Working More

If the younger generation works more (higher labor force participation, more weekly hours), the revenues of the pension system increase. A back-of-the-envelope calculation suggests that one needs to extend a 40-hour week to 48 hours in order to increase the volume of labor enough to offset the negative impacts of a productivity slowdown. This increase is large, in particular for France and some Mediterranean countries.

Attracting Well-Trained Migrants

France has a workforce of 30 million, Germany 43 million, and Italy 26 million. A back-of-the-envelope calculation indicates that increasing this workforce by 0.6 percent a year to offset a productivity decline of the same magnitude would require that France attract 180,000, Germany 260,000, and Italy 160,000 well-trained migrants annually from 2020 to 2050. During the unusual year of 2015, France received 190,000, Germany 950,000, and Italy 200,000 migrants (Eurostat data). Only a small fraction were well trained, however, and the year was a political shock for Europe. This option therefore seems entirely unrealistic.

Saving More

Saving more in a PAYG system is tantamount to creating a new pillar that compensates for the loss in real wages and related pension benefits. This strategy was one of the backbones in many pension reforms between 1990 and 2010 in Europe (e.g., the mandatory "premium pension" in Sweden, the voluntary "Riester pensions" in Germany, and recent nudging approaches in the United Kingdom). A saving rate of 4 percent of earnings during the entire working life offsets the loss in pension benefits displayed in figure 5.8 for the German hybrid system, based on a modest (but currently hard to achieve) real rate of return of 1.5 percent. The above back-of-the-envelope calculation suggests increasing this saving rate to about 5 percent in order to compensate for an even lower rate of return because of the productivity slowdown.

Whether this option is realistic in a voluntary system is unclear and depends very much on the underlying assumptions about saving behavior. These assumptions (e.g., are humans behaving like the forward-looking neoclassical paradigm or do they procrastinate, will they react to changes in the interest rate or are they solely oriented toward a saving target?)

are controversial. The current participation rate for Riester pensions in Germany is slightly less than 50 percent and stagnant. Alternative investments, such as occupational and unsubsidized private pensions, cover an additional quarter of the German population. Full coverage has not been achieved; it appears to have fallen rather than risen. It is much easier to fulfill this aim in a mandatory system, such as Sweden's, or a nudging system, such as the United Kingdom's.

Higher saving has several feedback effects that cannot be ignored. Higher forced saving (in mandatory funded systems, both public and private) may crowd out other saving. The literature provides contradictory results.[18] A transition to more funding and less PAYG depresses interest rates even farther. Börsch-Supan, Ludwig, and Winter (2006) use an overlapping generations macro model to estimate this effect. If funds are invested globally, the effect is negligible. The effect can become significant if home bias incentivizes people to invest predominantly in their own country. The effects also depend on whether the additional savings are invested in government bonds (which increase the effect) or productive capital (which reduces the effect).

Improving Education

Better education has direct and indirect effects. It directly mitigates the productivity decline and improves the budget of the pension system through higher earnings. Very little is known about the elasticity of changes in the education system with respect to labor productivity, however, and even less is known about the cost-effectiveness of investing in education.

Conclusion

A productivity slowdown is like a falling tide: It lowers all the boats. If pension benefits are consistently indexed to wages, neither financial stability nor relative adequacy is endangered, but the entire system shrinks in proportion to the wage bill. Depending on whether the system is based on a defined benefit or a defined contribution, the decline in absolute terms will make the older or younger generation worse off than the preceding generation relative to the baseline at historical productivity growth rates.

Absolute pension benefits would not decline, however. Even slower growth of labor productivity of about 0.9 percent a year is more than the annual loss in resources because of population aging (about 0.5 percent a year). Under historical growth rates of labor productivity (about 1.5 percent a year), annual benefits rose by a full percentage point. The increase is now

---

18. Börsch-Supan et al. (2015) provide a review. Corneo, Keese, and Schröder (2009) present a decidedly different view.

substantially less (0.4 percent a year) but still positive. If this increase is politically unacceptable, policymakers have to increase the volume of labor or capital.

This discussion shows clearly that one needs a policy mix. No single policy action is sufficient to carry the entire burden of keeping pension benefits and contribution rates at the preslowdown level. What is needed is a policy mix consisting of working longer, working more, attracting well-trained migrants, saving more, and improving education.

References

Auerbach, A.J., and L.J. Kotlikoff. 1987. *Dynamic Fiscal Policy*. New York: Cambridge University Press.

Boeri, T., A. Börsch-Supan, and G. Tabellini. 2001. Would You Like to Shrink the Welfare State? The Opinions of European Citizens. *Economic Policy* 32: 9–50.

Boeri, T., A. Börsch-Supan, and G. Tabellini. 2002. Would You Like to Reform the Pension System? The Opinions of European Citizens. *American Economic Review* 92: 396–401.

Börsch-Supan, A., T. Bucher-Koenen, M. Coppola, and B. Lamla. 2015. Savings in Times of Demographic Change: Lessons from the German Experience. *Journal of Economic Surveys* 29: 807–29.

Börsch-Supan, A., T. Bucher-Koenen, V. Kutlu-Koc, and N. Goll. 2018. Dangerous Flexibility: Retirement Reforms Reconsidered. *Economic Policy* (March): 1–36.

Börsch-Supan, A., K. Härtl, and D.N. Leite. 2016. Social Security and Public Insurance. *Handbook of the Economics of Population Aging* 1B: 781–863.

Börsch-Supan, A., A. Ludwig, and J. Winter. 2006. Aging, Pension Reform, and Capital Flows: A Multi-Country Simulation Model. *Economica* 73: 625–58.

Börsch-Supan, A., R. Schnabel, S. Kohnz, and G. Mastrobuoni. 2004. Micro-modeling of Retirement Decisions in Germany. In *Social Security Programs and Retirement around the World: Micro-Estimation*, ed. J. Gruber and D. Wise. Chicago: University of Chicago Press.

Börsch-Supan, A., and M. Weiss. 2016. Productivity and Age: Evidence from Work Teams at the Assembly Line. *Journal of the Economics of Ageing* 7: 30–42.

Börsch-Supan, A., and C.B. Wilke. 2005. The German Public Pension System: How It Will Become an NDC System Look-Alike. In *Pension Reform: Issues and Prospects for Non-Financial Defined Contribution (NDC) Schemes*, ed. R. Holzmann and E. Palmer. Washington: World Bank.

Buchheim, Christoph. 1997. *Einführung in die Wirtschaftsgeschichte*. Munich: Beck.

Corneo, G., M. Keese, and K. Schröder. 2009. The Riester Scheme and Private Savings: An Empirical Analysis Based on the German SOEP. *Schmollers Jahrbuch* 129: 321–32.

Franco, D., and N. Sartor. 2005. Notional Defined Contribution in Italy: Unsatisfactory Present, Uncertain Future. In *Pension Reform: Issues and Prospects for Non-Financial Defined Contribution (NDC) Schemes*, ed. R. Holzmann and E. Palmer. Washington: World Bank.

Galasso, V. 2007. *The Political Future of Social Security in Aging Societies*. Cambridge, MA: MIT Press.

German Federal Ministry of Labor and Social Affairs. 2015. *Pension Report*. Berlin.

Göbel, C., and T. Zwick. 2009. Age and Productivity: Evidence from Linked Employer Employee Data. *De Economist* 160: 35–57.

Graf, N., H. Hofer, and R. Winter-Ebmer. 2011. Labor Supply Effects of a Subsidized Old-Age Part-Time Scheme in Austria. *Zeitschrift für ArbeitsmarktForschung* 44: 217–29.

Holthausen, Annette, Johannes Rausch, and Christina Benita Wilke. 2012. *MEA-PENSIM 2.0: Weiterentwicklung eines Rentensimulationsmodells, Konzeption und Ausgewählte Anwendungen.* MEA Discussion Paper 03-2012. Munich: Max Planck Institute for Social Law and Social Policy.

Kotlikoff, L. 2002. Generational policy. In *Handbook of Public Economics*, vol. 4, ed. A. J. Auerbach and M. Feldstein. Amsterdam: North-Holland.

Lynch, J., and M. Myrskyl. 2009. Always the Third Rail? Pension Income and Policy Preferences in European Democracies. *Comparative Political Studies* 42: 1068–97.

OECD (Organization for Economic Cooperation and Development). 2015. *Pensions at a Glance.* Paris.

Palmer, E. 2002. Swedish Pension Reform: How Did It Evolve, and What Does It Mean for the Future? In *Social Security Pension Reform in Europe*, ed. M. Feldstein and H. Siebert. Chicago: University of Chicago Press.

Poterba, J.M. 2004. Impact of Population Aging on Financial Markets in Developed Countries. *Federal Reserve Bank of Kansas City Economic Review* 89: 43–53.

Queisser, M., and E. Whitehouse. 2006. *Neutral or Fair? Actuarial Concepts and Pension System Design.* OECD Social, Employment and Migration Working Paper 40. Paris: Organization for Economic Cooperation and Development.

Rausch, Johannes, and Martin Gasche. 2016. Beitragsentwicklung in der Gesetzlichen Krankenversicherung und der Sozialen Pflegeversicherung: Projektionen und Determinanten. *Zeitschrift für Wirtschaftspolitik* 65, no. 3: 195–238.

Settergren, O. 2001. The Automatic Balance Mechanism of the Swedish Pension System. *Wirtschaftspolitische Blätter* 2001/4.

Wilke, Christina Benita. 2004. *Ein Simulationsmodell des Rentenversicherungssystems: Konzeption und ausgewählte Anwendungen von MEA-PENSIM.* MEA Discussion Paper 048-04. Munich: Max Planck Institute for Social Law and Social Policy.

II

INTERNATIONAL
IMPLICATIONS

6

Productivity in Emerging-Market Economies: Slowdown or Stagnation?

JOSÉ DE GREGORIO

Since the global financial crisis, productivity growth in advanced economies has been sluggish and is expected to remain slow. Medium-term prospects have also been declining. Whether the slowdown reflects secular stagnation, caused by lack of aggregate demand (Summers 2014), or a long-term trend decline in productivity growth (Gordon 2016), the implications for emerging-market economies are far-reaching. These economies will face low global demand for their goods and services and weak tailwinds from the global economy. Closing the productivity gap with advanced economies could improve their growth prospects.

Total factor productivity (TFP) is central because it is the driver of growth in the long run in traditional models of economic growth. This chapter examines the main historical facts about productivity in emerging-market economies compared with the United States and other advanced economies. (Table 6A.1 in the appendix lists the 41 economies in the sample.)[1] The next section describes the outlook for a long-term decline in

José De Gregorio, nonresident senior fellow at the Peterson Institute for International Economics, is dean of the School of Economics and Business at the University of Chile. He was governor of the Central Bank of Chile and minister of the economy, mining, and energy of Chile. He thanks Egor Gornostay, Olivier Jeanne, Adam Posen, and Jeromin Zettelmeyer for their helpful comments. He is also grateful for comments and discussions during the preconference meeting and the conference at PIIE and a seminar at the University of Chile. Bernardo Candia and Mariana del Rio provided excellent research assistance.

1. I use the definition provided by the International Monetary Fund's *Fiscal Monitor*, which includes "emerging markets and middle-income economies." I include only countries for which sufficient data are available and that had GDP per capita greater than $5,000 in purchasing

growth and productivity and reviews the historical evolution of productivity and GDP across groups of countries. The following section examines the convergence of GDP in emerging-market economies and the evolution of factors and productivity gaps across emerging-market economies. The third section presents a development accounting exercise for a group of Asian, European, and Latin American emerging markets, which shows that low TFP explains most of the income gap with respect to the United States. The fourth section analyzes episodes of growth accelerations and compares growth decompositions during those episodes with the whole period covered by the Penn World Tables 9.0 for each country. The fifth section looks at the correlations between TFP in emerging-market economies and advanced economies and the frequency of growth accelerations with the global cycle. It shows a recent increase in the correlation of TFP growth between emerging-market economies and advanced economies and discusses potential factors that may explain the increase. The sixth section discusses factors affecting TFP in the long run. The last section summarizes the chapter's main conclusions.

The main findings of this chapter are:

- The GDP per capita gap between emerging-market economies and the United States has narrowed.

- The narrowing of the gap is explained by faster accumulation of physical and human capital than in the United States.

- In contrast, the TFP gap has not narrowed. In most countries, productivity has been growing slower than in the United States. Low productivity explains about two-thirds of the output gap.

- Emerging-market economies are characterized not by a smooth process of growth but by growth bursts followed by slowdowns. Periods when growth accelerates are also periods when the contribution to TFP growth is the largest.

---

power parity dollars and population of more than 3 million in 2010. I compare this definition with the *World Economic Outlook*'s classification of emerging-market economies, which adds Bulgaria. I excluded Kuwait, Saudi Arabia, and the United Arab Emirates, because total factor productivity data for these countries are too volatile, largely because of the importance of oil. Some countries would have been classified as emerging-market economies decades ago but are now classified as advanced economies. Looking at those countries is useful because they reveal the evolution of "successful" emerging-market economies. Advanced economies that in 1990 had per capita GDP of no more than 60 percent that of the United States were included in the emerging-market economies group. They are the Czech Republic, Greece, Israel, Korea, Lithuania, Portugal, the Slovak Republic, and Taiwan. Most data come from version 9.0 of the Penn World Tables.

- Productivity growth in emerging-market economies is correlated with that in advanced economies. Growth accelerates in emerging-market economies during periods of higher global growth.
- In recent years the correlation between TFP growth in emerging-market economies and that in advanced economies has increased.

Long-Term Decline in Growth and Productivity Outlook

Long-term prospects for growth and productivity increases have softened. The decline began before the global financial crisis and intensified thereafter. A simple way to gauge long-term growth prospects is to look at five-year-ahead forecasts produced by the International Monetary Fund (IMF) for each of its biannual *World Economic Outlook* reports, and how they have changed over time. Figure 6.1 shows the change in the five-year-ahead rate of GDP growth forecast in the IMF's *World Economic Outlook* of April 2008, April 2012, and April 2017.[2]

For the world economy as a whole, expected long-term growth declined from 4.9 percent in 2008 to 4.7 percent in 2012 and 3.8 percent in 2017. Most of the change thus came well after the crisis, for both the world as a whole and most country groupings. Only for the United States, five-year-ahead projections of growth increased from 3.2 percent in 2008 to 3.3 percent in 2012, but then fell to 1.7 percent in 2017. In the unweighted average for emerging-market economies used in this chapter, forecasted potential output growth fell from 4.9 percent in 2008 to 4.4 percent in 2012 to 3.2 percent in 2017.[3] The downward revision of China's expected growth—from 10 percent in 2008 to 8.5 percent in 2012 and 5.7 percent in 2017—drove the sharp decline in growth expectations in Asia. The euro area is the only region in which the downward forecast revision between 2008 and 2012 was greater than the revision between 2012 and 2017. The revisions made in the 2000s coincided with the productivity slowdown that started in that decade and deepened in the current decade.

Now, I turn to the historical evidence. Figure 6.2 shows the average of five-year median growth of GDP and TFP in emerging-market and advanced

---

2. The five-year-ahead forecast is not always an estimate of long-term potential, because some countries may be in a cyclical position that may affect growth forecast at longer horizons. However, the dates chosen for the comparisons as well as the fact that I look at country averages should provide a reasonable estimate of the IMF's assessment for long-term growth.

3. Averages in documents from international organizations are usually computed as weighted averages. My focus is on countries. I therefore use simple average or medians in the rest of this chapter. In figure 6.1 only the average of the sample of emerging-market economies used in this chapter is a simple one; the rest are weighted averages.

Figure 6.1 Changes in five-year-ahead growth forecasts

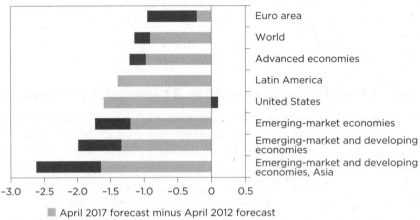

Note: This figure presents the difference between the five-year-ahead growth forecast of the IMF *World Economic Outlook* in 2017 and 2012 and in 2012 and 2008—that is, the difference between the forecast for 2022 made in 2017 and the forecast for 2017 made in 2012 and the difference between the former forecast and the forecast for 2013 made in 2008. The length of the bar represents the total change from 2008 to 2017. The figure for emerging-market economies is the simple average for the sample used in this paper.

Source: IMF *World Economic Outlook*, April 2008, April 2012, and April 2017.

Figure 6.2 Total factor productivity (TFP) and GDP growth in emerging-market and advanced economies, 1955–2014

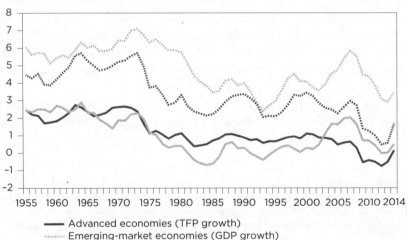

Source: Penn World Tables 9.0.

economies.[4] The rates are correlated, but the most striking fact is that GDP growth in emerging-market economies has generally been higher than that of advanced economies whereas TFP growth has been lower. Between 1951 and 2014, average annual GDP growth was 4.5 percent in emerging-market economies and 3.5 percent in advanced economies. In contrast, average TFP growth was 1.0 percent in emerging-market economies and 1.2 percent in advanced economies. TFP growth in emerging-market economies was consistently below that of advanced economies until the 2000s, the period of the commodity price boom, when TFP growth was significantly higher. That growth came to a halt with the global financial crisis.

Differences in TFP account for the bulk of the differences in levels of income across countries, as Klenow and Rodríguez-Clare (1997) and Hall and Jones (1999) show; I confirm these findings below. Clark and Feenstra (2003) show that the source of income divergence since the Industrial Revolution has been TFP divergence. I go one step farther, showing that even within countries that have been converging to high levels of income, TFP has been diverging.

Income, Factors, and Productivity Catch-Up

There is a significant income gap between emerging-market and advanced economies. I follow the convention of using the United States as the benchmark for comparisons.

The income gap has declined but remains significant. For the sample of countries I use, the simple average income gap (1 minus relative GDP per capita) was 71 percent in 1990. It declined to 65 percent in 2014. The decline may reflect the accumulation of factors and the more rapid growth of productivity in emerging-market economies than in the United States.

This section examines the evolution of the gaps in per capita GDP, per capita physical capital, per capita human capital, and TFP. All of the data are from the Penn World Tables 9.0. It compares these gaps in 2014 (the last year of the database) and 1990.[5]

---

4. The sample of advanced economies follows the classification of the IMF. I exclude a group of countries that were classified as emerging markets many years ago and are now advanced economies. Those countries are included in the sample of emerging market economies as described in the text. For each year I compute median growth and then the average of these medians over a five-year period.

5. The comparisons could have been made with 1980, but the 1980s were years of low growth in emerging-market economies, in particular in Latin America, where countries suffered the debt crisis ("the lost decade"). In 1980 Latin American countries had high levels of income, often fueled by the abundant liquidity in the global economy. In contrast, the 1990s marked the beginning of increased international financial integration and were a period of resurgence of capital flows to emerging-market economies (Calvo, Leiderman, and Reinhart 1993). In ad-

Figure 6.3 GDP per capita relative to the United States, 1990 and 2014

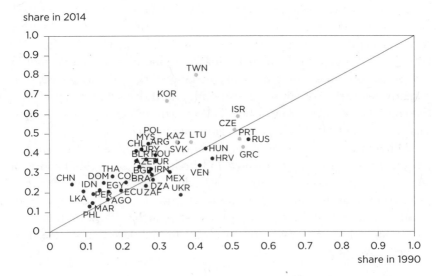

share in 2014

Note: Dark gray dots represent emerging-market economies; light gray dots are former emerging-market economies that are now classified as advanced economies. See table 6A.1 for country names.

Source: Penn World Tables 9.0.

Most countries increased their GDP per capita relative to the United States over this period (figure 6.3). Of the 41 countries studied, 31 had a larger ratio in 2014 than in 1990. The most successful cases were Korea, where the ratio rose from 32 percent to 67 percent, and Taiwan, where it rose from 40 percent to 80 percent. The ratio in China went from 6 percent to 24 percent. Russia, Greece, Venezuela, and Ukraine are among the countries that experienced declines in relative GDP. Mexico, which signed the North American Free Trade Agreement (NAFTA) in 1994, also experienced a decline in relative GDP per capita, which fell from 33 percent to 30 percent.

Figures 6.4 and 6.5 show the relative levels of physical and human capital, respectively. Most countries have been catching up to the United States with respect to physical capital ("capital" for short). The magnitudes are similar to those of relative GDP. The average stock of capital per capita rose from 29 percent of the United States' in 1990 to 40 percent in 2014. In 36 economies, the share increased; it declined in only 5. The cases of Korea and Taiwan are the most remarkable. The ratio in Korea rose from 27 percent to 83 percent; the ratio in Taiwan rose from 37 percent to 89 percent. Among

---

dition, the size of the sample increased after 1990 (by, for example, including members of the former Soviet Union). In any case, using 1980 or 1990 leads to broadly similar results.

Figure 6.4   Capital stock per capita relative to the United States, 1990 and 2014

share in 2014

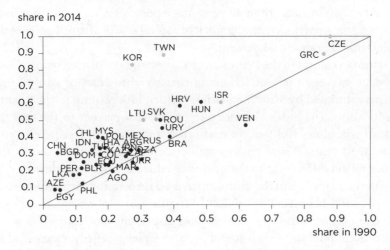

Note: Dark gray dots represent emerging-market economies; light gray dots represent former emerging-market economies that are now classified as advanced economies. See table 6A.1 for country names.

Source: Penn World Tables 9.0.

Figure 6.5   Human capital relative to the United States, 1990 and 2014

share in 2014

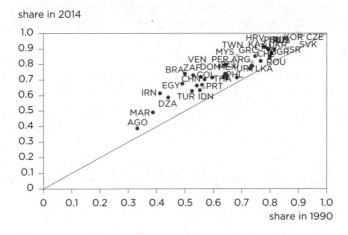

Note: Dark gray dots represent emerging-market economies; light gray dots represent former emerging-market economies that are now classified as advanced economies. See table 6A.1 for country names.

Source: Penn World Tables 9.0.

middle-income countries, Lithuania closed the gap by 20 percentage points. Chile and Malaysia, which started at lower income per capita levels, also narrowed the gap by more than 20 percentage points. China stands out in the lowest income portion, with the stock of capital soaring from 4 percent that of the United States to 31 percent.

Human capital in the Penn World Tables 9.0 is measured with an index based on average years of schooling that weights years of education by returns estimated by Mincer equations, which link earning to the quantity of education. The index assumes a return of 13.4 percent to the first four years of schooling, 10.1 percent to the next four years, and 6.8 percent to all subsequent years.[6] These returns are not country specific; the results thus do not reflect differences in the quality of education across countries.

All the countries in the sample increased their ratios with respect to the United States between 1990 and 2014 (figure 6.5). On average, these ratios rose from 66 percent to 77 percent, and dispersion was relatively low. The Slovak Republic, the Czech Republic, and Israel reached or exceeded the level of the United States, and Korea neared it.

The Penn World Tables include no data on the level of TFP at constant prices. They do include an index for TFP at constant national prices, on which 2011 is equal to 1. With this index, it is possible to compute the real rate of growth of TFP but not the level, preventing the computation of a gap with respect to the United States. However, the Penn World Tables also provide an index for TFP at current prices in which the United States equals 1 for each year. The ratio for 2011 can be used to compute relative values for TFP (figure 6.6).

The Penn World Tables calculate measures of TFP for every country using its own income shares. Using country-specific income shares may present some measurement anomalies for some countries. Later in this chapter, I present other evidence using identical income shares, which also provides a robustness check. The results are similar to the ones presented in this section.[7]

The results are striking. There is no pattern of catching up; on average the productivity gap increased. In 1990 average TFP was 67 percent that of the United States; by 2014 the figure had declined to 60 percent. The countries that enjoyed the largest GDP catch-up (Korea and Taiwan) experienced

---

6. For details on the measure of human capital in the Penn World Tables see www.rug.nl/ggdc/docs/human_capital_in_pwt_90.pdf.

7. Some countries, including Bulgaria, Egypt, Iran, and Turkey, enjoyed higher TFP than the United States. I exclude these countries from the comparisons because I have no explanation for this result, which seems to reflect a measurement problem. TFP data are not available for Algeria, Angola, Azerbaijan, and Belarus.

Figure 6.6 Total factor productivity relative to the United States, 1990 and 2014

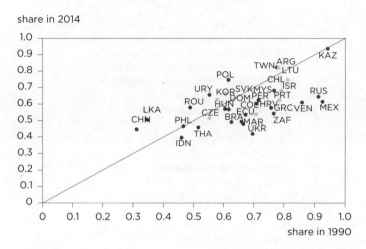

share in 2014

Note: Dark gray dots represent emerging-market economies; light gray dots represent former emerging-market economies that are now classified as advanced economies. See table 6A.1 for country names.

Source: Penn World Tables 9.0.

only a small productivity catch-up. Mexico, Russia, Ukraine, and Venezuela showed significant divergence. Of the 33 countries shown in figure 6.6, only 10 experienced productivity catch-up. In all of the others, the gap widened.

This widening does not necessarily reflect a decline in TFP; it merely shows that growth was slower than in the United States. Figure 6.7 shows the annual average growth in productivity during 1990–2014. China, Sri Lanka, Poland, and a handful of other countries experienced faster TFP growth than the United States. About a third of countries had slower but still positive growth. Other countries experienced negative TFP growth. This finding may reflect reallocation from more productive firms and sectors to less productive ones.

TFP is intrinsically difficult to measure,[8] and the figures from the Penn World Tables 9.0 often differ from more careful estimates made in each country. These comparisons should therefore be taken as broadly indicative of productivity developments across countries rather than as precise country by country figures.

---

8. Low productivity in Chile, for example, partly reflects low TFP in the mining sector that reflects geological rather than technological factors. Excluding mining, Chile's TFP growth was higher (Blagrave and Santoro 2016). In Uruguay agriculture played a key role: TFP in agriculture grew at about 7 percent during 2002–13 (Lema 2015).

Figure 6.7   Annual average change in total factor productivity between 1990 and 2014

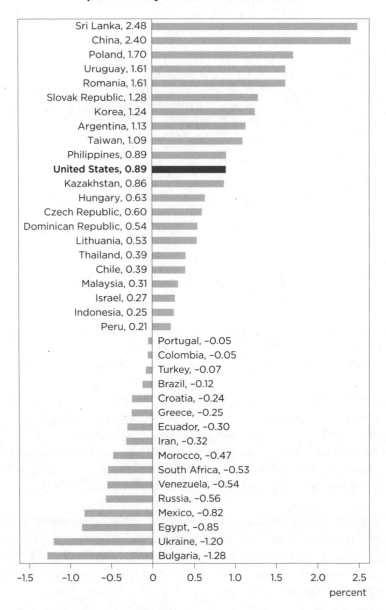

Source: Penn World Tables 9.0.

A puzzling case is Mexico, which experienced negative productivity growth. This finding is not an artifact of the Penn World Tables data: National sources (e.g., Torre and Colunga 2015) show that TFP contracted by an average annual rate of 0.4 percent between 1990 and 2011 (the Penn World Tables for the same period indicate a contraction of 0.8 percent a year). The only five-year period in which productivity growth was positive was 1996–2000, which corresponds to the recovery from the Tequila crisis and the first years of NAFTA.

Declining productivity in Mexico is puzzling, given NAFTA, the stabilization of inflation, and other important reforms, including in the energy sector. Openness increased. Exports rose from 6 percent of GDP in 1990 to 27 percent in 2014. Levy and Rodrik (2017) argue that dualism is an important explanation of the "Mexican paradox." After liberalization, the size of the informal sector widened, deepening dualism, as reflected in large growth disparities across Mexican regions (OECD 2017). The entrance of China into the global economy may also have reduced the potential benefits of NAFTA, although Mexican exports have been dynamic. Another contributing factor could be the weak rule of law and high levels of corruption.

According to Levy (2018), Mexico's problems stem from the misallocation of physical and human capital. Lack of competition in many sectors and the ability of too many inefficient and small firms, many of them informal, to survive, may account for the fact that the rise in investment has not been accompanied by TFP growth.

The closing of the GDP per capita gap between emerging-market economies and the United States has largely reflected the decline in the gap between the capital and human capital stocks, with no contribution from productivity. This evidence is reminiscent of the discussion generated by the findings of Young (1994), who showed that the Asian miracle was more "perspiration" than "inspiration"—the result of increased labor force participation and high levels of investment, with modest TFP growth. In Indonesia, Malaysia, and Thailand, TFP growth is below that of the United States, resulting in a widening of the gap. In the Philippines, the gap remains unchanged. Only Korea and Taiwan experienced a small decline in the gap.

This pattern is not particular to Asia; it characterizes most emerging-market economies. One important exception is China, where productivity growth has been close to 3 percent a year. With a labor share of 0.65 percent and annual TFP growth of 3 percent, the steady-state rate of growth of per capita GDP in the neoclassical growth model would be 4.6 percent, allowing for rapid catch-up. The question is how long can this TFP growth can be sustained.

Development Accounting

To obtain additional evidence on the closing of the GDP gap, I perform development accounting for a group of Asian, emerging European, and Latin American countries. Given the production function

$$Y = AK^{\alpha}H^{1-\alpha}, \tag{6.1}$$

where Y is output, A is TFP, K is capital, H is human capital (assumed to be a linear function of labor), and $H = hL$ (where h is human capital per worker, measured as a combination of years of schooling and returns and L is labor), GDP per capita can be expressed as

$$y = (k/y)^{\alpha/(1-\alpha)}hA^{1/(1-\alpha)}, \tag{6.2}$$

where lowercase letters represent per worker variables, which, assuming no changes in labor force participation, should be proportional to GDP per capita. Using a subscript i for emerging-market economies and u for the United States yields the following decomposition for the GDP per capita ratio:

$$\frac{y_i}{y_u} = \left(\frac{k_i/y_i}{k_u/y_u}\right)^{\alpha/(1-\alpha)} \left(\frac{h_i}{h_u}\right)\left(\frac{A_i}{A_u}\right)^{1/(1-\alpha)}. \tag{6.3}$$

This equation can be used to undertake a development accounting exercise. The first two terms capture gaps in physical and human capital, respectively; the third gap is for TFP.

In an alternative decomposition, the component of capital would be measured not as the relative capital-output ratio in equation (6.3) but as the ratio of capital per worker. In this case, the equation for development accounting becomes

$$\frac{y_i}{y_u} = \left(\frac{k_i}{k_u}\right)^{\alpha} \left(\frac{h_i}{h_u}\right)^{1-\alpha} \left(\frac{A_i}{A_u}\right). \tag{6.4}$$

Equation (6.3) is preferred, because, in the neoclassical growth model, capital per worker depends on the level of productivity; TFP therefore explains part of the differences in capital in equation (6.4). In contrast, the capital-output ratio is independent of TFP (for details, see Jones 2016). In the appendix I report the decomposition using equation (6.4) as an alternative to the traditional one. As the capital gap between emerging markets and the United States is larger than the gap in the capital-output ratio, equation (6.4) tends to indicate a smaller TFP gap than equation (6.3).

I assume that labor shares $(1-\alpha)$ are the same across countries and equal to 0.65. Data on GDP, physical capital, and human capital are taken from

Table 6.1 Development accounting

Region/year	GDP per worker (1)	Capital/ GDP (2)	Human capital (3)	TFP (4)	Share due to TFP (5)
Asia					
1990	0.127	0.799	0.595	0.266	64.1
2000	0.147	0.969	0.654	0.232	73.3
2010	0.208	1.024	0.694	0.293	70.8
Latin America					
1990	0.246	0.909	0.617	0.440	56.0
2000	0.242	1.025	0.668	0.354	65.9
2010	0.293	0.961	0.714	0.428	61.6
Emerging Europe					
1990	0.306	0.938	0.796	0.410	64.6
2000	0.307	1.034	0.846	0.351	71.4
2010	0.473	1.106	0.873	0.490	66.3

TFP = total factor productivity

Note: Asia: China, India, Indonesia, Korea, the Philippines, Malaysia, and Thailand. Latin America: Argentina, Brazil, Chile, Colombia, Mexico, Peru, and Venezuela. Emerging Europe: Czech Republic, Hungary, Latvia, Lithuania, Poland, and Romania.

Source: Data from Penn World Tables 9.0.

the Penn World Tables 9.0. In contrast to the previous figures, A is computed as a residual from equation (6.3) or (6.4), dividing the ratio of GDP per worker by the ratio of factors. Table 6.1 presents the results for equation (6.3); table 6A.2 presents the results for equation (6.4). To avoid giving excessive weight to large countries, I aggregate using geometric averages, so the multiplication of the averages of columns 2, 3, and 4 yields exactly 1. The last column is the share of the GDP per worker ratio explained by TFP.

As evident from the rising values in the first column of tables 6.1 and 6A.2, all groups of countries reduced their GDP per worker gap. The physical capital and human capital gaps also narrowed. The TFP gap declined in Asia and emerging Europe but increased in Latin American countries.

The last column of table 6.1 shows the share of the TFP gap explaining the GDP gap.[9] In all regions, the TFP gap explains 60–70 percent of the total gap in output per worker. From 2000 to 2010, the TFP gap increased its explanatory power of the GDP per worker gap.

---

9. If relative shares were equal to 1, a ratio equal to f1 = 1/[column (2) x column (3)] would be explained by factors and f2 = 1/[column (4)] would be explained by TFP. Hence the share explained by TFP is f2/(f1 + f2).

The results of this decomposition are similar to the results shown above, with the output and factors gaps declining. The pattern for TFP is less clear. The development accounting decomposition also illustrates another stylized fact—namely, that the TFP gap explains about two-thirds of the output gap.[10] In the decomposition presented in the appendix, the TFP gap is about 50 percent, and the capital gap increases its share. Which measure of the TFP gap is more relevant depends on how tightly capital is linked to productivity in the long run.

The main result of the decomposition, consistent with the rest of the evidence in this chapter, is that although there has been broad income convergence in emerging-market economies, TFP has diverged.

Evidence during Growth Accelerations

Economic growth is not a smooth process. Countries with high rates of average growth over long time spans have experienced long periods of moderate growth and some episodes of growth acceleration (growth spurts) before returning to more normal levels (Hausmann, Pritchett, and Rodrik 2005; Jones and Olken 2008; Berg, Ostry, and Zettelmeyer 2012). In this section I examine whether the patterns of TFP growth in normal times and during growth accelerations differ.

I focus on the period starting in 1950. The analysis serves as a robustness check on the results presented above, confirming that the low growth of TFP among emerging-market economies has been a long-standing problem, not one that appeared only after 1990. I also conduct standard Solow growth decompositions using a labor share of 0.65 and obtain TFP as a residual.[11] These decompositions are independent of the ones using the United States as a benchmark.

Most growth accelerations come after the implementation of reforms, and they seem to be more frequent in periods of high global growth. They are associated with faster TFP growth, which could indicate that more than single policies, what matters is the joint implementation of major reforms, such as macroeconomic stabilization and opening up to trade, as well as political transitions.

To define a growth acceleration, I extend the evidence from Hausmann, Pritchett, and Rodrik (2005) by endogenizing the length of the high growth

---

10. The results are not sensitive to the labor share. If the labor share were 0.5 instead of 0.35, the last column would be 58–74 percent instead of 56–73 percent.

11. The Solow decomposition looks at the contribution of factors and TFP to GDP growth. In the previous section, I performed development accounting that compares the output gap to the gaps in factors and TFP.

spell. They look at periods of acceleration lasting exactly eight years. I start searching for periods of seven-year growth accelerations and then extend them to estimate whether the period lasts longer.

The Hausmann, Pritchett, and Rodrik method proceeds by estimating log-linear regressions for GDP per capita on time. It assumes a fixed seven-year period for growth accelerations, an assumption that I relax. The coefficient of time in the regression is the average rate of growth, denoted by $g(t, t + n)$, where $n = 7$.[12] The change in the rate of growth is defined as $\Delta g = g(t, t + n) - g(t - n, t)$, that is, the difference between growth in a seven-year period and the previous seven years. A growth acceleration is defined when the following three conditions hold:

- $g(t, t + n) > 3.5$ percent.

- $\Delta g \geq 2$ percent.

- Per capita GDP at the end of the episode is greater than or equal to the maximum growth before the episode (meaning that no recoveries from big slumps are considered).

The year that maximizes the F-statistic of a spline regression is assumed to be the year of the break in growth.[13] To define the last year of the acceleration without being constrained to exactly seven years, I consider whether average growth for three years following the seven-year episode is greater than or equal to 2.5 percent (i.e., whether growth is still high). The idea is that growth can decelerate but only by 1 percentage point in a three-year average. A three-year period is chosen to avoid sensitivity to a single year's growth rate.

Table 6A.3 in the appendix presents the periods of growth accelerations identified using this method. For each country, I conduct Solow growth decompositions and compare the results of during accelerations and during the whole period for which data are available. Figure 6.8 summarizes the results. The basic data from the Penn World Tables cover the period 1950–2014. I use the longest period of data available for each country.[14]

In most cases, the contribution of TFP growth was larger during accelerations (the average was 32 percent during the whole period and 55

---

12. As it considers seven years of growth, it must use eight years for the level of per capita GDP.

13. The Matlab files used to estimate seven-year growth accelerations are those of Buera and Shin (2017).

14. There are 53 episodes of growth acceleration. For graphical convenience, I exclude the six cases (in Croatia, Morocco, Russia, and Uruguay) in which productivity during the episode or the whole period was negative. These episodes are in table 6A.3. I also exclude Azerbaijan and Belarus, because no data were available on which to perform growth decompositions.

Figure 6.8 Contribution of total factor productivity to changes in GDP per worker, 1990 and 2014

period of growth acceleration (percent)

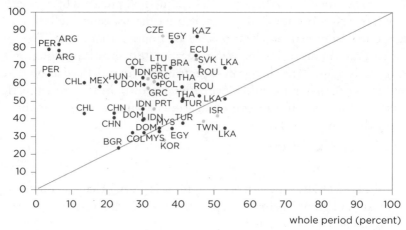

whole period (percent)

Note: Dark gray dots represent emerging-market economies; light gray dots represent former emerging-market economies that are now classified as advanced economies. See table 6A.1 for country names.

Source: Author's calculations.

percent during periods of acceleration). In Korea and Taiwan, TFP growth was higher in the whole period, but these economies had one of the longest periods of growth acceleration (and the longer the episode, the more similar is the period of growth acceleration to the whole period). In both economies, the contribution of TFP to growth during accelerations was somewhat smaller than in the nonacceleration period.

For Korea the growth acceleration lasted from 1963 to 1995; for Taiwan it ran from 1960 to 2000. China also experienced a long period of high growth, from 1978 to 2014, except for 1988–91. It has not ended. The contribution of TFP was 42 percent during periods of growth and 22 percent during the 1952–2014 period, where data for China are available. Thailand also had a long growth spell, from 1957 to 1995. The contribution of TFP growth was 50 percent during this period, compared with 41 percent for the whole period.

Some growth accelerations end in large recessions. These episodes are likely to include ones that originated in transitory factors, such as financial liberalizations, massive capital inflows that end with sudden stops, or booms caused by exchange rate–based stabilizations.

To distinguish between sustainable and unsustainable accelerations, I compare the level of per capita GDP four and five years after the end of the episode. If per capita GDP in some of those years is below the level at the end of the spell, I call it unsustainable. The evidence, shown in table 6A.3, shows no significant differences between types of accelerations. All accelerations, whether sustainable or not, tend to coincide with a larger contribution of TFP growth. There are, of course, difficulties in defining unsustainable episodes, in particular after the global financial crisis, when external shocks largely caused the slump. Good external conditions and financial liberalization often drive unsustainable episodes; sustainable ones are associated with large increases in trade, real depreciations, and economic reforms. They also start after political changes (Hausmann, Pritchett, and Rodrik 2005). Berg, Ostry, and Zettelmeyer (2012) also endogenize the duration of the spells in episodes of growth spurts. They find them to be positively related to export orientation, openness to foreign direct investment, democratic institutions, and, particularly, equality levels. More work could be done on a larger sample of countries to study more carefully the distinction between sustainable and unsustainable growth accelerations. In the episodes studied here, relatively few were unsustainable.[15]

These results suggest that many economies take off after the implementation of reforms, most of them related to trade and stabilization. Buera and Shin (2017) show how reforms that remove distortions trigger growth accelerations and TFP growth.[16] Before the reforms, capital is misallocated across sectors; reallocation is what causes TFP to grow. The question is why TFP subsequently decelerates. An interpretation is that growth accelerations are periods in which the economy may be reaching its potential level of productivity, after which growth becomes more difficult.

Rather than removing basic distortions, countries need to move their own frontier. Many observers have argued in favor of second-generation reforms, such as increasing transparency and improving governance. But there is little evidence suggesting which of those reforms spur growth.

---

15. An alternative definition for growth acceleration is that used in a report by the European Bank for Reconstruction and Development (EBRD 2017), which refers to such episodes as "periods of exceptionally strong growth." It computes episodes in which the rate of growth in some countries is significantly higher than in a group of similar countries. Growth accelerations may therefore not show up in a period in which global growth is strong. I focus on episodes of absolute growth accelerations, which also reveal how they are related to growth in advanced economies.

16. In their model, savings rise before investment takes off. At the beginning of the period, there are thus capital outflows.

Productivity in Emerging-Market Economies and the Global Economy

Will the slowdown in productivity growth in the advanced economies result in a drag on productivity in emerging-market economies? To answer this question, I examine the relationship between productivity in the two groups of countries for the longest available period.

Aggregate productivity growth in the two country groups (measured as five-year averages) is correlated (see figure 6.2). Figure 6.9 shows the correlation of median TFP growth of emerging-market economies with respect to advanced economies for 10- and 20-year rolling data. The 20-year correlation was low before the first oil shock, increased until the early 1990s, and declined in the decade that followed. The correlations increased again in more recent years. These correlations are similar when the sample is broken down by region. Therefore, without examining the causal links or the mechanisms for this correlation, the decline in advanced economy productivity should be associated with a decline in potential TFP growth among emerging-market economies. This result is also consistent with the worldwide decline in growth prospects reported in figure 6.1. The increased correlation of TFP growth is consistent with the evidence reported in Adler et al. (2017), who observe that "the drop in total factor productivity (TFP) growth following the global financial crisis has been widespread and persistent across advanced, emerging, and low-income countries."

Is the frequency of growth accelerations correlated with global growth? Figure 6.10 shows the number of accelerations and two measures of global growth: the rate of growth of advanced economies and the simple average rate of growth from the Penn World Tables. The figure starts in 1960 because the first growth accelerations are detected only by the end of the 1950s. In order to avoid biasing the results by including new countries, I include only countries for which data are available for the whole period.

Until the early 1970s, global growth was robust and accelerations frequent. The number of episodes declined thereafter, before picking up again in the 1990s, during which the correlation between productivity in emerging-market economies and advanced economies declined. After the global financial crisis, the number of growth accelerations declined.

Gruss, Nabar, and Poplawsky-Ribeiro (2018) examine the relationship between growth accelerations and external conditions in emerging and developing economies. They find that strong country-specific external conditions increase the probability of experiencing a growth acceleration. This finding reveals the relevance of a good external environment for growth, in particular in inducing growth accelerations. Their measure is country specific and not driven by common global factors.

Figure 6.9 Ten- and 20-year correlation between median total factor productivity growth in advanced and emerging-market economies, 1970–2014

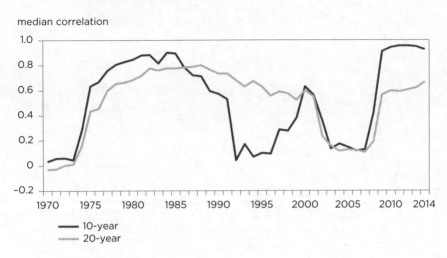

median correlation

Source: Data from Penn World Tables 9.0.

If productivity growth in emerging-market economies consists mostly of adopting technologies from the frontier in advanced economies, one should not expect correlations as high as those seen in the data, particularly in recent years. In the rest of this section, I discuss some potential explanations for these correlations, leaving the discussion of long-term headwinds and opportunities in emerging-market economies for the next section.

Business Cycle Synchronization

One possible reason why the correlation is high is that business cycles in the world are synchronized. TFP tends to be procyclical, suggesting that standard measures do not take into account the utilization of production factors. Hence a global deceleration of GDP should be reflected in a global deceleration of measured TFP. Another reason is that periods of high (low) growth are periods that are most (least) conducive to the adoption of better technologies.

Did the business cycle became more synchronized after the global financial crisis? The evidence suggests that although there was more synchronization in the financial cycle (see, e.g., Rey 2014), there was no increase in business cycle co-movements as a result of greater financial and trade globalization (Cesa-Bianchi, Imbs, and Saleheen 2016; Monnet and Puy 2016). Indeed, financial integration could desynchronize national levels of activity from world output. The worldwide decline in TFP growth does not appear

Figure 6.10 Number of growth accelerations and world and advanced economies rates of growth, 1960–2014

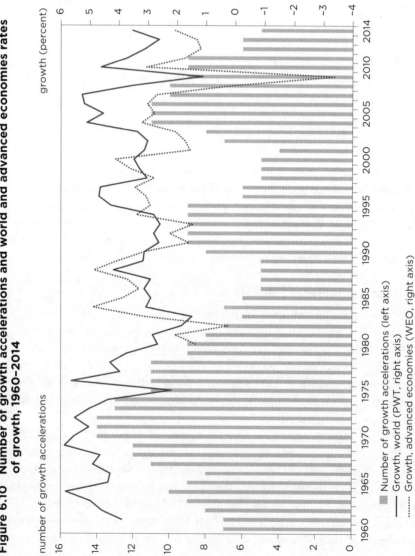

number of growth accelerations

growth (percent)

▨ Number of growth accelerations (left axis)
— Growth, world (PWT, right axis)
⋯⋯ Growth, advanced economies (WEO, right axis)

Sources: Data from the IMF *World Economic Outlook* (WEO), October 2017, and Penn World Tables (PWT) 9.0.

Figure 6.11 Synchronization of output growth, 1981–2016

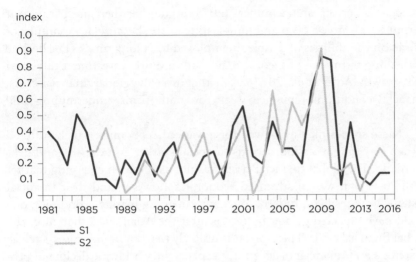

Note: Sample includes all countries for which data were available in the IMF *World Economic Outlook* database that had GDP per capita in 2010 of at least 5,000 in purchasing power parity dollars and population of more than 3 million. See text for explanation of figure.

Source: Data from the IMF *World Economic Outlook* database, October 2017.

to be the result of an increase in the correlation of domestic cycles with that of the global economy.

Cesa-Bianchi, Imbs, and Saleheen (2016) compute the inverse of the pairwise differences in GDP growth in absolute value. I compute two alternative measures of whether growth is moving in the same direction across countries. I assign a value of 1 when growth between two years is rising and a value of –1 when growth is falling. For each year, I then compute the absolute value of the sum of these variables divided by the number of countries, S1, which takes a value of 0 when countries with rising and declining growth are evenly split and 1 when all move in the same direction. An alternative measure is S2, which compares the growth rate in a given year with the average of the previous five years. The greater the index, the greater the synchronization. Both measures increased, displaying similar trends (figure 6.11). ·

During the commodity price boom, synchronization rose, reaching a peak in 2009 with the Great Recession. For the period as a whole, however, synchronization of growth rates did not increase, ruling out synchronization as a major explanation for the global decline in productivity.

Crises, Legacies, and Hysteresis

Blanchard, Cerutti, and Summers (2015) argue that there are permanent output losses after a deep and long-lasting crisis—because, for example, of effects on the abilities of people unemployed for a long time.[17] The decline in the long-term level of income may result in lower investment rates and TFP growth. Adler et al. (2017) argue that after the global financial crisis, financial conditions remained weak for many firms, undermining TFP growth.

These stories may work well for advanced economies, which suffered from a very long recession, serious financial market dislocations, and debt overhang. The global financial crisis was not as severe in emerging-market economies as it was in advanced economies, however, and their financial systems were resilient. Indeed, for many emerging-market economies, one could have expected greater hysteresis after the Asian crisis than after the global financial crisis. Therefore, it is unlikely that common causes, such as hysteresis and financial dislocations, explain the worldwide decline in productivity.

Trade

Between 1990 and 2007, real trade grew twice as rapidly as real GDP; before 1990 it grew about 1.5 times as quickly. Since 2011 trade has been growing at about the same rate as GDP. In 2018–19 trade is expected to grow faster, about 1 percentage point more than GDP, which is projected to increase at 3.9 percent. This rate is much slower than the average rate of global trade growth of 7 percent a year in 1990–2008.

This slowdown does not appear to be related to increased protectionism (Freund 2016). It probably reflects the decline in growth in China, the halt in the expansion of global value chains, and the cyclical downturn in global investment, as trade in capital goods is an important component of global trade. The trade slowdown is a potential explanation for low TFP growth in emerging-market economies.

Openness has been shown to be one of the most robust determinants of long-term economic growth, with some caveats. Trade integration allows the transmission of knowledge and requires efficiency to compete in global markets. Trade is no longer the only means of interconnection across economies, however. Technological diffusion may take many other forms. Nevertheless, the decline in trade growth may dent technology adoption and hold down efficiency gains in small open economies.

---

17. A stronger proposition is that of Cerra and Saxena (2008), who present evidence from a broad sample of countries that all recessions have negative permanent effects on output.

Although the empirical evidence is still inconclusive, sector-level evidence suggests that trade could be one of the reasons for the global decline in TFP growth. Comparing the change in TFP growth before and after the crisis for a sample of 28 countries, Jeanne (2017) finds that it is unrelated to the degree of trade and financial openness. Aggregate correlations are persuasive. However, Adler et al. (2017) show that among advanced economies, the spillovers from a decline in TFP growth in the United States are greater the more exposed the country is to the frontier. They also show that countries and sectors that benefited the most from increasing trade with China also enjoyed faster productivity growth. The decline in China's rate of growth is one of the reasons why trade growth declined after the global crisis. Therefore, the links are more likely to be at the sectoral than the country level, which may explain why the aggregate evidence is inconclusive.

The worldwide decline in TFP growth may have to do with the decline in trade and spillovers from the slowdown in TFP growth in the frontier economies, which suffered a deep and protracted recession. As a result of globalization, spillovers from the global economy into emerging markets are stronger than they once were. The mechanism of transmission is not a simple correlation of the business cycle, as there is no evidence that such correlation increased after the crisis, but more likely the diffusion of knowledge through trade and other channels.

Factors Affecting Total Factor Productivity in the Long Run

There are reasons to be pessimistic about productivity growth in advanced economies. Gordon (2014, 2016) points to three factors—inequality, education, and demographics—that can explain the slowdown of labor productivity growth in the United States to about 1.3 percent in the next two to four decades.[18] The question is whether they are also relevant for emerging-market economies and whether other factors could hinder TFP growth there.

Inequality

High levels of inequality not only raise concerns about social justice but also hamper potential growth (Berg and Ostry 2017) and may adversely affect productivity. High or rising inequality can induce increases in taxation to provide transfers and equalizing government expenditure, with consequent

---

18. Gordon (2014) also notes the high level of public debt in the United States, which will impose a heavy burden on public debt service. This issue is not relevant in emerging market economies, which have lower (albeit rising) levels of public debt. However, the situation is quite heterogeneous among emerging market economies.

distortions. It can negatively affect public finances and inflation. More generally, it induces bad policies and weakens institutions (De Gregorio and Lee 2004). Inequality causes a waste of potential human resources. It could also exacerbate the financial cycle, by, for example, increasing demand for financial aid in the housing.[19] Rising inequality may generate social demands that cannot be met in a manner that is consistent with maintaining an environment that is conducive to economic growth.

For emerging-market economies, the evidence is mixed, but it can be summarized, with some caveats, as follows. In less unequal areas (emerging Asia and Europe), inequality has increased since the early 1990s.[20] In Latin America, where inequality is relatively high, it declined (De Gregorio 2015, figure 14). Inequality has thus become an issue everywhere. When inequality is high or rising but growth is also high, demands for greater redistribution diminish. At times of low growth, they increase, possibly weakening growth prospects. Tackling high and rising income inequality is important to foster productivity growth.

Demographics

Population aging may be a drag on growth in the United States and other advanced economies. Emerging-market economies are also experiencing this phenomenon.

Population aging reduces income per capita for a given level of labor productivity, as older people work shorter hours or not at all. The change in the age composition of the labor force may also affect TFP, as older people have more experience while younger ones bring more knowledge to the labor force. The net effect may have reduced TFP growth by 0.1 percent a year in emerging-market economies (Adler et al. 2017).

Another important development in advanced economies in the postwar period was the entry of women into the labor force. Female participation in the labor force in the United States rose from 40 percent in 1960 to 57 percent in 2017. There are no comparable long-term data for Latin America, but in 1990 it was 40 percent, just like in the United States 30 years before, and reached 52 percent in 2017. Whereas in the United States female participation in the labor force remained broadly the same between 1990 and

---

19. Rajan (2010) argues that rising inequality in the United States led to subsidized mortgages, which were a central cause of the financial crisis. Bordo and Meissner (2012) do not find evidence of the link between inequality and crisis in a broad sample of countries.

20. Lee and Lee (2017) show that in Asia, fast economic growth, globalization, and technological change explain the rise in inequality, which has occurred despite the equalizing effects of higher and less unequal educational attainment.

2017, it rose 12 percentage points in Latin America.[21] Although there are disparities across emerging-market economies, increasing female participation in the labor force can overcome some of the demographic headwinds, but the scope for increase has diminished.

Another policy implication of the demographic drag are the benefits of allowing greater migration around the world, so that labor can be reallocated more efficiently. Greater migration flows may create political and social tensions that need to be attended to before they result in a ban on immigration, the populist welfare-reducing solution.

Education

There has been catch-up in terms of relative human capital. In 1990 the level of human capital in emerging-market economies was 66 percent that of the United States; in 2014 it increased to 76 percent (see figure 6.5). All countries partially closed the gap in recent decades.

According to Gordon (2016), coverage rates in the United States plateaued, and completion rates stagnated or even declined. As measured by international tests, the quality of secondary school in the United States is lower than in other advanced economies. The data in figure 6.5 do not correct human capital by quality of education, which is at least as important as school enrollment in fostering economic growth (Barro and Lee 2015). Most measures of quality of education are based on test scores, and the gaps between emerging-market economies and advanced economies are significant. Not just increasing school attainment but also improving quality could provide opportunities for productivity catch-up.

Other areas of educational quality are also relevant, but broad worldwide evidence is scant. Preschool, for example, is central for developing cognitive skills and an important determinant of the returns to education. The distinction between vocational and technical education and training on the one hand and general education on the other is also relevant, however there is no evidence to assess their relative importance for TFP growth. Reducing inequality in education also reduces income inequality. Improvements in all of these areas could help catch-up. The benefits come only in the long term, however, because it takes time for better-educated workers to become a relevant share of the labor force.

---

21. For the United States the data come from OECD.Stat and for Latin America from data. worldbank.org. They refer to the percentage of the female population aged 15 and older.

Rule of Law and Institutions

The weakness of institutions, which is pervasive in emerging-market economies, hinders growth (Acemoglu and Robinson 2012). Like inequality, weak institutions are related to bad policymaking, often driven by the interests of particular groups, including groups prone to illegal activities. Weak institutions also lead to weak protection of property rights—reducing incentives for investment and productivity-enhancing activities—and high levels of corruption. Corruption and weak institutions are negatively correlated with income. Causation runs both ways, but strengthening institutions would help increase economic growth.

Firm-Level Evidence

Andrews, Criscuolo and Gal (2016) look at firm-level evidence in 23 OECD countries since the early 2000s. They find that the productivity slowdown reflects a widening of the gap between firms at the productivity frontier and laggards rather than a slowing of productivity growth at the frontier. For example, while frontier firms increased labor productivity by about 2.8 percent in manufacturing and 3.6 percent in services, productivity growth in all other firms was about 0.5 percent in both sectors. The differences in labor productivity growth are not the result of capital deepening but a widening gap in TFP growth across firms.

Some technological factors may be behind this evidence. Technological progress in many high-tech and information technology (IT)-intensive industries may be of the winner takes all form. In addition, diffusion may be more limited, particularly in IT-intensive sectors. Technological adoption is costly and may require complementary factors, such as human capital, which may explain why, although new technologies may be readily available, diffusion is limited. It may also explain low turnover and the persistence of firms at the frontier.

These ideas are consistent with aggregate, very long-run, cross-country evidence that shows that technological adoption between rich and poor countries has converged but that the intensity of adoption differs across countries (Comin and Mestieri 2018). This evidence could help explain the TFP gap between frontier and emerging-market economies.

Frontier firms have higher sales, pay higher wages, and charge higher mark-ups than other firms (Andrews, Criscuolo and Gal, 2016). In the services sector, the persistence of firms at the frontier has increased. Both phenomena could indicate weak competition, in particular in the services and less tradable sectors, where regulation is also heavier than in other sectors. Procompetition policies and regulatory reform could hence potentially increase technological diffusion.

Figure 6.12   Real interest rates in Chile and the United States, 1993–2017

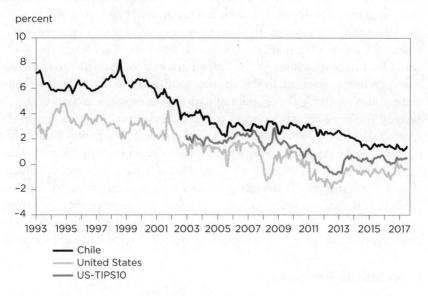

TIPS-10 = 10-year Treasury Inflation-Protected Securities

Sources: Central Bank of Chile; Federal Reserve Economic Data, Federal Reserve Bank of St. Louis.

Interest Rates

In this somewhat gloomy outlook, an important positive development for emerging-market economies has been the systematic decline in global interest rates since the late 1980s, which is expected to persist (Rachel and Smith 2017). Lower long-term sovereign rates have also been passed through to market rates, helping explain the massive increase in corporate debt in emerging markets.

To compare real rates in emerging-market economies and the United States, I use an estimate of the real rate in the United States based on the Michigan survey of inflation expectations and the 10-year bond yield as well as the 10-year Treasury Inflation-Protected Securities (TIPS) yield, which may be a better estimate of long real rates (this series is somewhat shorter).[22] I compare these rates with the indexed interest rate for a 10-year bond in Chile, which has had a deep market in indexed paper for several decades (figure 6.12). Since the early 1990s, real rates have declined by 400–500 basis points.

---

22. On average, the TIPS yield is 1,000 basis points higher than the rate I constructed, but the trend is very similar.

This decline in the cost of capital is good news for investment, still the main driver of output growth. Moreover, investment, foreign and domestic, may bring in technologies, spurring further growth in productivity.[23]

Low interest rates and investment booms also create macroeconomic tensions in emerging-market economies, however. The search for yield could lead to booms in capital inflows, current account widening, and exchange rate appreciation. In this context countries need to safeguard financial stability by using prudential regulation. Allowing the exchange rate to float to facilitate adjustment and using exchange rate intervention in exceptional cases may also help. The use of capital controls may be another option, but the experience of emerging-market economies that already have significant financial integration shows that such measures are broadly ineffective and may add distortions. However, economies with relatively low levels of financial integration need to be cautious when opening the capital account, and the discussion should be about how and when to open up to capital inflows, an issue that is more relevant for lower-income economies.[24]

Concluding Remarks

Emerging-market economies have reduced their income gap with respect to the United States. In many cases, progress has been remarkable. However, except in China and a few other countries, the TFP gap has not declined significantly—and in most cases it has widened.

The evidence also shows that TFP growth has been a bigger driver of income catch-up in periods of growth acceleration and that TFP growth among emerging-market economies is correlated with that of advanced economies, suggesting that persistently low productivity growth in advanced economies is likely to affect emerging-market economies, through trade channels and diffusion of knowledge.

Prospects for TFP growth in emerging-market economies are not very promising, although some economists are more sanguine than Gordon (2016). Brynjolfsson and McAfee (2016), for example, argue that it will take time for the technological revolution to spread broadly across economic activities, as it did in the case of other great inventions.

---

23. Adoption of frontier technologies does not necessarily result in higher growth. The effect depends on the skill intensity of these technologies as well as the absorptive capacity of the economy (Mies 2017). This issue may be more relevant in lower-income countries, where the skill gap may be large.

24. For a discussion of the Latin American experience during the global financial crisis, see De Gregorio (2014). Capital controls do not help explain better performance during the global financial crisis, as Alvarez and De Gregorio (2014) show.

This chapter does not explore the important question of whether statistics are measuring GDP and productivity appropriately. If there is a downward bias in the measures of GDP, TFP may be underestimated. Progress in health, IT, and other sectors may not have been properly measured. Moreover, free goods such as WhatsApp and Wikipedia do not add to GDP but have enormous welfare gains, especially in emerging-market and low-income economies.

There may be opportunities for productivity catch-up in emerging-market economies. In the current context of low interest rates, the cost of investment and productivity-enhancing technologies is low. The productivity slowdown in advanced economies and the decline in global trade growth are a drag on productivity growth in emerging-market economies, however—although the problem seems to pre-date this slowdown. Emerging-market economies have not enjoyed robust TFP growth for a long time, despite having taken important steps to stabilize and reform their economies.

References

Acemoglu, Daron, and James A. Robinson. 2012. *Why Nations Fail?* New York: Crown.

Adler, Gustavo, Romain Duval, Davide Furceri, Sinem Kilic Celik, Ksenia Koloskova, and Marcos Poplawski-Ribeiro. 2017. *Gone with the Headwinds: Global Productivity*. IMF Staff Discussion Note SDN/17/04. Washington: International Monetary Fund

Alvarez, Roberto, and José De Gregorio. 2014. Understanding Differences in Growth Performance in Latin America and Developing Countries between the Asian and the Global Financial Crises. *IMF Economic Review* 62, no. 4: 494–525.

Andrews, Dan, Chiara Criscuolo, and Peter Gal. 2016. *The Global Productivity Slowdown, Technology Divergence and Public Policy: A Firm Level Perspective*. Global Forum on Productivity. Republica Portuguesa and OECD.

Barro, Robert J., and Jong-Wha Lee. 2015. *Education Matters*. Oxford: Oxford University Press.

Berg, Andrew G., and Jonathan D. Ostry. 2017. Inequality and Unsustainable Growth: Two Sides of the Same Coin. *IMF Economic Review* 65, no. 4: 792–815.

Berg, Andrew G., Jonathan D. Ostry, and Jeromin Zettelmeyer. 2012. What Makes Growth Sustainable? *Journal of Development Economics* 98, no. 2: 149–166.

Blagrave, Patrick, and Marika Santoro. 2016. *Estimating Potential Output in Chile: A Multivariate Filter for Mining and Non-Mining Sectors*. IMF Working Paper WP/16/201. Washington: International Monetary Fund.

Blanchard, Olivier, Eugenio Cerutti, and Lawrence Summers. 2015. *Inflation and Activity: Two Explorations and Their Monetary Policy Implications*. NBER Working Paper 21726. Cambridge, MA: National Bureau of Economic Research.

Bordo, Michael D., and Christopher M. Meissner. 2012. Does Inequality Lead to a Financial Crisis? *Journal of International Money and Finance* 31, no. 8: 2147–61.

Brynjolfsson Erik, and Andrew McAfee. 2016. *The Second Machine Age. Work, Progress, and Prosperity in a Time of Brilliant Technologies*. New York: W.W. Norton and Company.

Buera, Francisco J., and Yongseok Shin. 2017. Productivity Growth and Capital Flows: The Dynamics of Reforms. *American Economic Journal: Macroeconomics* 9, no. 3: 147–85.

Calvo, Guillermo, Leonardo Leiderman, and Carmen Reinhart. 1993. Capital Inflows and Real Exchange Rate Appreciation in Latin America: The Role of External Factors. *IMF Staff Paper* 40, no. 1: 108–51.

Cerra, Valerie, and Sweta C. Saxena. 2008. Growth Dynamics: The Myth of Economic Recovery. *American Economic Review* 98, no. 1: 439–57.

Cesa-Bianchi, Ambrosio, Jean M. Imbs, and Jumana Saleheen. 2016. *Finance and Synchronization.* CEPR Discussion Paper 11037. London: Centre for Economic Policy Research.

Clark Gregory, and Robert C. Feenstra. 2003. Technology in the Great Divergence. In *Globalization in Historical Perspective,* ed. Michael D. Bordo, Alan M. Taylor, and Jeffrey G. Williamson. Chicago: University of Chicago Press for the National Bureau of Economic Research.

Comin, Diego, and Martí Mestieri. 2018. If Technology Has Arrived Everywhere, Why Has Income Diverged? *American Economic Journal: Macroeconomics* 10, no. 3: 137-178.

De Gregorio, José. 2014. *How Latin America Weathered the Global Financial Crisis.* Washington: Peterson Institute of International Economics.

De Gregorio, José. 2015. *From Rapid Recovery to Slowdown: Why Recent Economic Growth in Latin America Has Been Slow.* PIIE Policy Brief 15-6. Washington: Peterson Institute for International Economics.

De Gregorio, José, and Jong-Wha Lee. 2004. Growth and Adjustment in East Asia and Latin America. *Economia* 5, no. 1: 69–134.

EBRD (European Bank for Reconstruction and Development). 2017. *Transition Report 2017–18. Sustaining Growth.* London: European Bank for Reconstruction and Development.

Freund, Caroline. 2016. Global Trade Growth: Slow but Steady. In *Reality Check for the Global Economy,* ed. Olivier Blanchard and Adam Posen. PIIE Briefing 16-3. Washington: Peterson Institute of International Economics.

Gordon, Robert J. 2014. *The Demise of US Economic Growth: Restatement, Rebuttal, and Reflections.* NBER Working Paper 19895. Cambridge, MA: National Bureau of Economic Research.

Gordon, Robert J. 2016. *The Rise and Fall of American Growth. The U.S. Standard of Living since the Civil War.* Princeton, NJ: Princeton University Press.

Gruss, Bertrand, Mahlar Nabar, and Marco Poplawsky-Ribeiro. 2018. *Growth Accelerations and Reversals in Emerging Market and Developing Economies: The Role of External Conditions.* IMF Working Paper WP/18/52. Washington: International Monetary Fund.

Hall, Robert E., and Charles I. Jones. 1999. Why Do Some Countries Produce So Much More Output per Worker than Others? *Quarterly Journal of Economics* 114, no. 1: 83–116.

Hausmann, Ricardo, Lant Pritchett, and Dani Rodrik. 2005. Growth Accelerations. *Journal of Economic Growth* 10, no. 4: 303–29.

Jeanne, Olivier. 2017. Secular Stagnation and Asia: International Transmission and Policy Spillovers. Manuscript, Johns Hopkins University.

Jones, Benjamin F., and Benjamin A. Olken. 2008. The Anatomy of Start-Stop Growth. *Review of Economics and Statistics* 90, no. 3: 582–587.

Jones, Charles I. 2016. The Facts of Economic Growth. *Handbook of Macroeconomics,* vol. 2A, 3–69. Amsterdam: Elsevier.

Klenow, Peter, and Andrés Rodríguez-Clare. 1997. The Neoclassical Revival in Growth Economics: Has It Gone Too Far? *NBER Macroeconomics Annual 1997*, vol. 12: 73–114.

Lee, Jong-Wha, and Hanoi Lee. 2017. Human Capital and Income Inequality. Unpublished manuscript, Korea University.

Lema, Daniel. 2015. Crecimiento y productividad total de factores en la agricultura: Argentina y países del cono sur 1961–2013. *Serie de informes técnicos del Banco Mundial en Argentina, Paraguay y Uruguay*. Washington: World Bank.

Levy, Santiago. 2018. *Under-Rewarded Efforts. The Elusive Quest for Prosperity in Mexico*. Washington: Inter-American Development Bank.

Levy, Santiago, and Dani Rodrik. 2017. *The Mexican Paradox*. Project Syndicate, August 10.

Mies, Veronica. 2017. Technology Adoption during the Process of Development: Implications for Long Run Prospects. *Macroeconomic Dynamics*, 1-36. doi:10.1017/S1365100517000074.

Monnet, Eric, and Damien Puy. 2016. *Has Globalization Really Increased Business Cycle Synchronization?* IMF Working Paper WP/16/54. Washington: International Monetary Fund.

OECD (Organisation for Economic Co-operation and Development). 2017. *OECD Economic Surveys: Mexico 2017*. Paris: OECD Publishing.

Rachel, Lukasz, and Thomas D. Smith. 2017. Are Low Interest Rates Here to Stay? *International Journal of Central Banking* 13, no. 3: 1–42.

Rajan, Raghuram. 2010. *Fault Lines: How Hidden Fractures Still Threaten the World Economy*. Princeton, NJ: Princeton University Press.

Rey, Hélène. 2014. Dilemma not Trilemma: The Global Financial Cycle and Monetary Policy Independence. In *Global Dimensions of Unconventional Monetary Policy*, 2013 Jackson Hole Symposium Proceedings. Kansas City, MO: Federal Reserve Bank of Kansas City.

Summers, Lawrence H. 2014. U.S. Economic Prospects: Secular Stagnation, Hysteresis, and the Zero Lower Bound. *Business Economics* 49, no. 2: 66–73.

Torre, Leonardo, and Luis Colunga. 2015. *Patterns of Total Factor Productivity Growth in Mexico: 1991–2011*. Working Paper 2015-24. Mexico City: Banco de México.

Young, Alwyn. 1994. Lessons from the East Asian NICs: A Contrarian View. *European Economic Review* 3–4: 964–73.

Appendix 6A Tables

Table 6A.1 Emerging-market economies included in the study

Economy	Abbreviation	Economy	Abbreviation
Algeria	DZA	Korea[a]	KOR
Angola	AGO	Lithuania[a]	LTU
Argentina	ARG	Malaysia	MYS
Azerbaijan	AZE	Mexico	MEX
Belarus	BLR	Morocco	MAR
Brazil	BRA	Peru	PER
Bulgaria	BGR	Philippines	PHL
Chile	CHL	Poland	POL
China	CHN	Portugal[a]	PRT
Colombia	COL	Romania	ROU
Croatia	HRV	Russia	RUS
Czech Republic[a]	CZE	Slovak Republic[a]	SVK
Dominican Republic	DOM	South Africa	ZAF
Ecuador	ECU	Sri Lanka	LKA
Egypt	EGY	Taiwan[a]	TWN
Greece[a]	GRC	Thailand	THA
Hungary	HUN	Turkey	TUR
Indonesia	IDN	Ukraine	UKR
Iran	IRN	Uruguay	URY
Israel[a]	ISR	Venezuela	VEN
Kazakhstan	KAZ		

a. Currently classified as advanced economy, but in 1990 they had income per capita less than 60 percent of the United States and could have been considered emerging markets. When comparisons are made with the advanced-economy aggregate of the International Monetary Fund, these countries are excluded from the sample of emerging-market economies.

Table 6A.2   Development accounting using equation (6.4)

Region/year	GDP per worker (1)	Capital/ GDP (2)	Human capital (3)	TFP (4)	Share due to TFP (5)
Asia					
1990	0.127	0.42	0.714	0.423	41.4
2000	0.147	0.501	0.759	0.386	49.6
2010	0.208	0.586	0.788	0.450	50.7
Latin America					
1990	0.246	0.576	0.730	0.586	41.8
2000	0.242	0.618	0.769	0.509	48.3
2010	0.293	0.634	0.803	0.576	46.9
Emerging Europe					
1990	0.306	0.634	0.862	0.560	49.4
2000	0.307	0.676	0.897	0.506	54.5
2010	0.473	0.822	0.915	0.629	54.4

TFP = total factor productivity

Note: This table covers the same set of countries as in table 6.1 and uses equation (6.4) instead of (6.3).

Source: Author's calculations.

Table 6A.3 Episodes of growth acceleration (percent)

Country/period	Share of		
	Capital per worker	Education per worker	Total factor productivity
Argentina			
1990–1997[a]	14.3	7.5	78.1
2003–2011	7.6	10.6	81.8
1950–2014	49.7	43.8	6.5
Brazil			
1967–1978[a]	31.7	–0.2	68.5
1950–2014	25.1	37.0	37.9
Bulgaria			
2000–2007	66.5	10.1	23.3
1970–2014	64.5	12.2	23.3
Chile			
1974–1981[a]	26.9	30.4	42.7
1990–1997	33.2	6.6	60.2
1951–2014	59.7	26.5	13.7
China			
1978–1987	38.8	18.2	43.0
1992–2014	48.9	10.7	40.4
1952–2014	55.1	22.8	22.1
Colombia			
1967–1974	17.8	13.6	68.6
2002–2014	29.7	38.3	31.9
1950–2014	29.5	43.2	27.3
Croatia			
1997–2006[a]	33.7	31.0	35.3
1990–2014	81.4	40.6	–21.9
Czech Republic			
2001–2008[a]	10.2	3.4	86.4
1990–2014	41.6	22.7	35.8
Dominican Republic			
1968–1975	27.4	13.6	59.1
1991–2000	46.9	21.2	31.9
2004–2014	29.0	31.3	39.7
1951–2014	36.3	33.2	30.5

(table continues)

Table 6A.3 Episodes of growth acceleration (percent) (continued)

Country/period	Share of		
	Capital per worker	Education per worker	Total factor productivity
Ecuador			
1970–1978[a]	12.6	12.0	75.5
1950–2014	17.7	37.3	45.0
Egypt			
1958–1965	9.1	7.8	83.1
1977–1985	47.5	18.1	34.4
1950–2014	32.6	29.0	38.4
Greece			
1959–1972	36.4	6.4	57.2
1998–2006[a]	19.5	18.2	62.3
1951–2014	41.7	26.6	31.7
Hungary			
1999–200[a]	24.8	14.5	60.7
1970–2014	59.1	18.3	22.6
Indonesia			
1967–1984	32.4	28.5	39.1
1988–1995[a]	37.3	17.5	45.2
2002–2014	28.9	8.2	62.9
1960–2014	38.7	31.1	30.2
Israel			
1967–1974[a]	48.0	10.6	41.4
1950–2014	32.4	16.7	51.0
Kazakhstan			
1997–2014	6.3	7.6	86.1
1990–2014	30.4	24.2	45.3
Korea			
1963–1995	52.0	20.0	28.0
1950–2014	47.2	16.7	36.1
Lithuania			
1997–2006	20.1	9.5	70.4
1990–2014	48.5	17.2	34.2

(table continues)

Table 6A.3 Episodes of growth acceleration (percent)
(continued)

Country/period	Capital per worker	Education per worker	Total factor productivity
	Share of		
Malaysia			
1967–1982	41.4	24.1	34.6
1988–1995	43.4	24.1	32.5
1955–2014	36.8	28.4	34.8
Mexico			
1962–1973	23.7	18.2	58.0
1950–2014	38.2	43.7	18.1
Morocco			
1957–1964[a]	–4.4	2.0	102.3
1970–1977[a]	68.6	38.6	–7.2
1999–2011	133.9	843.5	–877.5
1950–2014	23.1	41.6	35.3
Peru			
1959–1966	10.5	10.7	78.8
2002–2013	31.9	3.7	64.3
1950–2014	36.5	59.8	3.7
Poland			
1993–2000	29.2	11.5	59.3
1970–2014	45.8	19.8	34.4
Portugal			
1959–1972	30.6	8.5	60.9
1984–1991	24.9	29.8	45.3
1950–2014	42.2	24.4	33.4
Romania			
1970–1979	36.9	12.5	50.6
2001–2008[a]	26.9	3.8	69.2
1960–2014	40.4	13.6	45.9
Russia			
1999–2006	0.2	7.2	92.6
1990–2014	95.7	105.5	–101.2
Slovak Republic			
2001–2008	12.7	14.0	73.3
1990–2014	39.2	15.6	45.2

(table continues)

Table 6A.3 Episodes of growth acceleration (percent) (continued)

Country/period	Share of		
	Capital per worker	Education per worker	Total factor productivity
Sri Lanka			
1976–1984	40.7	24.9	34.5
1990–1998	22.0	26.9	51.1
2004–2014	32.2	–0.8	68.6
1950–2014	24.3	22.7	53.0
Taiwan			
1960–2000	45.4	16.2	38.3
1951–2014	36.6	16.3	47.1
Thailand			
1957–1995[a]	34.9	15.3	49.7
2001–2008	13.4	28.9	57.7
1950–2014	36.1	22.7	41.2
Turkey			
1964–1976[a]	39.4	9.4	51.2
2002–2011	37.5	25.1	37.4
1950–2014	36.8	21.8	41.4
Uruguay			
1973–1980[a]	39.7	18.6	41.6
2004–2014	13.6	9.7	76.8
1950–2014	74.6	36.6	–11.2

a. Unsustainable episode, as defined in the text.

Note: The last row for each economy is the Solow decomposition for the entire period, based on data available in Penn World Tables 9.0.

Source: Author's calculations.

7

Living with Lower Productivity Growth: Impact on Exports

FILIPPO DI MAURO, BERNARDO MOTTIRONI,
GIANMARCO OTTAVIANO, AND
ALESSANDRO ZONA-MATTIOLI

This chapter investigates the impact of sustained lower productivity growth on exports, by looking at the role of the productivity distribution and allocative efficiency as drivers of export performance. It follows and goes beyond the work of Barba Navaretti et al. (2017), analyzing the effects of productivity on exports depending on the dynamics of allocative efficiency.

Low productivity growth is a well-documented stylized fact in Western countries—and possibly a reality likely to persist for some time. What could be the impact of persistent sluggish growth of productivity on exports? To shed light on this question, this chapter examines the relationship between the productivity distribution of firms and sectoral export performance.

The structure of firms within countries or even sectors matters tremendously for the nexus between productivity and exports at the macroeconomic level, as the theoretical and empirical literature documents. For instance, whether too few firms at the top (lack of innovation) or too many firms at the bottom (weak market selection) drives slow average productivity

Filippo di Mauro is visiting professor at the Business School at the National University of Singapore and an external consultant of the Monetary Authority of Singapore and of the Singapore Economic Development Board. He is also chairman of CompNet, a large research network on competitiveness and productivity among EU institutions, and coordinator of the Productivity Research Network, a similar initiative based in Singapore and covering the Asia-Pacific region. Bernardo Mottironi is a former research assistant at the European Central Bank and currently a PhD student at London School of Economics. Gianmarco Ottaviano is full professor in the Department of Economics at Bocconi University; research fellow at the Centre for Economic Policy Research, London; and senior nonresident fellow at Bruegel, Brussels. Alessandro Zona-Mattioli is a trainee at the European Central Bank. The opinions expressed in this chapter are of the authors and do not necessarily reflect those of the institutions for which they work. The authors are thankful to Emanuele Forlani of Bologna University for his help in the analysis.

at the macro level has very different implications and therefore demands different policy responses.

The findings in this chapter relate to the literature that uses firm-level data to explore the relation between export and productivity, starting with Melitz (2003). In particular, the chapter elaborates on the results of Mayer and Ottaviano (2011) and Gabaix (2011), who show that aggregate economic outcomes are related mostly to the behavior of a small set of large and highly productive firms (the right tail of the productivity distribution).

The chapter is organized as follows. The first section presents econometric attempts to quantify the productivity-export nexus for a sample of countries in the European Union, taking into consideration higher moments of the productivity distribution. The second section introduces the role of allocative efficiency and provides some initial results on its possible drivers. The third section pulls the results together and provides initial estimates of a novel specification of export performance that accounts for different moments of the productivity distribution as well as allocative efficiency. The fourth section uses the results to construct alternative export scenarios, based on alternative hypotheses about future productivity. The last section provides concluding remarks.

Estimating the Export-Productivity Nexus

The basic intuition emerging from the literature is that because of fixed export costs, firms have to be productive in order to export. The right tail of the productivity distribution of firms is thus what matters most for the export prowess of an economy.

Testing such a simple theory presents some difficulties, because many factors may confound the effect of productivity dispersion on exports. To overcome this bias, this chapter relies on a gravity approach, based on the two-step methodology discussed below.

Data come from the Competitiveness Research Network (CompNet), a unique micro-aggregated database that provides a rich set of information on the variables' distribution at the granular level, together with micro-founded indicators such as the level of allocation efficiency. They are based on firm-level balance sheet information drawn from 16 European countries.[1] These data are of particular interest because they provide the moments of the distributions of the variables of interest. Detailed information on the structure and the methodology of CompNet is available in Lopez-Garcia, di Mauro, and CompNet Task Force (2015).

---

1. See appendix 7A for the list of countries and their time coverage.

Figure 7.1 Correlation between median export levels and median total factor productivity decile in selected countries

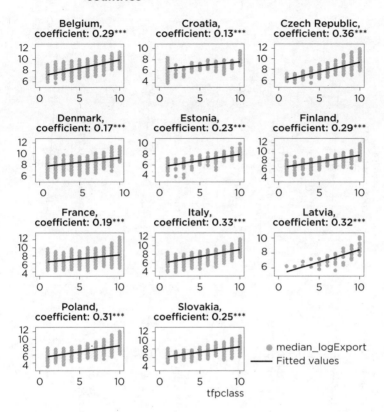

Note: The figure presents the relationship between the logarithm of exports of the median firm (vertical axis) and the total factor productivity decile of each sector-year combination (horizontal axis), by country. The distribution of exports is computed over the population of firms in the given sector-year combination. Each point is a sector-year observation. ***$p < 0.01$.

Source: Authors' calculations based on CompNet data.

Starting with stylized facts, the data show that both the level and the growth rate of exports are higher in the highest deciles of the productivity distribution. This relation holds at different levels of aggregation, with a positive and significant correlation across countries, sectors, and years (figures 7.1 and 7.2), at both the country and sector levels.

The potential role of the higher moments of the productivity distribution is explored by examining the correlation between export competitiveness and a set of dispersion measures: the skewness index, the Pearson's coefficient, and the ratios between percentiles (p80/p20, p90/p10). Evidence on these correlations is provided based on a two-step procedure.

Figure 7.2 Correlation between median export levels and median total factor productivity decile in selected sectors

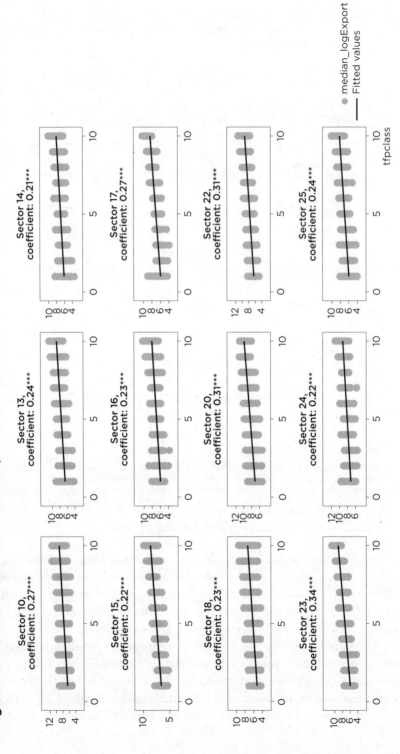

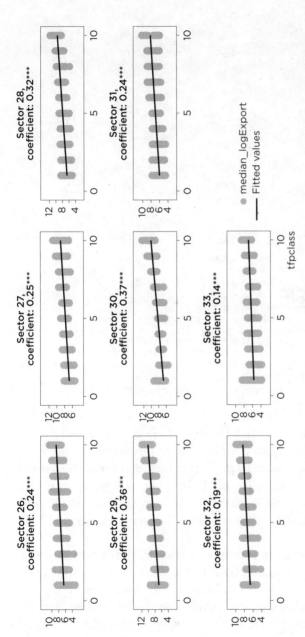

Note: The figure presents the relationship between the logarithm of exports of the median firm (vertical axis) and the total factor producivity decile of each country-year combination (horizontal axis), by sector. The distribution of exports is computed over the population of firms in the given country-year combination. Each point is a country-year observation. The numbers identifying the sectors follow the NACE Rev. 2 sector classification. ***$p < 0.01$.

Source: Authors' calculations based on CompNet data.

Table 7.1 Export competitiveness of selected countries

Country	Mean	Standard deviation
Austria	3.55	2.53
Belgium	4.27	2.42
Croatia	0.49	2.75
Estonia	0.94	2.84
Finland	2.95	2.74
France	5.14	2.39
Germany	5.93	2.50
Hungary	2.41	2.60
Italy	5.35	2.37
Lithuania	1.11	2.85
Poland	3.3	2.73
Portugal	2.88	2.71
Romania	2.02	2.81
Slovakia	1.81	2.63
Slovenia	1.35	2.62
Spain	4.59	2.46
Average for all countries in sample	3.05	3.02

Note: Figures represent the logarithm of export competitiveness fixed effects, estimated in a two-step procedure following Helpman, Melitz, and Rubinstein (2008). The analysis covers a sample of bilateral export flows from OECD countries to destination countries for several manufacturing sectors from 2001 to 2012. Both CompNet and other countries are included.

Source: Authors' calculations based on CompNet and OECD data.

In the first step, an index of export competitiveness is computed using a gravity equation approach: a two-stage estimation procedure uses an equation for selection into trade partners in the first stage and a trade flow equation in the second (Helpman, Melitz, and Rubinstein 2008; see appendix 7A for details on the procedure). As expected, the highest values correspond to Europe's largest and most central countries: Germany, France, and Italy (table 7.1).

In the second step, the index of competitiveness is used in its logarithmic transformation, as a dependent variable, to test the roles of the mean and the dispersion of the productivity distribution in the presence of a large set of control variables (market size, wage levels, and fixed effects by country, sector, and year). Three alternative dispersion indexes are used: the p90/p10

Table 7.2 Effect of different moments of the total factor productivity distribution on export competitiveness

	(1)	(2)	(3)	(4)	(5)	(6)
Variable	Export Comp_t	Export Comp_t	Export Comp_t	Export Comp_t	Export Comp_t	Export Comp_t
$\text{logTFP(Median)}_{t-1}$	0.028*** (0.009)	0.022** (0.009)	0.027*** (0.009)			
$\text{logTFP(Mean)}_{t-1}$				0.028*** (0.009)	0.023** (0.009)	0.027*** (0.010)
$\text{logTFP(p90/p10)}_{t-1}$	0.073*** (0.018)	0.081*** (0.018)	0.086*** (0.018)	0.072*** (0.018)	0.08*** (0.018)	0.084*** (0.018)
Asymm_{t-1}		0.042 (0.041)			0.04 (0.041)	
Skewness_{t-1}			0.051** (0.025)			0.052** (0.025)
Log Firms_{t-1}	0.492*** (0.049)	0.53*** (0.042)	0.521*** (0.042)	0.492*** (0.049)	0.53*** (0.042)	0.52*** (0.042)
$\text{Log Labor Cost}_{t-1}$	0.65*** (0.052)	0.662*** (0.054)	0.672*** (0.055)	0.649*** (0.052)	0.661*** (0.055)	0.669*** (0.055)
Constant	−3.2*** (0.618)	−3.559*** (0.596)	−3.691*** (0.598)	−3.191*** (0.618)	−3.556*** (0.596)	−3.668*** (0.599)
Observations	1,685	1,629	1,644	1,685	1,629	1,643
R-squared	0.97	0.97	0.97	0.97	0.97	0.97

Note: Country, year, and sector fixed effects are included. Robust standard errors in parentheses. *** $p < 0.01$, ** $p < 0.05$, * $p < 0.1$.

Source: Authors' calculations based on CompNet data.

ratio, the skewness index, and the asymmetry index (Pearson's second skewness coefficient).[2] The coefficients of productivity dispersion are retrieved through the following regression equation:

$$Export\ Competitiveness_{i,s,t} = \alpha_0 + \alpha_1 LogTFP(Median)_{i,s,t-1} +$$
$$\alpha_2 LogTFP(Mean)_{i,s,t-1} + [\alpha_3 TFP(\tfrac{p90}{p10})_{i,s,t-1}] + \alpha_4 Log\ LaborCost_{i,s,t-1} + \quad (7.1)$$
$$\alpha_5 Log\ Firms_{i,s,t-1} + \alpha_6 Disp_{i,s,t-1} + C_i + S_s + T_t + u_{i,s,t} \quad (7.1)$$

where $Disp_{i,s,t-1}$ is one of the two dispersion indexes other than p90/p10, and C_i, S_s, and T_t are country, sector, and year fixed effects, respectively. (The third section discusses the term $[\alpha_2 TFP(\tfrac{p90}{p10})_{i,s,t-1}]$.)

Table 7.2 reports the regression results. The productivity dispersion as measured by the p90/p10 index is always significant in explaining export performance.

---

2. Asymmetry is defined as $Pears._{i,s,t} = \frac{mean_{i,s,t} - median_{i,s,t}}{st.dev._{i,s,t}}$.

Interaction between Productivity Dispersion and Allocative Efficiency

Having established that productivity dispersion matters, it is time to look at its drivers, including their interaction with allocative efficiency. One can conjecture a variety of drivers of the asymmetry of the distribution, including the following:

■ Innovation can push the frontier of productivity outward, stretching the right tail of the distribution as innovators increase the distance between them and other firms. The rate at which other firms are able to follow the innovators defines the skewness of productivity. If technological change is able to spread out in the economy, skewness may not increase dramatically; if technology remains limited to a restricted share of firms, skewness will increase, as the rest of the distribution will lag behind.

■ Labor market institutions (e.g., bargaining mechanisms and workers' unions) play a role in determining the efficiency of the allocation of laborers among firms. If these institutions are effective, they will channel workers toward more productive firms, which will increase in size, thickening the right tail of the distribution.

■ Financial markets can help increase allocative efficiency by awarding resources to the most productive firms.

■ Insolvency laws are among the factors that operate on the selection side of firms' demography. The extent to which distressed or unproductive firms are allowed to stay on the market can have important effects on aggregate productivity figures. Allowing distressed or unproductive firms to stay in the market (e.g., by subsidizing them) may indeed increase the misallocation of resources and reduce export competitiveness.

What matters for aggregate productivity growth is whether resources are efficiently reallocated toward the most productive segment of the economy. We first define *allocative efficiency* according to the method of Olley and Pakes (1996), by computing the extent to which firms with higher productivity have a larger market share (the so-called OP gap, computed as the covariance of the change in productivity and firm size with respect to the mean).[3]

We regress the two main indexes used to proxy productivity dispersion (P80/P20 and P90/P10; figure 7.3) on the OP gap. The correlation between these variables is robust and positive after controlling for country and year

---

3. The OP gap is defined as $\sum_i^N (s_{it} - \hat{s}_t)(\varphi_{it} - \widehat{\varphi}_t)$, where s_{it} represents the single firm's market share, such that $s_{it} \in (0,1)$, $\sum_i^N s_{it}=1$, φ_{it} is the single firm's level of productivity, $\hat{s}_t = \frac{1}{N}\sum_i^N s_{it}$ is the mean market share, and $\widehat{\varphi}_t = \frac{1}{N}\sum_i^N \varphi_{it}$ is the unweighted mean productivity.

Figure 7.3 Correlation between productivity asymmetry and allocative efficiency

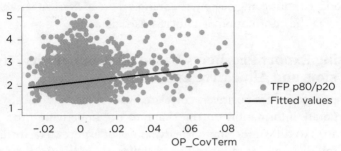

P80/P20, coefficient: 8.55***

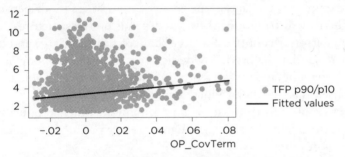

P90/P10, coefficient: 17.32***

OP = Olley-Pakes covariance term; TFP = total factor productivity
Note: Each point is a sector-year observation. ***$p < 0.01$.
Source: Authors' calculations based on CompNet data.

Table 7.3 Coefficients on productivity asymmetry and allocative efficiency

	P80/P20	P80/P20	P90/P10	P90/P10
Olley-Pakes	8.5***	3.58***	17.32***	4.18*
Constant	Yes	Yes	Yes	Yes
Country fixed effects	No	Yes	No	Yes
Year fixed effects	No	Yes	No	Yes

***$p < 0.01$, **$p < 0.05$, *$p < 0.1$.
Source: Authors' calculations based on CompNet data.

fixed effects (table 7.3). This finding suggests a crucial role for reallocation policies, which can increase growth not only by affecting aggregate productivity but also by strengthening the export channel.

These results add a new perspective to the question about the effects of the slowdown in productivity on exports. If the productivity path becomes slower for the average firm but does not change for the right tail of the distribution, an increase in allocative efficiency may reinforce aggregate exports, regardless of the productivity of the average firm. This feature cannot be understood without going beyond the standard use of average variables (i.e., exploiting all the information of a micro-based dataset).

Assessing Export Prospects Based on Productivity, Its Dispersion, and Allocative Efficiency

Average productivity is positively correlated with trade, but one also needs to incorporate information on the shape of the underlying productivity distributions to fully understand the dynamics of exports. The intuition is that behind the same average productivity there may be distributions with very different shapes: Indeed, for a given level of average productivity, the share of exporters will be larger the greater the skewness (or dispersion) of the productivity distribution. Skewness depends on the structure of firms within the sector or country. If a large share of firms are large and highly productive (so that the productivity distribution of the economy is characterized by a long and thick right tail), more firms will be able to position themselves above the productivity cutoff that allows them to export, increasing exports. In contrast, in an economy in which productivity is normally distributed, the effects of higher average productivity on exports would be more muted.

This section applies this approach to exports. It explores the extent to which productivity dispersion mediates the effect of a change in median productivity on exports. When median productivity slows, the implications for trade will depend strongly on the productivity dispersion: Exports could decrease in the presence of lower productivity dispersion and increase if dispersion is sufficiently greater.

This section also examines the potential role of allocative efficiency in influencing such mediation effects, shedding light on the potential gains from increased allocative efficiency on export competitiveness. It identifies the main channels of interaction between the median and the dispersion of the relevant productivity distribution and uses them to project exports.

The choice of the terms representing different moments of the productivity distribution is not as straightforward as one might think. Indeed, it can lead to biases driven by spurious or trivial relations. We argue that the first moment should be represented by median total factor productivity (TFP), because it is more stable than mean TFP and not necessarily affected by changes in outliers. Skewness cannot be used as a dependent variable, because its formula contains the mean (which enters with a negative sign) and by construction will therefore always display a negative correlation with average TFP. By the same line of reasoning, the asymmetry index (or Pearson coefficient) is constructed using the difference between the mean and the median over the standard deviation and is therefore equally unusable. All this considered, the rest of the analysis therefore uses the p90/p10 and p80/p20 ratios, which are not susceptible to these biases, to represent skewness and asymmetry.

The econometric strategy is as follows:

- We estimate the relation between productivity dispersion and median productivity.

- We augment this relationship by adding the OP gap (a proxy for allocative efficiency) to determine whether it modifies the impact of median productivity on dispersion.

- We use the estimated parameters to construct fitted values for the p90/p10 term in equation 7.1 in order to understand the implications of different productivity growth scenarios for export competitiveness.

Stylized Facts

The data in the sample reveal heterogeneity across countries in the change in median and average TFP between 2006 and 2013 (figure 7.4). This heterogeneity reflects a wide array of factors—from labor market to competition policy, from openness toward foreign competition to the presence of multinationals—that affect the spectrum of firms in existence and their contribution to overall productivity growth. As expected, average productivity is much more variable than median productivity, as it is mechanically influenced by the other moments of the distribution. As a consequence, the median is chosen as the most suitable variable for detecting a nontrivial relation between central moments of productivity and its dispersion.

Figure 7.5 presents a scatter plot showing the correlation between lagged median productivity and productivity dispersion (in the form of changes in p90/p10 and p80/p20 ratios). Each observation represents a sector-country-year combination. The results reveal a very small but strongly significant positive relationship. This measure is very raw, however; additional tests are needed.

Results of Initial Tests

We used ordinary least squares (OLS) regression to test the relation between productivity growth and its dispersion. The dependent variable is the productivity dispersion, defined by either the p90/p10 or the p80/p20 ratio of the TFP distribution. The main independent variable of interest is the median TFP (because the median is more stable and less sensitive to variations at the extremes of the distribution).

Figure 7.4   Absolute difference between mean and median total factor productivity (TFP) between 2006 and 2013 in selected countries

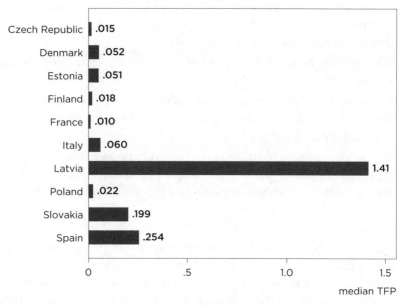

a. Median TFP

Czech Republic	.015
Denmark	.052
Estonia	.051
Finland	.018
France	.010
Italy	.060
Latvia	1.41
Poland	.022
Slovakia	.199
Spain	.254

median TFP

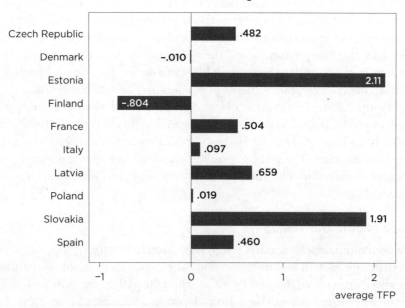

b. Average TFP

Czech Republic	.482
Denmark	-.010
Estonia	2.11
Finland	-.804
France	.504
Italy	.097
Latvia	.659
Poland	.019
Slovakia	1.91
Spain	.460

average TFP

Source: Authors' calculations based on CompNet data.

Figure 7.5 Correlation between lagged median total factor productivity and productivity dispersion indexes

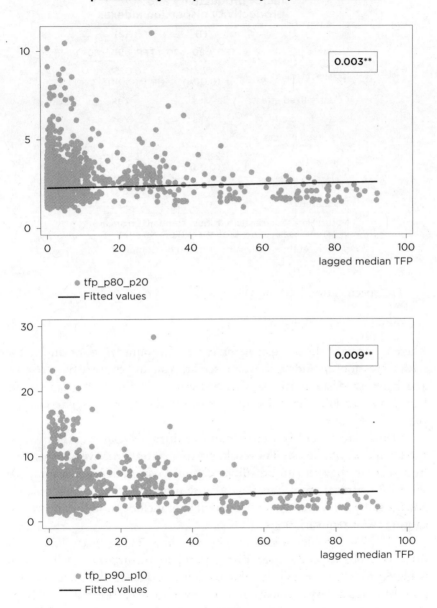

Note: Each point is a country-sector-year observation.

Source: Authors' calculations based on CompNet data.

Table 7.4 Effect of lagged median total factor productivity and productivity dispersion indexes

Variable	(1) TFP_p80_p20	(2) TFP_p90_p10
logTFP(Median)$_{t-1}$	0.027*** (0.004)	0.075*** (0.010)
Country fixed effects	Yes	Yes
Sector fixed effects	Yes	Yes
Year fixed effects	Yes	Yes
Constant	2.226*** (0.087)	3.302*** (0.169)
Observations	4,905	4,907
R-squared	0.53	0.53

Notes: Heteroskedasticity-robust standard errors are in parentheses. *** $p < 0.01$, ** $p < 0.05$, * $p < 0.1$.

Source: Authors' calculations based on CompNet data.

The specification is as follows:

$$Y_{ist} = \alpha_1 + S_s + C_i + T_t + \beta_1 X_{ist-1} + \epsilon_{ist} \tag{7.2}$$

where Y_{ist} is one of the two dispersion indexes in country i, year t, and sector s. All regressions include a constant; sector, year, and country fixed effects; and heteroskedasticity-robust standard errors. The term X_{ist-1} stands for lagged median TFP, the main explanatory variable of interest, in country i, year t, and sector s.

Median lagged TFP is positively and significantly related to the two dispersion indexes (table 7.4). The results are robust to alternative time periods. In particular, they remain broadly unchanged when adding a dummy for the 2008 financial crisis—possibly because productivity trends vary slowly and the sample does not go far back enough or include enough countries to capture consistent variations.

Table 7.4 provides initial insight into how TFP growth affects the dispersion of the productivity distribution, suggesting that such growth is higher for the right tail than for the left tail. This finding does not yet provide a satisfactory explanation of the heterogeneity shown in the figures above, however, as it establishes only the existence of an average correlation. The temporal dimension does not seem to be sufficient to explain such heterogeneity, as the coefficient of median productivity does not change with the sample period used. We need to find other variables to motivate such heterogeneity.

Table 7.5 Contribution of allocative efficiency to the effect of median total factor productivity on productivity dispersion

Variable	(1) TFP_p80_p20	(2) TFP_p80_p20	(3) TFP_p90_p10	(4) TFP_p90_p10
High allocative efficiency dummy$_t$	0.029 (0.023)	0.033 (0.024)	0.083 (0.062)	0.096 (0.062)
logTFP(Median)$_{t-1}$	0.027*** (0.004)	0.022*** (0.004)	0.075*** (0.009)	0.059*** (0.009)
Interaction		0.02** (0.009)		0.08*** (0.002)
Constant	2.224*** (0.087)	2.222*** (0.087)	3.3*** (0.169)	3.288*** (0.171)
Observations	4,905	4,905	4,907	4,907
R-squared	0.53	0.53	0.53	0.53

Note: Country, year, and sector fixed effects are included. Robust standard errors are in parentheses. *** $p < 0.01$, ** $p < 0.05$, * $p < 0.1$.

Source: Authors' calculations based on CompNet data.

Adding Allocative Efficiency

In order to further explore the nexus between average productivity and its dispersion, we introduce allocative efficiency, which we measure by computing the extent to which labor is located in the most productive firms using the OP gap. Given the institutional framework in a given country or sector, reallocation of labor from less productive to more productive sectors may increase productivity dispersion, given the same variation in median productivity.

To incorporate this new variable in the regression framework, we modify equation 7.2 as follows:

$$Y_{ist} = \alpha_1 + S_s + C_i + T_t + \beta_1 X_{ist-1} + \beta_2 D_{ist} + \beta_3 D_{ist} * X_{ist-1} + \epsilon_{ist} \qquad (7.3)$$

This equation adds the dummy variable D_{ist}, which takes the value 1 if the observation presents an OP covariance term that is equal to or greater than the 90th percentile of the overall distribution. The dummy is added in order to identify that part of the sample characterized by high allocative efficiency. We also add an interaction term between this allocative efficiency dummy and median productivity growth, X_{ist-1}. The coefficient estimate β_3 gives an idea of whether allocative efficiency can explain heterogeneity in the relation between TFP growth and dispersion (table 7.5).

The high allocative efficiency dummy does not seem to have a significant effect on productivity dispersion per se, but its interaction with median productivity is striking. The coefficient is positive and statistically significant for both specifications, as is the coefficient of median TFP. These results suggest that the positive relationship between median TFP and dispersion is much stronger in the presence of high allocative efficiency.

The coefficient estimates for the interaction terms show the potential additional effect on productivity dispersion of an intervention designed to increase allocative efficiency from the sample average to the top 10 percent of the sample. Column (3) shows that on average, a unitary increase in median TFP would result in a 0.075 point increase in the p90/p10 ratio. In the high allocative efficiency scenario (column 4), the same variation in median TFP increases the p90/p10 ratio by up to 0.14 point on average (0.059 + 0.08), about doubling its size. This difference is remarkable, with important policy implications, particularly for export dynamics. Depending on allocative efficiency (by country and/or sector), the same rate of productivity growth (increasing or declining) implies a different reaction of productivity dispersion and thus export performance.

Impact of Alternative Productivity Scenarios on Export Performance

Having provided more clarity on the possible drivers of heterogeneity in the relationship between productivity growth and dispersion, we can put all the elements together to investigate how a change in productivity growth affects export performance. Using the computed coefficients, we construct two scenarios for export performance: a baseline growth scenario, in which median TFP rises by 1.2 percent (the Congressional Budget Office's baseline scenario), and a low-growth scenario, in which it rises by just 0.8 percent.

For both scenarios we assume either baseline allocative efficiency (computed using the coefficient of median TFP in column 4 of table 7.5) or high allocative efficiency (computed using the coefficients of median TFP and the interaction term in column 4 of table 7.5). We multiply the initial increase in median productivity by these coefficients to assess the impact on the productivity distribution. We then multiply the resulting number by the coefficient of p90/p10 on export competitiveness (from column 1 of table 7.2) to estimate the effect of the assumed increase in median TFP on exports, as mediated by productivity dispersion and the degree of allocative efficiency. Table 7.6 summarizes the results.[4] For the baseline allocative efficiency case,

---

4. As an illustration, the number in the upper right cell (0.5 percent) is obtained by multiplying the 1.2 percentage point increase by the baseline coefficient of 0.059 (the effect of median TFP on the p90/p10 ratio in the absence of allocative efficiency, from column (4) of table 7.5) and then by the second stage coefficient 0.073 (the effect of p90/p10 on "export competitiveness," from column (1) of table 7.2). Analogously, the effect in the upper left cell (1.2 percent; high TFP growth and high allocative efficiency) is obtained by multiplying the increase of productivity of 1.2 percentage points by 0.14 (the effect of median TFP on p90/p10 in the case of

Table 7.6 Impact of total factor productivity (TFP) growth and allocative efficiency on export competitiveness

TFP growth\Olley-Pakes covariance term	High allocative efficiency scenario	Baseline allocative efficiency case
Baseline TFP growth scenario (1.2 percent)	1.2 percent	0.5 percent
Low TFP growth scenario (0.8 percent)	0.8 percent	0.3 percent

Note: Coefficients in percentage point variations. See footnote 4 for derivation of scenarios.

table 7.6 suggests that a slowdown in annual productivity growth from 1.2 percent to 0.8 percent would slow the annual increase in export competitiveness from 0.5 percent to 0.3 percent. It also shows that allocative efficiency can modify this result significantly. For a country that is in the top 10 percent of allocative efficiency (the high allocative efficiency scenario), the impact of slowing productivity growth on exports is more pronounced, on the order of 0.4 percent a year (1.2 percent minus 0.8 percent). A reform that moves a country from the baseline allocative efficiency case to the high scenario would initially have a much larger impact than the productivity slowdown, raising export competitiveness by 0.7 percent (1.2 percent minus 0.5 percent). For a country with average allocative efficiency, an efficiency-enhancing reform could thus offset the impact of slowing productivity growth on export competitiveness for as long as three and a half years.

Concluding Remarks

An economy's allocative efficiency conditions affect the nexus between productivity and exports. Using a novel framework, we set up four illustrative alternative scenarios by interacting two alternative productivity growth assumptions (high and low) with two allocative efficiency scenarios (average and high). In all the scenarios, a reduction in productivity growth relative to the baseline reduces export competitiveness, by both shifting the productivity distribution to the left and shrinking the tail of productive firms that tend to export. However, this effect can be offset, for up to three and a half years, by reforms that take countries from the average to the higher allocative efficiency scenario.

These preliminary calculations show how policies aimed at improving the allocation of resources could modify the relation between productivity growth and export activity. Allocative efficiency plays an important role in

high allocative efficiency, that is, 0.06 + 0.08 in column (4) of table 7.5) and then by 0.073 (the effect of p90/p10 on "export competitiveness," from column (1) of table 7.2).

explaining the heterogeneity embedded in the evolution of the distribution of productivity and in the relation between median productivity and dispersion, which determines the share of firms that are productive enough to export.

In an environment of slowing productivity growth, policies that raise allocative efficiency are hence important for two reasons. First, they may mitigate the productivity slowdown. Second, even if they do not, they will reduce its impact on export competitiveness, by increasing productivity dispersion (creating a longer and thicker right tail of the distribution). The larger and more competitive firms that are able to face global competition would then play a key role in increasing export volumes. Targeted policies to achieve such a goal should be a priority for countries that aim to stimulate export activity and remain competitive in an increasingly globalized economy.

References

Barba Navaretti, G., M. Bugamelli, E. Forlani, and G. Ottaviano. 2017. *It Takes (More Than) a Moment: Revisiting the Link between Firm Productivity and Aggregate Exports*. London: London School of Economics.

Gabaix, X. 2011. The Granular Origins of Aggregate Fluctuations. *Econometrica* 79, no. 3: 733–72.

Helpman, E., M. Melitz, and Y. Rubinstein. 2008. Estimating Trade Flows: Trading Partners and Trading Volumes. *Quarterly Journal of Economics* 123, no. 2: 441–87.

Lopez-Garcia, P., F. di Mauro, and the CompNet Task Force. 2015. *Assessing European Competitiveness: The New CompNet Database*. Working Paper 1764. Frankfurt: European Central Bank.

Mayer, T., and G. Ottaviano. 2011. *The Happy Few: The Internationalisation of European Firms*. Bruegel Blueprint Series, November 11. Available at http://bruegel.org/wp-content/uploads/imported/publications/BP_Nov2008_The_happy_few.pdf.

Melitz, M. 2003. The Impact of Trade on Intra-Industry Reallocations and Aggregate Industry Productivity. *Econometrica* 71, no. 6: 1695–725.

Olley, G., and A. Pakes. 1996. The Dynamics of Productivity in the Telecommunications Equipment Industry. *Econometrica* 64, no. 6: 1263–97.

Appendix 7A Estimating Export Competitiveness Using the Helpman, Melitz, and Rubinstein Methodology

The procedure involves two steps, following Helpman, Melitz, and Rubinstein (2008). In the first, we estimate firms' selection into the export market based on the probability that firms meet an implied zero-profit condition. The probability of selection into trade is measured by estimating a linear probit model over a sample of bilateral export flows from OECD countries (i) to export countries (d) for several manufacturing sectors (s) from 2001 to 2012. The sample includes both CompNet and other countries (table 7A.1). For each sector, we estimate the following equation:

$$\Pr\left(Export_{i,d,t}\right) = \varphi_{i,d,t} = \Phi\left(\alpha_0 + \alpha_{i,t} + \beta_{d,t} - \gamma D_{i,d} + z_{i,d,t} + \eta_{i,d,t}\right) \qquad (7A.1)$$

where $a_{i,t}$ represent origin*year fixed effects; $\beta_{d,t}$ represent destination*year fixed effects; and $D_{i,d}$ is a vector of standard trade cost variables (such as distance, common border, common language, etc.). We also include bilateral indicators for regulation costs in the foreign market ($z_{i,d,t}$) and an error term ($\eta_{i,d,t}$).

Table 7A.1 Countries included in the analysis

Country	Years covered
Belgium	2001–13
Croatia	2002–13
Czech Republic	2002–13
Denmark	2001–13
Estonia	2001–13
Finland	2001–13
France	2001–13
Italy	2001–13
Latvia	2006–13
Poland	2005–13
Slovakia	2001–13
Spain	2001–12

We use the estimated probability to create a set of controls to estimate the second-step model using a nonlinear least squares estimator. These controls are the inverse Mills ratio and a polynomial expansion of $\hat{\varphi}_{i,d,t}$ of degree three designed to control for sample selection bias and unobserved firm heterogeneity.[5] The resulting equation is

$$Export_{i,d,t} = \beta_0 + \alpha_{i,t} + \beta_{d,t} - \gamma D_{i,d} + invMill_{i,d,t} + \pi(\hat{\varphi}_{i,d,t}) + \varepsilon_{i,d,t} \quad (7A.2)$$

where $\alpha_{i,t}, \beta_{d,t}$, and $\gamma D_{i,d}$ follow the same notation as before; $invMill_{i,d,t}$ is the inverse Mills ratio of $\hat{\varphi}_{i,d,t}$; $\pi(\hat{\varphi}_{i,d,t})$ represents its polynomial expansion; and $\varepsilon_{i,d,t}$ is an error term. The resulting $\alpha_{i,t}$ represents what we then define as export competitiveness.

---

5. See Helpman, Melitz, and Rubinstein (2008) for details of the model on which these assumptions are based.

III

IMPLICATIONS FOR WAGES, DISTRIBUTION, AND POLITICS

8

Productivity and Pay: Is the Link Broken?

ANNA STANSBURY AND LAWRENCE H. SUMMERS

After growing in tandem for nearly 30 years after World War II, average labor productivity and the compensation of the typical American worker diverged beginning in 1973. Between 1973 and 2016, median compensation grew by only 11 percent in real terms, and compensation of production/nonsupervisory workers rose by only 12 percent; over the same period, labor productivity rose by 75 percent. Since 2000 average compensation has also diverged from labor productivity (figure 8.1).

What does this stark divergence imply for the relationship between productivity and typical compensation? A range of views are compatible with the data presented in figure 8.1.

At one end of the spectrum, it is possible that productivity growth has delinked from typical compensation, casting doubt on the common aphorism that a rising tide lifts all boats. Factors may be blocking the transmission mechanism from productivity to pay such that increases in productivity growth do not systematically translate into increases in typical workers' compensation ("strong delinkage"). On the other hand, just as two time series growing in tandem does not mean that one causes the other,

Anna Stansbury is a PhD candidate in economics at Harvard University. Lawrence H. Summers is the Charles W. Eliot University Professor at Harvard University. In addition to serving as the 71st Secretary of the US Treasury in the Clinton administration, Summers served as director of the White House National Economic Council in the Obama administration, as president of Harvard University, and as chief economist of the World Bank. The authors thank Jared Bernstein, Josh Bivens, John Coglianese, Jason Furman, Egor Gornostay, Larry Katz, John Komlos, Robert Lawrence, Eben Lazarus, Larry Mishel, Adam Posen, Jaana Remes, Jim Stock, and Jeromin Zettelmeyer for comments; the participants at the Peterson Institute for International Economics conference on "The Policy Implications of Sustained Low Productivity Growth" in November 2017 and the preconference in July 2017; and Philipp Schellhaas, for excellent research assistance.

Figure 8.1 Labor productivity, average compensation, and compensation of production/nonsupervisory workers, 1948–2016

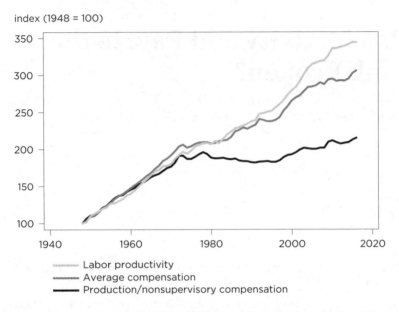

index (1948 = 100)

········ Labor productivity
━━━━━━ Average compensation
━━━━━━ Production/nonsupervisory compensation

Note: Labor productivity = total real output per hour. Average compensation = total real compensation per hour, calculated using the consumer price index research series using current methods (CPI-U-RS) deflator. Production/ nonsupervisory compensation = real hourly compensation of production and nonsupervisory workers, calculated using the CPI-U-RS deflator.

Source: Authors' calculations using data from Bureau of Labor Statistics, Bureau of Economic Analysis, and Economic Policy Institute.

two series diverging may not mean that the causal link between the two has broken down. Productivity growth may have been acting to raise pay while at the same time other orthogonal factors acted to reduce it, creating a divergence between productivity and pay despite the two series being causally linked ("strong linkage"). Between these two ends of the spectrum lies a range of possibilities in which some degree of linkage between productivity and typical compensation exists.

Several observers have questioned the degree of linkage between productivity and compensation in the United States. Harold Meyerson wrote in *American Prospect* in 2014 that "for the vast majority of American workers, the link between their productivity and their compensation no longer exists." The *Economist* wrote in 2013 that "unless you are rich, GDP growth isn't doing much to raise your income anymore."

The divergence between productivity and compensation has also led to questions about the extent to which faster productivity growth would boost typical incomes. Bernstein (2015), for example, writes that "Faster productivity growth would be great. I'm just not at all sure we can count on it to lift middle-class incomes." Bivens and Mishel (2015, 2) note that "although boosting productivity growth is an important long-run goal, this will not lead to broad-based wage gains unless we pursue policies that reconnect productivity growth and the pay of the vast majority."

Establishing where the productivity-compensation relationship falls on the linkage-delinkage spectrum is important not only to gain a better understanding of the mechanisms causing middle-income stagnation and the productivity-pay divergence but also to design the most effective policy solutions.

This chapter estimates the extent of linkage or delinkage by investigating the comovement of productivity growth and typical compensation growth, using the natural quasi-experiment provided by the fact that productivity growth fluctuates over time. Under the strongest linkage view, marginal increases in productivity growth will translate one for one into increases in typical worker compensation even without any changes to policy. Under the strongest delinkage view, given the current structure of the economy, marginal increases in productivity growth will not translate into increases in typical workers' pay.[1] Between these views is a transmission of productivity growth to compensation growth that is positive but less than one.

Most of the debate on the productivity-pay divergence has focused on the divergence between *typical* workers' pay (median or production/nonsupervisory workers) and productivity. It is also possible to examine the gap between *average* compensation and labor productivity. This gap has grown since about 2000, as labor's share of income started to fall. The chapter investigates the evidence on the linkage/delinkage question for both typical and average compensation.

Periods of faster productivity growth over the last seven decades have in general coincided with faster real compensation growth for the typical American worker.[2] The regression results show that since 1973, a 1 percentage point increase in productivity growth has been associated with 0.65 to 1 percentage point higher real compensation growth for the median worker, with almost none of the coefficient estimates significantly different from 1 and all significantly different from 0. For average production/nonsuper-

---

1. Finding support for delinkage would not necessarily imply that productivity growth can never translate into pay. It would most likely imply that given the current structure of the economy, the transmission mechanism from productivity growth to typical pay is blocked but that with certain reforms transmission could be restored.

2. A strong relationship between productivity growth and median compensation growth can be compatible with divergence of the series in levels if other factors that have been suppressing median compensation are orthogonal to productivity growth.

visory compensation, a 1 percentage point increase in productivity growth has been associated with 0.4 to 0.6 percentage point higher real compensation growth.

For average compensation, since both 1948 and 1973 a 1 percentage point increase in productivity growth has been associated with 0.7 to 1 percentage point higher real compensation growth, with the coefficients in most specifications significantly different from 0. The coefficient estimates are slightly lower since 2000 (0.4 to 0.8, depending on the specification).

This evidence suggests that the relationship between median compensation and productivity since 1973 has been very substantial and close to one for one, even while the two series diverged in levels. For production/nonsupervisory compensation, the evidence suggests that there is substantial linkage between productivity growth and compensation growth but that this linkage is likely less than one for one. As median and production/nonsupervisory compensation grew by the same amount over the period, the difference in these coefficient estimates is interesting and bears further investigation. For average compensation, there has been substantial and close to one-for-one linkage in the relationship with productivity over the postwar period; whether the degree of linkage has fallen somewhat since 2000 is not clear.

The evidence is supportive of substantial linkage between productivity and both typical and average compensation. Rather than the link having broken down, it appears that factors not associated with productivity growth have caused typical and average compensation to diverge from productivity.

What are these factors that are causing productivity and typical pay to diverge? A large body of research has sought to understand both the divergence between median and average pay (a manifestation of rising income inequality) and the divergence between average pay and productivity (the falling labor share). Explanations include technological progress, education and skills, globalization, unions, and market power. Technology-focused theories have a testable implication: If technological change is the primary driver of the divergence and more rapid technological change causes faster productivity growth, periods of faster productivity growth should coincide with more rapid divergence between productivity and pay.

The analysis in this chapter examines the comovement of labor productivity with the labor share and with the mean-median compensation ratio, finding little support for a pure technology-based cause of the productivity-pay divergence. It finds little evidence of a significant relationship between productivity growth and changes in the labor share for any period except since 2000, and no evidence of a relationship between productivity growth and changes in the mean-median ratio.

The chapter is organized as follows. The next section reviews the literature on the relationship between compensation and productivity. Section three describes the model and the data and presents the baseline results. It also discusses robustness (testing alternate specifications and considering the effect of productivity mismeasurement) and presents regressions for different deciles of the wage distribution in the United States and other G-7 countries. Section four examines the comovement of productivity growth with the pay-productivity divergence and its implications for technology-based theories of the divergence. The last section summarizes the chapter's main findings.

Literature on the Relationship between Compensation and Productivity

The divergence between median compensation and productivity can be decomposed into various components (figure 8.2). Doing so reveals the following trends:[3]

- Gross labor productivity grew more rapidly than net labor productivity, because of rising depreciation.[4]

- Net labor productivity grew more rapidly than average compensation deflated by a producer price index (PPI), as the labor share fell.

- Average compensation deflated by a PPI grew more rapidly than average compensation deflated by a consumer price index (CPI), as the consumer and producer price indexes diverged.[5]

- Average compensation grew more rapidly than median compensation, as income inequality in the top half of the distribution rose.

- Median compensation grew more rapidly than median wages, as non-wage benefits increased their share of total compensation (not shown in figure 8.2).

---

3. Bivens and Mishel (2015) and Lawrence (2016) present similar figures. Baker (2007); Fleck, Glaser, and Sprague (2011); and Pessoa and Van Reenen (2013) demonstrate similar divergences.

4. Baker (2007), Sherk (2013), Bivens and Mishel (2015), and Lawrence (2016) discuss the importance of this trend in the productivity-compensation divergence.

5. See Lawrence and Slaughter (1993), Bosworth and Perry (1994), Feldstein (2008), Sherk (2013), and Lawrence (2016). According to the Bureau of Labor Statistics (BLS), this divergence exists partly because the consumer price index uses Laspeyres aggregation and the GDP deflator uses Fisher ideal aggregation. In addition, the CPI includes import prices and does not include goods and services purchased by businesses, governments, or foreigners (Church 2016). Extensive work has been done on the divergence between different deflators; see Triplett (1981); Fixler and Jaditz (2002); McCully, Moyer, and Stewart (2007); and Bosworth (2010).

Figure 8.2 Decomposition of divergence between productivity and compensation in the United States, 1970–2016

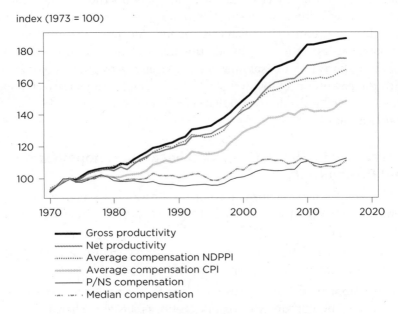

index (1973 = 100)

— Gross productivity
— Net productivity
········· Average compensation NDPPI
········· Average compensation CPI
— P/NS compensation
–·· –·· · Median compensation

Note: Average compensation NDPPI = average compensation deflated by the net domestic product (NDP) price index. Average compensation CPI = average compensation deflated by the consumer price index research series using current methods (CPI-U-RS) deflator. P/NS compensation = average production/nonsupervisory worker compensation. Median and P/NS compensation are deflated by the CPI-U-RS. All compensation measures refer to compensation inclusive of nonwage benefits.

Source: Authors' calculations using data from Bureau of Labor Statistics, Bureau of Economic Analysis, and Economic Policy Institute.

Many researchers have investigated different aspects of the productivity-pay divergence. Bivens and Mishel (2015) document the divergence between productivity and the typical worker's compensation, comparing net labor productivity in the total economy with two measures of typical worker compensation: median compensation and average production/nonsupervisory compensation, deflated by consumer price deflators. They argue that production/nonsupervisory compensation is both a good measure of typical compensation (representing about 80 percent of the private sector workforce) and a good proxy for trends in median compensation before 1973 (a period for which median compensation data are not available). They use a consumer price deflator to reflect consumers' experienced change in living standards. Dew-Becker and Gordon (2005), Baker (2007), and Pessoa and Van Reenen (2013) carry out similar analyses, using median household income, production/nonsupervisory compensation, and median compensation, respectively.

Another line of inquiry is the divergence between productivity and average compensation, which is conceptually equivalent to the decline in the labor share.[6] Feldstein (2008) compares labor productivity and average compensation in the nonfarm business sector, as deflated by a producer price deflator, over 1948–2006. He uses a producer price deflator to reflect the real cost to firms of employing workers. Lawrence and Slaughter (1993) and Bosworth and Perry (1994) carried out similar analyses in the 1990s.

Lawrence (2016) compares average compensation to net productivity, a more accurate reflection of the increase in income available for distribution to factors of production. Because depreciation accelerated in recent decades, using gross productivity reveals a misleadingly large divergence between productivity and compensation. Lawrence finds that net labor productivity and average compensation grew together until 2001, when they started to diverge (labor's share of income started to fall). Many other studies also find a decline in the U.S. labor share of income since about 2000, though the timing and magnitude are disputed (see, for example, Elsby, Hobijn, and Şahin 2013; Pessoa and Van Reenen 2013; Karabarbounis and Neiman 2014; Lawrence 2015; Rognlie 2015; and Grossman et al. 2017).

Model and Results

The analysis in this chapter examines the divergence of productivity from both typical and average compensation. It tries to establish the extent to which labor productivity growth feeds through into worker compensation.

The measure of productivity used is net output per hour for the total economy, in order to capture trends affecting all workers. Net (rather than gross) output is used to reflect only the extra output that is available for distribution to factors of production.[7]

Typical compensation is measured using median compensation. Results are also reported for average production/nonsupervisory compensation, both as an interesting measure in itself and because it enables analy-

---

6. In the special case of Cobb-Douglas technology, examination of this divergence also tests the marginal productivity theory of labor (whether workers are paid their marginal product by firms).

7. Productivity is difficult to measure accurately for the entire economy, because it includes government and nonprofit institutions, whose output is difficult to measure (as it is not usually traded on markets). Productivity of the nonfarm business sector is likely to be easier to measure than productivity of the economy as a whole, but it captures only 75 percent of GDP and only a gross measure of productivity is available. Repeating the baseline regressions with nonfarm business sector productivity yielded little change in the results (results available on request).

sis of the pre-1973 period, for which median data are not available (as in Bivens and Mishel 2015).

Median compensation is the measure that is most clearly interpretable as revealing trends for middle-income workers. It captures trends for the middle of the income distribution, in contrast to average production and nonsupervisory compensation, which captures compensation for roughly 80 percent of the private sector workforce. Median compensation is consistently lower than average production/nonsupervisory compensation (in 2015, for example, median hourly compensation was $22.04 and average production/nonsupervisory compensation $26.61). As the average production/nonsupervisory compensation figure is a mean, it can be skewed by large changes at the top or bottom of its distribution. In addition, there is some evidence that the average production/nonsupervisory compensation measure does not cover all of the workers it is intended to cover and that this group may be growing (Barkume 2007).[8]

Although the two series cover different workers, they move in a similar fashion over most of 1973–2016, except during the 1980s, when real production/nonsupervisory compensation fell significantly more than median compensation. The divergence during the 1980s may have been driven partly by the substantial fall in incomes at the lowest end of the distribution, which would have pulled down the average production/nonsupervisory measure, and partly by the reduction in well-paid blue-collar jobs and the increase in middle-income white-collar jobs (the former covered in the production/nonsupervisory measure, the latter possibly missed).

For average compensation, we look at mean compensation in the total economy. We deflate all compensation series using consumer price deflators to reflect the changes in standards of living experienced by workers.[9]

Feldstein (2008) investigates the linkage between productivity and average compensation by regressing the change in log average compensation on the current and lagged change in log productivity, finding a close to one-for-one relationship. We use a similar approach to investigate the linkage between typical compensation and productivity and to update

---

8. Abraham, Spletzer, and Stewart (1998) and Champagne, Kurmann, and Stewart (2017) suggest that many service sector establishments surveyed for the Bureau of Labor Statistics' Current Employment Statistics (from which production/nonsupervisory wages are calculated) interpret the "production and nonsupervisory" category to include workers paid by the hour and/or nonexempt workers (under the Fair Labor Practices Act) but to exclude other types of salaried or exempt workers even if they are nonsupervisory.

9. We deflate using the CPI-U-RS. Repeating the baseline regressions with compensation deflated by the personal consumption expenditures (PCE) and net domestic product (NDP) price indexes had little effect on the results (results available on request).

Feldstein's estimates of the linkage between average compensation and productivity.

Empirical Estimation

At the simplest level, a linear model can relate productivity and typical or average compensation growth, as shown in equation (8.1).[10] Under the strongest "linkage" view, $\beta = 1$. Under the strongest "delinkage" view, $\beta = 0$. A value of β between 0 and 1 suggests a point on the linkage-delinkage spectrum. Many other factors affect compensation growth besides productivity. As long as they are orthogonal to productivity growth, however, they will not affect the estimation of β:

$$compensation\ growth_t = \alpha + \beta\ productivity\ growth_t \tag{8.1}$$

We can estimate β using the substantial variation in productivity and compensation growth rates since 1948. We look at three measures of compensation: median, production/nonsupervisory, and average. As we run the same tests for all three measures, for brevity we refer to them as simply "compensation."

In our baseline specification (equation 8.2), we regress the three-year moving average of the change in log compensation on the three-year moving average of the change in log labor productivity and the current and lagged three-year moving average of the unemployment rate:[11]

$$\frac{1}{3}\Sigma_0^2 \Delta \log comp_{t-i} = \alpha + \beta\ \frac{1}{3}\Sigma_0^2 \Delta \log prod_{t-i} + \gamma \frac{1}{3}\Sigma_0^2 unemp_{t-i} +$$
$$\delta \frac{1}{3}\Sigma_0^2 unemp_{t-i-1} + \varepsilon_t \tag{8.2}$$

The time horizon over which any productivity-compensation relationship would hold depends on both the wage-setting process and the degree to which productivity changes are correctly perceived and anticipated. If the average firm changes pay and benefits infrequently, or if it takes some time for firms and workers to discern the extent to which an increase in output reflects a rise in productivity rather than other factors, productivity increases will translate into compensation only with a lag. In contrast, if firms and workers correctly anticipate that there will be a productivity

---

10. We use the change in logged values of compensation and productivity, rather than their levels, as compensation and productivity are both nonstationary unit-root processes but their first differences appear to be stationary (as suggested by Dickey-Fuller tests).

11. To account for the autocorrelation introduced by the moving-average specification, we use Newey-West heteroskedasticity and autocorrelation robust standard errors, with a lag length of twice the length of the moving average.

increase in the near future, the rise in compensation may precede the actual rise in productivity.

To take this uncertainty into account, alongside our baseline three-year moving average regressions we present results for regressions without a moving average and with two-, four-, and five-year moving averages. We also repeat our regressions with a distributed-lag specification with up to four years of lagged productivity. The results are similar to the results in our moving-average regressions (results available on request).

We control for the level of unemployment for two reasons. First, it is likely to affect bargaining dynamics: For a given rate of productivity growth, a higher unemployment rate should enable employers to raise compensation by less, because more unemployed workers are searching for jobs.

Second, unemployment is likely to reflect broader cyclical economic fluctuations that may affect compensation in the short term. Higher unemployment may reflect a downturn, which could mean lower pay rises for a given rate of productivity growth. If unemployment is also related to changes in productivity growth—if, for example, the least productive workers are likely to be laid off first—then excluding unemployment would bias the results.

By controlling for the current and one-year lagged moving average of the unemployment rate, we allow for both the level and the change in unemployment to affect compensation growth. We use the unemployment rate of 25- to 54-year-olds, in order to avoid capturing the effects of demographic shifts, such as an aging population. Using the total unemployment rate instead had almost no effect on our results (available on request).

Data

We primarily use publicly available data from the Bureau of Labor Statistics (BLS), the Bureau of Economic Analysis (BEA), and the Economic Policy Institute's State of Working America Data Library, as well as the BLS total economy productivity dataset, which is available on request from BLS.[12]

Our measure of labor productivity for the total economy is calculated by dividing net domestic product, deflated by the net domestic product price index, by the total hours worked in the economy, following Bivens and Mishel (2015). Average compensation for the total economy is from the BLS total economy productivity dataset; it is deflated by the CPI-U-RS. The median and production/nonsupervisory compensation series are from the Economic Policy Institute's State of Working America Data Library. They

12. For a detailed list of data sources, see the working paper version of this chapter (Stansbury and Summers 2017).

are constructed from median wages from the Current Population Survey Outgoing Rotation Group (CPS-ORG) and average production/nonsupervisory wages from the BLS *Current Employment Statistics*, respectively, and deflated by the CPI-U-RS. They are then adjusted to include nonwage compensation using the average real compensation/wage ratio, which is calculated from BEA national income and product accounts data on the composition of workers' compensation. All components of compensation are deflated by personal consumption expenditures (PCE) except health and life insurance, which are deflated by the PCE healthcare index (details are available in Bivens and Mishel 2015).[13]

Our analysis of different percentiles of the wage distribution uses data on real wages from the Economic Policy Institute's State of Working America Data Library. The data are constructed from the CPS-ORG and deflated by the CPI-U-RS.

For our analysis of the other major advanced economies, for all countries except Germany we use OECD data on unemployment, labor productivity per hour, and average compensation per hour, deflated by the CPI for the country in question. For Germany before and after reunification, we use data on hourly labor productivity, hourly compensation, and unemployment from the German Federal Statistical Office (Statistiches Bundesamt Deutschland).

Baseline Results

Figures 8.3 and 8.4 illustrate the relationship between compensation growth and productivity growth in the U.S. economy by plotting the three-year moving average of productivity growth and median, production/nonsupervisory, and average compensation growth (in change in log form). While median and production/nonsupervisory compensation consistently grew more slowly than productivity since the 1970s, the series move largely together. Average compensation and productivity move closely together, particularly since the 1970s.

Table 8.1 displays our baseline regression results.[14] For average and production/nonsupervisory compensation, we show coefficients for the entire

---

13. We are grateful to Larry Mishel and Josh Bivens for providing us with the raw data alongside the publicly available versions.

14. In all tables, the year is listed as the middle year of the moving average (a regression over 1950–2015 implies that the first observation is the three-year moving averages of the change in logged variable in 1949, 1950, and 1951 and the last observation is the three-year moving averages of the change in logged variable in 2014, 2015, and 2016).

Figure 8.3 Change in log labor productivity, median compensation, and average production/ nonsupervisory compensation in the United States, 1951–2016

change in log, 3-year moving average

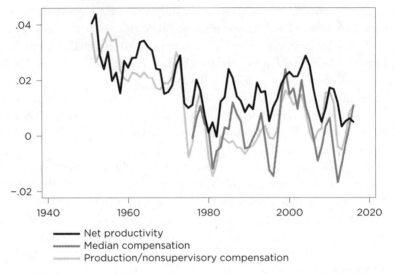

——— Net productivity
·········· Median compensation
············ Production/nonsupervisory compensation

Note: Series are three-year backward-looking moving averages of change in logs.

Source: Authors' calculations using data from Bureau of Labor Statistics, Bureau of Economic Analysis, and Economic Policy Institute.

postwar period and on either side of 1973.[15] The year 1973 is often identified as the beginning of the modern productivity slowdown, as well as the year when median and production/nonsupervisory compensation began to diverge from productivity.[16] Breakpoint tests also identify a structural break at 1973 for both average and production/nonsupervisory compensation.[17] As our median compensation data go back only to 1973, showing results for average and production/nonsupervisory compensation since 1973 also

15. We break the regressions so that the last data point in the 1950–73 regressions is the three-year moving average of the change in log productivity/compensation for 1972, 1973, and 1974 and the first data point in the 1975–2015 regressions is the three-year moving average for 1974, 1975, and 1976.

16. Bosworth and Perry (1994), Baker (2007), Bivens and Mishel (2015), and the Economic Report of the President (US Government Printing Office 2015) identify a break at 1973 when discussing trends in productivity and compensation.

17. For regressions of the change in log productivity with either average or production/ nonsupervisory compensation, a Wald test is significant at the 0.1 percent level for a break at 1973.

Figure 8.4   Change in log labor productivity and average compensation in the United States, 1951–2016

change in log, 3-year moving average

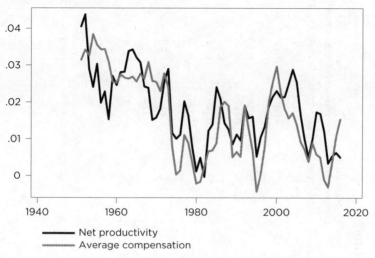

——— Net productivity
············ Average compensation

Note: Series are three-year backward-looking moving averages of change in logs.

Source: Authors' calculations using data from Bureau of Labor Statistics, Bureau of Economic Analysis, and Economic Policy Institute.

makes it easier to compare the results. For average compensation, we also show a split from 2000 onward, the period over which average compensation and productivity began to diverge.

The results in table 8.1 suggest that over 1975–2015, the period during which productivity and median compensation diverged in levels, a 1 percentage point increase in productivity growth was associated with a 0.73 percentage point increase in the growth rate of median compensation. The coefficient is strongly significantly different from 0 and not significantly different from 1, suggesting substantial linkage between productivity and median compensation. The strong linkage hypothesis of a one-for-one relationship between productivity and compensation cannot be rejected.

Over 1975–2015, a 1 percentage point increase in productivity growth was associated with a 0.53 percentage point increase in the growth rate of average production/nonsupervisory compensation. The coefficient is significantly different from both 0 and 1. The result suggests substantial linkage between productivity and production/nonsupervisory compensation but does not support the strong linkage hypothesis of a one-for-one relationship.

Table 8.1 Baseline regression results on compensation and productivity

Dependent variable is 3-year moving average of the change in log compensation	Average compensation				Median compensation	Production/ nonsupervisory compensation		
	1950–2015 (1a)	1950–1973 (1b)	1975–2015 (1c)	2000–2015 (1d)	1975–2015 (1e)	1950–2015 (1f)	1950–1973 (1g)	1975–2015 (1h)
Change in log productivity	0.77*** (0.10)	0.58** (0.25)	0.74*** (0.14)	0.40** (0.14)	0.73*** (0.16)	0.84*** (0.11)	0.69*** (0.19)	0.53*** (0.19)
Unemployment among people 25–54	−0.19 (0.15)	0.36** (0.16)	−0.24* (0.14)	−0.23* (0.12)	−0.15 (0.18)	0.06 (0.25)	0.69* (0.34)	0.09 (0.33)
Lagged unemployment	−0.17 (0.18)	−0.73*** (0.25)	0.02 (0.12)	−0.05 (0.06)	−0.10 (0.15)	−0.40 (0.28)	−0.99*** (0.31)	−0.21 (0.31)
Constant	0.02*** (0.01)	0.03*** (0.01)	0.01*** (0.00)	0.02** (0.01)	0.01 (0.01)	0.01* (0.01)	0.02* (0.01)	0.00 (0.01)
Number of observations	66	24	41	16	41	66	24	41
F-test: Is coefficient on productivity significantly different from 1?								
Test statistic	4.85**	3.00*	3.43	18.5***	2.71	1.95	2.61	5.87**
Prob > F	0.03	0.10	0.07	0.00	0.11	0.17	0.12	0.02

Note: Newey-West standard errors (HAC) in parentheses, *** $p < 0.01$, ** $p < 0.05$, * $p < 0.1$.

Notation: The year is listed as the middle year of the moving average. A regression over "1950–2015" implies the first observation is the three-year moving average of the change in logged variable in 1949, 1950, and 1951 and the last observation is the three-year moving average of the change in logged variable in 2014, 2015, and 2016.

F-test null hypothesis: Coefficient on productivity is *not* significantly different from one.

Source: Authors' calculations.

A 1 percentage point increase in productivity growth was associated with a 0.77 percentage point increase in the growth rate of average compensation in 1950–2015 and a 0.74 percentage point increase in 1975–2015. The estimates are strongly significantly different from 0 and not significantly different from 1. Over 2000–15 the coefficient estimate is smaller, at 0.40; it remains significantly different from 0 but is also significantly different from 1.

Testing for significant differences in coefficients between the pre- and post-2000 period yields mixed results. In an unrestricted regression allowing all coefficients to differ between the two periods, we find significantly different coefficients on productivity at the 5 percent level. But a regression that allows the productivity coefficients to differ but restricts unemployment coefficients and the constant to be the same across the whole 1950–2015 period gives a larger coefficient on productivity over 2000–15 (0.56 rather than 0.4), and the difference between the two periods is nonsignificant (see Stansbury and Summers 2017, table A11).

These results suggest substantial linkage between productivity and average compensation. The strong linkage hypothesis cannot be rejected for most of the period. For the period since 2000, over which the labor share declined, there is some suggestion that the degree of linkage may have fallen (though strong delinkage is still rejected).

Alternate Specifications

As a robustness check, we repeat these regressions for a number of other specifications:

- excluding the unemployment control,
- including a time trend,
- including dummy variables for each decade, and
- varying the moving average bandwidth.

Table 8.2 summarizes the results for the coefficient on the change in log productivity (the full regressions are shown in Stansbury and Summers 2017, tables A1–A7).[18] The results are generally robust across specifications and largely supportive of the hypothesis that for middle-class workers, increases in productivity growth led to substantial increases in real compensation growth.

---

18. We also repeated the regressions using distributed lags instead of moving averages, using nonfarm business sector productivity instead of total economy productivity, and deflating the compensation series with the PCE and net domestic product price index rather than the CPI-U-RS. The overall picture from these regressions is not substantially different from the results presented here (results available on request).

Table 8.2 Coefficients on productivity from various specifications of productivity-compensation regressions

Regression specification	Average compensation				Median compensation	Production/nonsupervisory compensation		
	1949–2016	1949–73	1974–2016	1999–2016	1974–2016	1949–2016	1949–73	1974–2016
(2a) Initial regression (tables 8.1 and 8.3)	0.77*** (0.10)	0.58** (0.25)	0.74*** (0.14)	0.40** (0.14)	0.73*** (0.16)	0.84*** (0.11)	0.69*** (0.19)	0.53*** (0.19)
(2b) Without unemployment	0.96*** (0.08)	0.29 (0.20)	0.79*** (0.17)	0.55*** (0.14)	0.80*** (0.2)	1.00*** (0.11)	0.35* (0.18)	0.58*** (0.17)
(2c) With time trend	0.68*** (0.16)	0.26 (0.28)	0.73*** (0.14)	0.79*** (0.21)	0.73*** (0.17)	0.73*** (0.17)	0.38 (0.32)	0.51*** (0.15)
(2d) With decade dummy variables	0.69*** (0.17)	0.38 (0.25)	0.91*** (0.16)	0.57*** (0.08)	1.00*** (0.16)	0.60*** (0.15)	0.45* (0.25)	0.59*** (0.13)
(2e) Contemporaneous only	0.63*** (0.09)	0.39 (0.23)	0.56*** (0.16)	0.48*** (0.14)	0.33** (0.16)	0.61*** (0.08)	0.24 (0.16)	0.41*** (0.12)
(2f) Two-year moving average	0.73*** (0.11)	0.30 (0.19)	0.70*** (0.15)	0.45** (0.16)	0.72*** (0.17)	0.82*** (0.12)	0.43* (0.24)	0.55*** (0.18)
(2g) Four-year moving average	0.83*** (0.10)	0.72*** (0.18)	0.73*** (0.12)	0.42** (0.14)	0.72*** (0.17)	0.87*** (0.12)	0.95*** (0.20)	0.50*** (0.18)
(2h) Five-year moving average	0.88*** (0.09)	0.78*** (0.26)	0.77*** (0.11)	0.46** (0.17)	0.65*** (0.16)	0.92*** (0.12)	0.99*** (0.29)	0.44*** (0.13)

Note: Newey-West (HAC) standard errors in parentheses. Cells that are significantly different from 1 at the 5 percent level are highlighted in grey. Underlying regressions are in table 8.1 and in Stansbury and Summers (2017, tables A1–A7). Except where otherwise indicated, regressions use three-year moving averages. *** $p < 0.01$, ** $p < 0.05$, * $p < 0.1$.

Source: Authors' calculations.

The coefficient estimates for median compensation are in the range of 0.65 to 1 for all but the contemporaneous regression. They are significantly different from 0 at the 1 percent level and mostly not significantly different from 1, suggesting substantial linkage between productivity and median compensation. In almost all specifications, the strong linkage hypothesis cannot be rejected.

For production/nonsupervisory compensation since 1973, the coefficient estimates are in the range of 0.4 to 0.6, significantly different from 0 at the 1 percent level and also significantly different from 1, suggesting a high degree of linkage between productivity and production/nonsupervisory compensation. However, both the strong linkage and strong delinkage hypotheses are rejected. The fact that the coefficients are significantly lower than for median compensation bears further investigation. Average compensation growth for production/nonsupervisory workers does not appear to reflect productivity growth to the same extent as compensation growth for the median worker, although the levels of the two series are similar throughout the postwar period.[19]

For average compensation since 1973, the coefficient estimates are in the range of 0.70 to 0.91 for all but the contemporaneous regression. They are strongly significantly different from 0 and mostly not significantly different from 1. Over 1999–2016, the estimates are 0.40 to 0.79 and mostly strongly significantly different from both 0 and 1. These results suggest substantial linkage between productivity and average compensation, with some possibility of a reduction in the degree of linkage since about 2000.

Three additional features of these results are worth noting. First, estimating only the contemporaneous relationship between productivity growth and compensation reduces the magnitude of the estimated coefficient in almost all regressions. This specification may allow insufficient time for firms to pass productivity growth on to workers' compensation.

Second, the coefficient estimates on productivity before 1973 are not as high as one might expect for either average or production/nonsupervisory compensation, considering that the levels of productivity and both compensation measures moved largely together during that period. The coefficient estimates rise significantly as the moving average bandwidth is extended, suggesting that the responsiveness of compensation to productivity growth may have been slower in the earlier period. The period 1956–65 was one of particularly low variation in both compensation and productivity growth, which may magnify the effect of noise. The coeffi-

---

19. The difference in coverage of the two series and the likely change in this difference over time (as discussed in Abraham, Spletzer, and Stewart 1998 and Champagne, Kurmann, and Stewart 2017) may go some way to explaining the difference in the coefficient estimates.

cient estimates rise significantly if that period is excluded when running the pre-1973 regressions (to 0.82 for average and 0.80 for production/nonsupervisory compensation in the baseline specification).

Third, the coefficient estimates for production/nonsupervisory compensation are higher for the whole postwar period than for either of the two subperiods. Looking at the periods before and after 1973 separately makes sense, as there is strong evidence of a structural break in the relationship around 1973. The strong relationship over the whole period appears to be a combination of two separate and somewhat weaker relationships over the two subperiods.

Possible Mismeasurement of Productivity

There has been substantial debate over the extent to which productivity statistics are mismeasured (see, for example, Byrne, Fernald, and Reinsdorf 2016; Feldstein 2017; Groshen et al. 2017; and Syverson 2017). Mismeasurement may occur, for example, if technological innovations are undermeasured or quality improvements or new goods and services are hard to value.

The degree of mismeasurement in the productivity statistics should not substantially affect our conclusions, however, because we compare real output per hour (labor productivity) with real compensation per hour. Each of these series is calculated from a nominal measure (net domestic product, total compensation) divided by a price deflator and by hours worked. We have no reason to believe that there is substantial mismeasurement in the nominal series, and as both series are divided by the same metric of hours worked, we need not be concerned that mismeasurement in hours affects our conclusions. The only major causes for concern with mismeasurement are the price deflators, but as we are investigating the relationship between changes in productivity and changes in real compensation, mismeasurement should not affect our conclusions as long as the relative degree of mismeasurement in the price deflators for output and consumption did not change.[20]

Results for the Rest of the Income Distribution

The evidence suggests that growth in median, average, and production/nonsupervisory compensation is strongly positively related to productivity growth. What about other parts of the income distribution?

---

20. This argument is stronger if we deflate both the productivity and compensation series by the same price deflator, as in this case the underlying relationship between the two should remain despite any mismeasurement. We repeated our baseline regressions deflating compensation by the net domestic product price index. There was no substantial effect on our results (results available on request).

To answer this question, we estimate the relationship between productivity and wages at each decile of the wage distribution, using data from the Economic Policy Institute's State of Working America Data Library. The results show substantial differences in the comovement of productivity and wages by decile (tables 8.3 and 8.4). Wages at the 20th and 40th to 90th percentiles comove significantly with productivity, with coefficients between 0.3 and 0.7.

A significant caveat in interpreting these regressions is that these data are for wages, not total compensation. As benefits grew faster than wages for much of the postwar period, our wage growth measure underestimates total real compensation growth (see, among others, Bosworth and Perry 1994, Feldstein 2008, Bivens and Mishel 2015, and Lawrence 2016). Growth in nonwage benefits is probably correlated with both wage growth and aggregate productivity growth. As a result, our estimates are likely to be biased downward.

Comparing the coefficient estimates in the median wage and median compensation regressions can help quantify this bias, at least for the middle of the distribution. The coefficient in the regression of the median wage on productivity is 0.60, compared with 0.73 for the regression of median compensation on productivity, suggesting that the bias is about 20 percent of the coefficient size.

Nonwage benefits make up a vastly different share of total compensation for workers at different points of the wage distribution (see Stansbury and Summers 2017, figure A1), and these shares grew at different rates for different parts of the wage distribution over recent decades (Pierce 2010, Monaco and Pierce 2015). This bias estimate cannot therefore be extrapolated to the entire wage distribution. Evidence from BLS does suggest, however, that at least over the periods 1987–97, 1997–2007, and 2007–14, the ratio of wage to nonwage compensation grew similarly for the middle of the income distribution (between about the 40th and 60th percentiles) (Pierce 2010, Monaco and Pierce 2015). This evidence suggests that we may be able to extrapolate the rough magnitude of the bias at the 50th percentile to the 40th and 60th percentiles. It implies that the regression coefficients of 0.37 and 0.48 should be considered lower bounds on the true relationship between productivity and compensation in the 40th and 60th percentiles, respectively, and that the true coefficients could be about 20 percent higher.

Other Countries

In the cross-section, countries with higher labor productivity tend to have higher typical and average compensation. Lawrence (2016) finds a close to one-for-one correlation between labor productivity and average manu-

Table 8.3 Wage and productivity regression results for 10th to 50th percentile of wages

Dependent variable is 3-year moving average of the change in log wage	Wage percentile (1975–2015)				
	(3a) 10th	(3b) 20th	(3c) 30th	(3d) 40th	(3e) Median
Change in log productivity	0.34 (0.39)	0.69** (0.26)	0.18 (0.28)	0.37** (0.16)	0.60*** (0.16)
Unemployment among people 25–54	-1.05* (0.54)	-0.63* (0.37)	-0.53 (0.36)	-0.42 (0.34)	-0.43* (0.22)
Lagged unemployment	0.29 (0.44)	0.04 (0.32)	-0.04 (0.30)	0.03 (0.32)	0.14 (0.19)
Constant	0.04*** (0.01)	0.02*** (0.01)	0.03*** (0.01)	0.02*** (0.01)	0.01 (0.01)
Number of observations	41	41	41	41	41
F-test: Is coefficient on productivity significantly different from 1?					
Test statistic	2.80	1.48	8.82***	15.3***	5.89**
Prob > F	0.10	0.23	0.01	0.00	0.02

Note: Newey-West standard errors (HAC) in parentheses. The year is listed as the middle year of the moving average. *** $p < 0.01$, ** $p < 0.05$, * $p < 0.1$.

F-test null hypothesis: Coefficient on productivity is not significantly different from one.

Source: Authors' calculations.

Table 8.4 Wage and productivity regression results for 60th to 95th percentile of wages

Dependent variable is 3-year moving average of the change in log wage	Wage percentile (1975–2015)				
	(4a) 60th	(4b) 70th	(4c) 80th	(4d) 90th	(4e) 95th
Change in log productivity	0.48** (0.19)	0.33** (0.13)	0.35** (0.13)	0.38** (0.17)	0.30 (0.23)
Unemployment among people 25–54	-0.28 (0.27)	-0.16 (0.27)	-0.18 (0.24)	-0.25 (0.23)	-0.44 (0.27)
Lagged unemployment	-0.03 (0.29)	-0.09 (0.26)	-0.04 (0.24)	0.05 (0.24)	0.25 (0.24)
Constant	0.01 (0.01)	0.01** (0.00)	0.01** (0.01)	0.01* (0.01)	0.01 (0.01)
Number of observations	41	41	41	41	41
F-test: Is coefficient on productivity significantly different from 1?					
Test statistic	7.74***	25.8***	23.6***	13.6***	9.38***
Prob > F	0.01	0.00	0.00	0.00	0.00

Note: Newey-West standard errors (HAC) in parentheses. The year is listed as the middle year of the moving average. *** $p < 0.01$, ** $p < 0.05$, * $p < 0.1$.

F-test null hypothesis: Coefficient on productivity is not significantly different from one.

Source: Authors' calculations.

facturing compensation for 32 countries. We find a correlation coefficient between labor productivity and median household equivalized disposable income of 0.8 in 34 OECD countries.[21]

Although the cross-country relationship between productivity and compensation is strong, median compensation diverged from productivity in most OECD countries over the past two decades, with rising mean and median income inequality and a falling labor share (ILO 2015; Nolan, Roser, and Thewissen 2016; Schwellnus, Kappeler, and Pionnier 2017; Sharpe and Uguccioni 2017).[22] This finding suggests that there may have been a delinkage of productivity from compensation in some of these countries.

To test whether this might be the case, we repeat our regressions for average compensation for the G-7 economies (table 8.5). We do not show results for median compensation, because most countries lack comparable median hourly compensation data over a sufficiently long period.

The regressions show a mixed picture. The relationship between average compensation and productivity in Canada, West Germany (before reunification), the United Kingdom, and the United States appears to reflect a strong degree of linkage: Coefficients on the change in log of productivity are strongly significant, close to 1, and not significantly lower than 1. France, Germany after reunification, Italy, and Japan have positive but smaller coefficients.

Taken as a whole, these results support the view that productivity growth has positive impacts on average compensation, but they do not support the view that the relationship is necessarily one to one. The surprisingly high degree of variation across countries deserves further exploration.

Technological Change and the Divergence between Productivity and Compensation

The gap between net labor productivity and median real compensation can be thought of in terms of three separate divergences: between mean compensation and productivity (equivalent to a fall in the labor share of income), between median and mean compensation (one aspect of rising

---

21. We use 2007 data from the OECD on labor productivity and household equivalized disposable income. Household equivalized disposable income takes into account taxes and social security contributions paid by households as well as the value of government services provided; it reflects a country's redistributive policies as well as its underlying labor market dynamics. We use this measure because there is no good comparable measure of median hourly compensation (our preferred measure across countries). A scatter plot is shown in Stansbury and Summers (2017, figure A2).

22. For comparative international evidence on the labor share decline, see Bentolila and Saint-Paul (2003); Blanchard and Giavazzi (2003); Azmat, Manning, and Van Reenen (2011); Karabarbounis and Neiman (2014); and Cho, Hwang, and Schreyer (2017).

Table 8.5 Regression results on average compensation and productivity in G-7 countries

Dependent variable is 3-year moving average of the change in log average compensation	Canada 1972–2015 (5a)	France 1972–2015 (5b)	West Germany 1972–90 (5c)	Germany 1993–2015 (5d)	Italy 1985–2015 (5e)	Japan 1997–2014 (5f)	United Kingdom 1996–2015 (5g)	United States 1950–2015 (5h)
Change in log productivity	0.95*** (0.23)	0.32** (0.13)	0.88*** (0.29)	0.23 (0.39)	0.42 (0.26)	0.20** (0.08)	1.55*** (0.22)	0.77*** (0.10)
Unemployment among people 25–54	−0.20 (0.20)	−0.62* (0.34)	−1.17*** (0.35)	0.18 (0.34)	−0.79** (0.35)	0.42 (0.34)	−0.41** (0.15)	−0.19 (0.15)
Lagged unemployment	−0.30 (0.22)	0.15 (0.36)	1.01** (0.40)	−0.64* (0.35)	0.59 (0.37)	−0.84*** (0.15)	−0.23 (0.23)	−0.17 (0.18)
Constant	0.04*** (0.01)	0.05*** (0.01)	0.01 (0.01)	0.04*** (0.01)	0.02* (0.01)	0.01 (0.01)	0.04** (0.01)	0.02*** (0.01)
Number of observations	44	44	19	23	31	18	20	66
F-test: Is coefficient significantly different from 1?								
Test statistic	0.04	27.4***	0.17	3.89*	5.11**	126.1***	6.45**	4.85**
Prob > F	0.84	0.00	0.68	0.06	0.03	0.00	0.02	0.03

Note: Newey-West standard errors (HAC) in parentheses. *** $p < 0.01$, ** $p < 0.05$, * $p < 0.1$.

Notation: The year is listed as the middle year of the moving average.

F-test null hypothesis: Coefficient on productivity is *not* significantly different from one.

Source: Authors' calculations.

labor income inequality), and between consumer and producer price deflators (Bivens and Mishel 2015).

Several theories focus on technological change to explain the first two of these three divergences: the falling labor share and rising labor income inequality in the top half of the distribution. This section summarizes these theories and tests them using short-term fluctuations in productivity growth.

Falling Labor Share (Divergence between Productivity and Mean Compensation)

The growing wedge between labor productivity and mean compensation is equivalent to a falling labor share of income:

$$percent\Delta \frac{Labor\ productivity}{Mean\ compensation} = percent\Delta \left(\frac{output}{hours\ worked} \middle/ \frac{total\ compensation}{hours\ worked} \right)$$
$$= percent\Delta \frac{1}{labor\ share}$$

Several theories of this decline focus on changes in technology. They include capital-augmenting technological change, which enables the mechanization and automation of production (Brynjolfsson and McAfee 2014, Acemoglu and Restrepo 2016); capital deepening, as a result of falling prices of investment goods, together with an elasticity of substitution between labor and capital greater than one (Karabarbounis and Neiman 2014); and labor-augmenting technological change combined with an elasticity of substitution of less than one, which leads to a fall in the effective capital-labor ratio (Lawrence 2015). The IMF's 2017 *World Economic Outlook* attributes about half the fall in the labor share in advanced economies to technological progress; the decline in the price of investment goods and advances in information and communications technology encouraged automation of routine tasks.

Grossman et al. (2017) argue that the productivity slowdown itself may have reduced the labor share by slowing technological progress on human capital accumulation.

Other authors argue that technological change is not the primary driver of the decline in the labor share. Nontechnology-focused theories of the decline in the labor share include offshoring of labor-intensive production tasks (Elsby, Hobijn, and Şahin 2013); capital accumulation (Piketty 2014, Piketty and Zucman 2014); reductions of worker bargaining power as a result of changing labor market institutions (Levy and Temin 2007, Bental and Demougin 2010, OECD 2012, Mishel and Bivens 2015, Solow 2015); industrial structure explanations, including increased firm concentration in "winner-take-most" markets (Autor et al. 2017, see also chapter 9 in this volume); increased markups (Barkai 2016); and the dynamics of the housing market (Rognlie 2015).

Rising Labor Income Inequality in the Top Half of the Distribution (Divergence between Mean and Median Compensation)

The growing wedge between mean and median compensation reflects rising income inequality in the top half of the income distribution. The gap between the 90th percentile wage and the median has risen steadily since about 1980; over the same period, the income shares of the top 1 percent and top 0.1 percent rose rapidly (see, for example, Goldin and Katz 2008; Autor, Katz, and Kearney 2008; Lemieux 2008; and Atkinson, Piketty, and Saez 2011).

As with the fall in the labor share, a number of pure technology-based explanations of rising labor income inequality have been put forward. They include capital-skill complementarity (Griliches 1969, Krusell et al. 2000); the increased pace of skill upgrading as a result of computerization (Autor, Katz, and Krueger 1998); the effect of routine-biased technological change on task demand and the hollowing out of middle-skill jobs (Autor 2010); and automation and the use of robots (Acemoglu and Restrepo 2017).

Nontechnological explanations of rising income inequality in the top half of the distribution include slower growth in educational attainment in the face of skill-biased technical change (Goldin and Katz 2008); declining unionization (Freeman et al. 2016; Rosenfeld, Denice, and Laird 2016)[23] lower top marginal tax rates (Piketty, Saez, and Stantcheva 2014); globalization, including rising trade with China and other low-cost manufacturing hubs (Autor, Dorn, and Hanson 2013); increased low-skill immigration (Borjas 2003); and the "superstar" effect, as globalization or technological change increase market size and returns to being the best (Rosen 1981, Gabaix et al. 2016, Jones and Kim forthcoming).

Implications of Technology-Based Theories of Rising Inequality

Pure technology-based theories of the falling labor share or rising wage inequality in the top half of the income distribution have a testable implication. If technological change caused the fall in the labor share and the mechanism operates over the short to medium term, one would expect the labor share to fall more quickly in periods in which labor productivity growth is more rapid, under the natural assumption that the technological

---

23. Freeman (1993); DiNardo, Fortin, and Lemieux (1996); and others argue that the decline in unionization significantly increased labor income inequality during the 1980s and 1990s.

Table 8.6 **Average annual productivity growth and changes in inequality in the United States** (percent)

Period	Average annual productivity growth	Average annual change in labor share	Average annual change in mean-median ratio
1950–73	2.58	0.10	n.a.
1973–96	1.16	–0.26	0.71
1996–2003	2.33	0.32	0.39
2003–14	1.15	–0.34	0.92

n.a. = not available

Sources: Data from Bureau of Labor Statistics, Bureau of Economic Analysis, Penn World Tables, and Economic Policy Institute Data Library.

change in question also increases labor productivity.[24] Similarly, if technological change caused the rise in the mean-median compensation ratio, one would expect that ratio to rise more rapidly in periods of faster labor productivity growth.[25]

Over a medium-term horizon, the opposite has occurred in the United States (table 8.6). During the productivity boom of 1996–2003, the labor share rose and the mean-median compensation ratio increased more slowly than in the periods of slower productivity growth before and afterward. Indeed, the labor share fell most and the mean-median ratio rose most in recent decades, during a period of productivity slowdown.

Mishel and Bivens (2017) argue that pure technology-based theories for rising US income inequality are weak. They argue that a number of indicators of the pace of automation—productivity growth, capital investment, and information technology and software investment—increased rapidly in the late 1990s and early 2000s, a period that saw "the best across-the-board wage growth for American workers in a generation." In periods of rapidly widening inequality (1973–95 and 2005 to the present), these indicators increased more slowly.

While the lack of medium-term correlations is suggestive, a relationship may exist over shorter horizons. Short-term fluctuations in productivity growth provide a simple natural quasi-experiment to test the implications of pure technology-based theories of rising income inequality: When

---

24. For theories in which the mechanism is longer term, one would not expect to observe a short-/medium-term relationship between productivity growth and changes in the labor share. One theory to which this may apply is that of Grossman et al. (2017), which operates through changed incentives for human capital accumulation.

25. The correlation between short- and medium-horizon changes in the mean-median ratio and changes in the labor share is relatively low (about 0.25 to 0.3) and not statistically significant, making it unlikely a priori that the same factor is causing both trends.

productivity growth is faster, the labor share should fall more quickly and the mean-median compensation ratio should increase more quickly.

To test this possibility, we run the following regressions:[26]

$$\frac{1}{3}\Sigma_0^2 \Delta \log labor\ share_{t-i} = \alpha + \beta\ \frac{1}{3}\Sigma_0^2 \Delta \log prod_{t-i} + \gamma \frac{1}{3}\Sigma_0^2 unemp_{t-i} +$$
$$\delta \frac{1}{3}\Sigma_0^2 unemp_{t-i-1} + \varepsilon_t \tag{8.3}$$

$$\frac{1}{3}\Sigma_0^2 \Delta \log \frac{mean}{median} compensation_{t-i} = \alpha + \beta\ \frac{1}{3}\Sigma_0^2 \Delta \log prod_{t-i} + \gamma \frac{1}{3}\Sigma_0^2 unemp_{t-i} +$$
$$\delta \frac{1}{3}\Sigma_0^2 unemp_{t-i-1} + \varepsilon_t \tag{8.4}$$

If pure technology-based theories of rising inequality are correct, one should see a negative and significant coefficient on the change in log productivity in the labor share regressions and a positive and significant coefficient in the change in log productivity in the mean-median compensation regressions.[27]

We use the Penn World Tables measure of the labor share, which covers labor compensation for the total US economy as a share of GDP. As Johnson (1954), Kravis (1959), and others note, the imputation of self-employed proprietors' income to labor or capital can matter significantly for labor share calculations. The Penn World Tables measure imputes mixed income of the self-employed to labor based on the average labor share in the rest of the U.S. economy. This measure appears to be the most plausible for the United States, based on the occupational demographics of the self-employed (Elsby, Hobijn, and Şahin 2013; Feenstra, Inklaar, and Timmer 2015), and it is consistent with much of the literature on the labor share.[28] For robustness, we repeated our regressions with the BLS measures of the labor share for the total economy and the nonfarm business sector,

---

26. We also ran distributed-lag versions of these regressions and versions with different measures of productivity growth. They did not show substantially different results (available on request).

27. In addition, specific technology-based theories may have specific testable implications. In Stansbury and Summers (2017), we tested the hypothesis that the labor share fell because a decline in the relative price of investment goods led to an increase in the capital-labor ratio (Karabarbounis and Neiman 2014). We were unable to find evidence to support it.

28. Gollin (2002) discusses three reasonable methods for imputing mixed income when calculating the labor share, of which this labor share–based imputation is one. Studies using this approach include Gomme and Rupert (2004); Caselli and Feyrer (2007); Valentinyi and Herrendorf (2008); Elsby, Hobijn, and Şahin (2013); and Koh, Santaeulàlia-Llopis, and Zheng (2016). Piketty and Zucman (2014) and Rognlie (2015) use a similar method, assuming that the noncorporate sector has the same net capital share as the corporate sector. Krueger (1999) describes a common convention, used since Johnson (1954), of imputing two-thirds of mixed income to labor, which approximates the US economywide labor share. Christensen (1971), Abel et al. (1989), and Geerolf (2013), among others, have used this approach.

as well as a net measure of the labor share.[29] The results were not substantially different from our baseline results (results available on request).

Results on Productivity and the Labor Share

Table 8.7 shows the results from our baseline specification (three-year moving average). Table 8.8 shows the coefficient estimates on productivity in regressions with varying moving average bandwidths. Most specifications show a negative relationship between changes in productivity growth and changes in the labor share, as predicted by technology-based theories of the labor share decline. One would also expect some mechanical negative relationship over short horizons, as a positive unanticipated productivity shock would translate into higher firm income in the current year but be unlikely to feed through to worker compensation until future years.

The coefficients tend to be small and insignificant for the postwar period and for the post-1973 period but large and strongly significant for the period since 2000, when the labor share declined. A Quandt likelihood ratio test identifies a structural break in the relationship at 2002, significant at the 1 percent level. The estimated coefficients for the post-2000 period imply that a 1 percentage point increase in the rate of productivity growth was associated with a 0.07 to 0.43 percentage point faster decline in the labor share. The labor share began to decline significantly in the early 2000s, falling 4.5 percentage points (6.5 percent) over 2001–14 (an annual rate of 0.49 percent); the average annual rate of labor productivity growth over 2001–14 was 1.3 percent.

The magnitude of the coefficient for the post-2000 period falls substantially as the moving average bandwidth increases (table 8.8), in line with the hypothesis that some of the short-term negative relationship between contemporaneous productivity growth and compensation growth could be mechanical; it should disappear over longer bandwidths. Testing for a significant difference between productivity coefficients in the pre- and post-2000 period using unrestricted regressions, we find significant differences at the 5 percent level for three-year moving averages and nonsignificant differences for two-, four-, and five-year moving averages. When restricting the coefficients on unemployment and the constant to be the same over both periods, the difference in productivity coefficients between the pre- and post-2000 period declines substantially and is not significant (see

---

29. BLS imputes the compensation of proprietors under the assumption that their hourly compensation is the same as that of the average employee in each sector (BLS 2008, Giandrea and Sprague 2017). Bentolila and Saint-Paul (2003) use a similar wage-based imputation. Bridgman (2014) shows that the use of gross rather than net labor shares can have a significant impact on calculations of the decline in the labor share in the United States.

Table 8.7   Regression results on productivity and labor shares

Dependent variable is 3-year moving average of change in log labor share	(7a) 1950–2013	(7b) 1950–73	(7c) 1975–2013	(7d) 2000–13
Change in log productivity	−0.10 (0.11)	−0.03 (0.24)	−0.11 (0.18)	−0.43*** (0.11)
Unemployment among people 25–54	−0.51*** (0.14)	−0.49* (0.26)	−0.47*** (0.16)	−0.20 (0.16)
Lagged unemployment	0.27** (0.13)	0.04 (0.25)	0.28** (0.12)	0.10 (0.18)
Constant	0.01*** (0.00)	0.02*** (0.00)	0.01* (0.01)	0.01 (0.01)
Number of observations	64	24	39	14

Note: Newey-West standard errors (HAC) in parentheses. The year is listed as the middle year of the moving average. *** $p < 0.01$, ** $p < 0.05$, * $p < 0.1$.

Source: Authors' calculations.

Table 8.8   Coefficients on productivity from productivity–labor share regressions for various moving average bandwidths

Dependent variable is X-year moving average of change in log labor share	(8a) 1950–2014	(8b) 1950–73	(8c) 1975–2014	(8d) 2000–14
Two years	−0.17* (0.09)	−0.31 (0.25)	−0.14 (0.17)	−0.43*** (0.11)
Three years	−0.10 (0.11)	−0.03 (0.24)	−0.11 (0.18)	−0.43*** (0.11)
Four years	−0.09 (0.12)	0.19 (0.25)	−0.12 (0.14)	−0.34** (0.11)
Five years	−0.11 (0.11)	0.08 (0.16)	−0.06 (0.12)	−0.07 (0.16)

Note: The independent variable is the X-year moving average of the change in the log of productivity. Regressions control for unemployment. Newey-West standard errors (HAC) are in parentheses. Underlying regressions are in table 8.7 and Stansbury and Summers (2017). *** $p < 0.01$, ** $p < 0.05$, * $p < 0.1$.

Source: Authors' calculations.

Stansbury and Summers 2017, table A12). It is not clear a priori whether one should expect the cyclicality of the productivity–labor share relationship or the constant term to have changed since 2000. If it did not, the restricted regressions are more appropriate.

Overall, these results on productivity and labor share present a mixed picture. As there is no apparent relationship between changes in the rate of productivity growth and changes in the labor share before 2000, the results do not tend to support theories that posit a long-term underlying relationship between technology and the labor share. The larger and negative coefficient estimates since 2000 provide some support for theories that attribute the labor share decline to a change in the technology–labor

Table 8.9 Regressions results on productivity and mean-median compensation

Dependent variable is 3-year moving average of change in log mean-median compensation ratio	(10a) 1975–2015	(10b) 1975–2015
Change in log productivity	-0.01 (0.10)	0.00 (0.10)
Unemployment among people 25–54		-0.09 (0.12)
Lagged unemployment		0.13 (0.10)
Constant	0.01*** (0.00)	0.01 (0.00)
Number of observations	41	41

Note: Newey-West standard errors (HAC) in parentheses. The year is listed as the middle year of the moving average. *** $p < 0.01$, ** $p < 0.05$, * $p < 0.1$.

Source: Authors' calculations.

share relationship since 2000, but these estimates are sensitive to the time horizon and methodology used.

Results on Productivity and the Mean-Median Ratio

If faster technological progress were responsible for the rising mean-median compensation ratio, one would expect periods of faster productivity growth to be associated with periods of faster increases in it. There is no significant relationship between productivity growth and changes in this ratio (which also holds with different moving-average bandwidths), casting doubt on pure technology-based theories of the rising mean-median compensation ratio (table 8.9).

Concluding Remarks

Over the past four decades, average compensation growth in the United States was slow and median compensation almost stagnant. Real average hourly compensation rose by 48 percent between 1973 and 2016, an annual rate of only 0.9 percent. Real hourly median compensation rose only 11 percent between 1973 and 2016 (real average hourly production/nonsupervisory compensation rose by 12 percent). During the same period, hourly labor productivity rose by 75 percent (1.3 percent a year).

In contrast, between 1948 and 1973, average pay for Americans rose much more quickly and more closely in line with productivity. Real average hourly compensation grew by 2.9 percent a year. Real hourly production/

nonsupervisory compensation—which is likely to have grown at a similar rate as median compensation (Bivens and Mishel 2015)—grew by 2.6 percent a year. Hourly labor productivity grew by 2.7 percent a year.

A period of slower productivity growth since 1973 has coincided with a period of even slower pay growth. Productivity has grown relatively slowly, average pay slower still, and median and production/nonsupervisory pay barely at all.

There is a spectrum of possible interpretations of this divergence between productivity and pay. At one end is the strong delinkage view, in which productivity growth did not systematically translate into growth in workers' compensation. At the other end is the strong linkage view, in which productivity growth translated one for one into compensation growth but a variety of other factors put downward pressure on workers' compensation at the same time.

Our regressions are supportive of substantial linkage between productivity and all three measures of compensation (median, production/nonsupervisory, and average). Over 1973–2016, a 1 percentage point increase in the rate of productivity growth was associated with an increase in compensation growth of 0.7 to 1.0 percentage point for median and average compensation and 0.4 to 0.6 percentage points for production/nonsupervisory compensation. Almost all specifications strongly reject the strong delinkage hypothesis. The strong linkage hypothesis of a one-for-one relationship cannot be rejected for either median or average compensation (it is rejected for production/nonsupervisory compensation). Evidence on different deciles of the wage distribution also shows large and significant positive comovement between productivity and wages for the middle deciles.

Our results suggest that productivity growth pushed up typical and average compensation significantly in recent decades. Other factors are likely to be responsible for the divergence between productivity and pay in the United States, suppressing typical workers' incomes even as productivity growth acted to increase them.

One of these factors could be technological change. Pure technology-based theories of the fall in the labor share or the rise in mean-median income inequality imply that in periods in which productivity growth is faster, productivity and median pay should diverge more rapidly. This hypothesis can be tested using the natural quasi-experiment of fluctuations in productivity growth. There is little evidence of significant comovement between productivity growth and the labor share in the United States over long periods (since 1948 and since 1973), but we find some evidence of a significantly negative relationship since 2000. We find no significant relationship between the mean-median ratio and productivity growth over the last four decades.

Taken together, these results tend not to provide strong support for purely technology-based theories of either the decline in the labor share or the rise in mean-median pay inequality. The factors suppressing median compensation over recent decades are more likely to have been factors that are orthogonal to productivity growth.

We can use the coefficient estimates from our regressions to roughly quantify the degree to which the productivity-median compensation divergence has been the result of a lack of pass-through of productivity growth to median compensation, as opposed to the suppression of median compensation by other factors orthogonal to productivity. Our baseline regression coefficient of 0.73 would suggest that if all else had been equal over 1973–2016, the productivity growth experienced in the United States would have resulted in median compensation growing by 51 percent instead of 11 percent. A lack of pass-through of productivity growth to median compensation can thus explain 38 percent of the divergence between the two series; other factors suppressing median compensation (which are orthogonal to productivity growth) can explain the other 62 percent. Using our full range of plausible coefficient estimates (from 0.65 to 1.00), 0 to 40 percent of the productivity-median compensation gap can be explained by lack of productivity pass-through; 60 to 100 percent of the gap can be explained by other factors suppressing median compensation. For production/nonsupervisory compensation, 40 to 50 percent of the gap with productivity can be explained by lack of productivity pass-through; 50 to 60 percent can be explained by other orthogonal factors suppressing production/nonsupervisory compensation.

The continued significance of productivity growth for compensation growth can be illustrated using some simple counterfactuals. If the ratio of the mean to median hourly compensation in 2016 had been the same as it was in 1973 and mean compensation had remained at its 2016 level, median compensation would have been about 33 percent higher, all else constant. If the ratio of labor productivity to mean compensation in 2016 had been the same as it was in 1973 (i.e., the labor share had not fallen), average and median compensation would have been 4 to 8 percent higher, all else constant. In contrast, assuming the relationship between compensation and productivity estimated in table 8.1 holds, if productivity growth had been as fast over 1973–2016 as it was over 1949–73 (2.7 percent rather than 1.3 percent a year), median and mean compensation would have been about 41 percent higher in 2016, all else constant.

These point estimates suggest that that the potential effect of raising productivity growth on the average American's pay may be as great as the effect of policies to reverse trends in income inequality. A continued productivity slowdown should therefore be a major concern for policy-makers hoping to increase real compensation for middle-income workers.

Our central conclusion is that the substantial variations in productivity growth that have taken place during recent decades have been associated with substantial changes in median and mean real compensation. If productivity accelerates for reasons relating to technology or to policy, the likely impact will be increased pay growth for the typical worker. Rather than productivity growth failing to translate into pay growth, our evidence suggests that other factors are suppressing typical workers' incomes, even as productivity growth acts to increase them.

Productivity growth still matters substantially for middle-income Americans. At the same time, the evidence of the past four decades suggests that in the face of rising inequality, productivity growth alone may not be enough to raise living standards substantially.

References

Abel, Andrew B., N. Gregory Mankiw, Lawrence H. Summers, and Richard J. Zeckhauser. 1989. Assessing Dynamic Efficiency: Theory and Evidence. *Review of Economic Studies* 56, no. 1: 1–19.

Abraham, Katharine G., James R. Spletzer, and Jay C. Stewart. 1998. Divergent Trends in Alternative Wage Series. In *Labor Statistics Measurement Issues*, eds. John C. Haltiwanger, Marilyn E. Manser, and Robert Topel. Chicago: University of Chicago Press, 293–324.

Acemoglu, Daron, and Pascual Restrepo. 2016. *The Race Between Machine and Man: Implications of Technology for Growth, Factor Shares and Employment.* NBER Working Paper 22252. Cambridge, MA: National Bureau of Economic Research.

Acemoglu, Daron, and Pascual Restrepo. 2017. *Robots and Jobs: Evidence from U.S. Labor Markets.* NBER Working Paper 23285. Cambridge, MA: National Bureau of Economic Research.

Atkinson, Anthony B., Thomas Piketty, and Emmanuel Saez. 2011. Top Incomes in the Long Run of History. *Journal of Economic Literature* 49, no. 1: 3–71.

Autor, David. 2010. *The Polarization of Job Opportunities in the U.S. Labor Market: Implications for Employment and Earnings.* Washington: Center for American Progress and the Hamilton Project.

Autor, David H., David Dorn, and Gordon H. Hanson. 2013. The China Syndrome: Local Labor Market Effects of Import Competition in the United States. *American Economic Review* 103, no. 6: 2121–68.

Autor, David H., Lawrence F. Katz, and Melissa S. Kearney. 2008. Trends in U.S. Wage Inequality: Revising the Revisionists. *Review of Economics and Statistics* 90, no. 2: 300–23.

Autor, David H., Lawrence F. Katz, and Alan B. Krueger. 1998. Computing Inequality: Have Computers Changed the Labor Market? *Quarterly Journal of Economics* 113, no. 4: 1169–213.

Autor, David, David Dorn, Lawrence F. Katz, Christina Patterson, and John Van Reenen. 2017. *The Fall of the Labor Share and the Rise of Superstar Firms.* Discussion Paper 1482. London: Centre for Economic Performance, London School of Economics.

Azmat, Ghazala, Alan Manning, and John Van Reenen. 2011. Privatization and the Decline of Labour's Share: International Evidence from Network Industries. *Economica*: 1–23.

Baker, Dean. 2007. *Behind the Gap between Productivity and Wage Growth*. Issue Brief, February. Washington: Center for Economic Policy and Research.

Barkai, Simcha. 2016. *Declining Labor and Capital Shares*. New Working Paper Series 2. Chicago: Stigler Center for the Study of the Economy and the State.

Barkume, Anthony J. 2007. *Some New Evidence on Overtime Use, Total Job Compensation and Wage Rates*. BLS Working Paper 402. Washington: Bureau of Labor Statistics.

Bental, Benjamin, and Dominique Demougin. 2010. Declining Labor Shares and Bargaining Power: An Institutional Explanation. *Journal of Macroeconomics* 32, no. 1: 443–56.

Bentolila, Samuel, and Gilles Saint-Paul. 2003. Explaining Movements in the Labor Share. *B.E. Journal of Macroeconomics* 3, no. 1: 1–33.

Bernstein, Jared. 2015. Faster productivity growth would be great. I'm just not at all sure we can count on it to lift middle-class incomes. On the Economy Jared Bernstein Blog, April 21.

Bivens, Josh, and Lawrence Mishel. 2015. *Understanding the Historic Divergence between Productivity and a Typical Worker's Pay: Why It Matters and Why It's Real*. Washington: Economic Policy Institute.

Blanchard, Olivier, and Francesco Giavazzi. 2003. Macroeconomic Effects of Regulation and Deregulation in Goods and Labor Markets. *Quarterly Journal of Economics* 118, no. 3: 879–907.

BLS (Bureau of Labor Statistics). 2008. *Technical Information about the BLS Major Sector Productivity and Costs Measures*, March 11. Washington: Bureau of Labor Statistics.

Borjas, George J. 2003. The Labor Demand Curve Is Downward Sloping: Reexamining the Impact of Immigration on the Labor Market. *Quarterly Journal of Economics* 118, no. 4: 1335–74.

Bosworth, Barry. 2010. *Price Deflators, the Trust Fund Forecast, and Social Security Solvency*. Center for Retirement Research Working Paper 2010-12. Chestnut Hill, MA: Boston College.

Bosworth, Barry, and Dean Perry. 1994. *Productivity and Real Wages: Is There a Puzzle?* Brookings Papers on Economic Activity. Washington: Brookings Institution.

Bridgman, Benjamin. 2014. *Is Labor's Loss Capital's Gain? Gross versus Net Labor Shares*. Washington: Bureau of Economic Analysis.

Brynjolfsson, Erik, and Andrew McAfee. 2014. *The Second Machine Age: Work, Progress, and Prosperity in a Time of Brilliant Technologies*. New York: W.W. Norton & Company.

Byrne, David M., J. Fernald, and Marshall Reinsdorf. 2016. *Does the United States Have a Productivity Slowdown or a Measurement Problem?* Brookings Papers on Economic Activity, March. Washington: Brookings Institution.

Caselli, Francesco, and James Feyrer. 2007. The Marginal Product of Capital. *Quarterly Journal of Economics* 122, no. 2: 535–68.

Champagne, Julien, André Kurmann, and Jay Stewart. 2017. Reconciling the Divergence in Aggregate US Wage Series. *Labour Economics* 49: 27–41.

Cho, T., S. Hwang, and P. Schreyer. 2017. *Has the Labour Share Declined? It Depends*. OECD Statistics Working Paper 2017/01. Paris: OECD Publishing.

Christensen, Laurits R. 1971. Entrepreneurial Income: How Does It Measure Up? *American Economic Review* 61, no. 4: 575–85.

Church, Jonathan D. 2016. Comparing the Consumer Price Index with the Gross Domestic Product Price Index and Gross Domestic Product Implicit Price Deflator. *Bureau of Labor Statistics Monthly Labor Review*, March. Washington: Bureau of Labor Statistics.

Dew-Becker, Ian, and Robert J. Gordon. 2005. *Where Did the Productivity Growth Go? Inflation Dynamics and the Distribution of Income.* NBER Working Paper W11842. Cambridge, MA: National Bureau of Economic Research.

DiNardo, John, Nicole M. Fortin, and Thomas Lemieux. 1996. Labor Market Institutions and the Distribution of Wages, 1973–1992: A Semiparametric Approach. *Econometrica* 64, no. 5: 1001–44.

Economic Policy Institute. 2017. Wages by Percentile. State of Working America Data Library. Washington.

The Economist. 2013. Inequality: A defining issue – for poor people. *Economist Blog – Democracy in America*, December 16.

Elsby, Michael W. L., Bart Hobijn, and Ayşegül Şahin. 2013. *The Decline of the U.S. Labor Share.* Brookings Papers on Economic Activity 2: 1–63. Washington: Brookings Institution.

Feenstra, Robert C., Robert Inklaar, and Marcel Timmer. 2015. The Next Generation of the Penn World Table. *American Economic Review* 105, no. 10: 3150–82.

Feldstein, Martin. 2008. Did Wages Reflect Growth in Productivity? *Journal of Policy Modeling* 30, no. 4: 591–94.

Feldstein, Martin. 2017. Underestimating the Real Growth of GDP, Personal Income, and Productivity. *Journal of Economic Perspectives* 31, no. 2: 145–64.

Fixler, Dennis, and Ted Jaditz. 2002. *An Examination of the Difference Between the CPI and the PCE Deflator.* BLS Working Paper 361. Washington: Bureau of Labor Statistics.

Fleck, Susan, John Glaser, and Shawn Sprague. 2011. The Compensation-Productivity Gap: A Visual Essay. *Bureau of Labor Statistics Monthly Labor Review*, January. Washington: Bureau of Labor Statistics.

Freeman, Richard B. 1993. How Much Has De-Unionization Contributed to the Rise in Male Earnings Inequality? In *Uneven Tides: Rising Inequality in America*, ed. Sheldon Danziger and Peter Gottschalk. New York: Russell Sage Foundation.

Freeman, Richard B., E. Han, B. Duke, and D. Madland. 2016. *How Does Declining Unionism Affect the American Middle Class and Inter-generational Mobility?* Federal Reserve System's Community Development Research Conference Publication, December: 451–80. Washington: Federal Reserve Board.

Gabaix, Xavier, Jean-Michel Lasry, Pierre-Louis Lions, and Benjamin Moll. 2016. The Dynamics of Inequality. *Econometrica* 84, no. 6: 2071–11.

Geerolf, François. 2013. *Reassessing Dynamic Efficiency.* Working Paper, Department of Economics, University of California, Los Angeles.

Giandrea, Michael D., and Shawn A. Sprague. 2017. Estimating the U.S. Labor Share. *Bureau of Labor Statistics Monthly Labor Review*, February. Washington: Bureau of Labor Statistics.

Goldin, Claudia Dale, and Lawrence F. Katz. 2008. *The Race between Education and Technology.* Cambridge, MA: Harvard University Press.

Gollin, Douglas. 2002. Getting Income Shares Right. *Journal of Political Economy* 110, no. 2: 458–74.

Gomme, Paul, and Peter Rupert. 2004. *Measuring Labor's Share of Income*. Policy Discussion Paper 04–07. Cleveland: Federal Reserve Bank of Cleveland.

Griliches, Zvi. 1969. Capital–Skill Complementarity. *Review of Economics and Statistics*: 465–68.

Groshen, Erica L., Brian C. Moyer, Ana M. Aizcorbe, Ralph Bradley, and David M. Friedman. 2017. How Government Statistics Adjust for Potential Biases from Quality Change and New Goods in an Age of Digital Technologies: A View from the Trenches. *Journal of Economic Perspectives* 31, no. 2: 187–210.

Grossman, Gene M., Elhanan Helpman, Ezra Oberfield, and Thomas Sampson. 2017. *The Productivity Slowdown and the Declining Labor Share: A Neoclassical Exploration*. NBER Working Paper 23853. Cambridge, MA: National Bureau of Economic Research.

ILO (International Labour Organization). 2015. *Global Wage Report 2014/15: Wage and Income Inequality*. Geneva.

IMF (International Monetary Fund). 2017 Understanding the Downward Trend in Labor Income Shares. *World Economic Outlook*, April. Washington.

Johnson, D. Gale. 1954. The Functional Distribution of Income in the United States, 1850–1952. *Review of Economics and Statistics* 36, no. 2: 175–82.

Jones, Charles I., and Jihee Kim. Forthcoming. A Schumpeterian Model of Top Income Inequality. *Journal of Political Economy*.

Karabarbounis, Loukas, and Brent Neiman. 2014. The Global Decline of the Labor Share. *Quarterly Journal of Economics* 129, no. 1: 61–103.

Koh, Dongya, Raül Santaeulàlia-Llopis, and Yu Zheng. 2016. *Labor Share Decline and Intellectual Property Products Capital*. Economics Working Papers ECO 2015/05. Florence: European University Institute.

Kravis, Irving B. 1959. Relative Income Shares in Fact and Theory. *American Economic Review* 49, no. 5: 917–49.

Krueger, Alan B. 1999. Measuring Labor's Share. *American Economic Review* 89, no. 2: 45–51.

Krusell, Per, Lee E. Ohanian, José-Víctor Ríos-Rull, and Giovanni L. Violante. 2000. Capital-Skill Complementarity and Inequality: A Macroeconomic Analysis. *Econometrica* 68, no. 5: 1029–53.

Lawrence, Robert Z. 2015. *Recent Declines in Labor's Share in U.S. Income: A Preliminary Neoclassical Account*. NBER Working Paper 21296. Cambridge, MA: National Bureau of Economic Research.

Lawrence, Robert Z. 2016. Does Productivity Still Determine Worker Compensation? Domestic and International Evidence. In *The U.S. Labor Market: Questions and Challenges for Public Policy*. Washington: American Enterprise Institute Press.

Lawrence, Robert Z., and Matthew J. Slaughter. 1993. *International Trade and American Wages in the 1980s: Giant Sucking Sound or Small Hiccup?* Brookings Papers on Economic Activity 1993, no. 2: 161–226.

Lemieux, Thomas. 2008. The Changing Nature of Wage Inequality. *Journal of Population Economics* 21, no. 1: 21–48.

Levy, Frank, and Peter Temin. 2007. *Inequality and Institutions in 20th Century America*. NBER Working Paper 13106. Cambridge, MA: National Bureau of Economic Research.

McCully, Clinton P., Brian C. Moyer, and Kenneth J. Stewart. 2007. Comparing the Consumer Price Index and the Personal Consumption Expenditure Price Index. *Survey of Current Business*, 26–33. Washington: Bureau of Economic Analysis.

Meyerson, Harold. 2014. How to raise Americans' wages. *American Prospect*, March 18.

Mishel, Lawrence, and Josh Bivens. 2017. *The Zombie Robot Argument Lurches On*. Washington: Economic Policy Institute.

Monaco, Kristen, and Brooks Pierce. 2015. Compensation Inequality: Evidence from the National Compensation Survey. *Monthly Labor Review,* July. Washington: Bureau of Labor Statistics.

Nolan, Brian, Max Roser, and Stefan Thewissen. 2016. *GDP Per Capita versus Median Household Income: What Gives Rise to Divergence over Time?* INET Oxford Working Paper 2016-03. Oxford: Institute of New Economic Thinking.

OECD (Organization for Economic Cooperation and Development). 2012. Labour Losing to Capital: What Explains the Declining Labour Share. In *OECD Employment Outlook*. Paris.

Pessoa, Joao Paolo, and John Van Reenen. 2013. *Decoupling of Wage Growth and Productivity Growth? Myth and Reality*. Centre for Economic Performance Discussion Paper 1246. London: London School of Economics.

Pierce, Brooks. 2010. Recent Trends in Compensation Inequality. In *Labor in the New Economy*, ed. Katharine G. Abraham, James R. Spletzer, and Michael Harper, 63–98. Chicago: University of Chicago Press.

Piketty, Thomas. 2014. *Capital in the Twenty-First Century*. Cambridge, MA: Belknap Press.

Piketty, Thomas, and Gabriel Zucman. 2014. Capital Is Back: Wealth–Income Ratios in Rich Countries 1700–2010. *Quarterly Journal of Economics* 129, no. 3: 1255–310.

Piketty, Thomas, Emmanuel Saez, and Stefanie Stantcheva. 2014. Optimal taxation of top labor incomes: A tale of three elasticities. *American Economic Journal: Economic Policy* 6, no. 1: 230–71.

Rognlie, Matthew. 2015. *Deciphering the Fall and Rise in the Net Capital Share: Accumulation or Scarcity*. Brookings Papers on Economic Activity 1: 1–69. Washington: Brookings Institution.

Rosen, Sherwin. 1981. The Economics of Superstars. *American Economic Review* 71, no. 5: 845–58.

Rosenfeld, Jake, Patrick Denice, and Jennifer Laird. 2016. *Union Decline Lowers Wages of Nonunion Workers*. Washington: Economic Policy Institute.

Schwellnus, Cyrille, Andreas Kappeler, and P. Pionnier. The Decoupling of Median Wages from Productivity in OECD Countries. *International Productivity Monitor* 32: 44–60.

Sharpe, Andrew, and James Uguccioni. 2017. Decomposing the Productivity-Wage Nexus in Selected OECD Countries, 1986-2013. *International Productivity Monitor* 32, Spring.

Sherk, James. 2013. *Productivity and Compensation: Growing Together*. Backgrounder 2825 on Labor. Washington: Heritage Foundation.

Solow, Robert. 2015. The Future of Work: Why Wages Aren't Keeping Up. *Pacific Standard Magazine*, August 11.

Stansbury, Anna M., and Lawrence H. Summers. 2017. *Productivity and Pay: Is the Link Broken?* NBER Working Paper 24165. Cambridge, MA: National Bureau of Economic Research.

Statistiches Bundesamt Deutschland. 2016. Volkswirtschaftliche Gesamtrechnungen: Inlandsproduktberechnung Lange Reihen ab 1970. Article 2180150167004. Wiesbaden.

Syverson, Chad. 2017. Challenges to Mismeasurement Explanations for the U.S. Productivity Slowdown. *Journal of Economic Perspectives* 31: 165–86.

Triplett, Jack E. 1981. Reconciling the CPI and the PCE Deflator. *Monthly Labor Review*, September 3–15. Washington: Bureau of Labor Statistics.

US Government Printing Office. 2015. *Economic Report of the President*. Washington.

Valentinyi, Akos, and Berthold Herrendorf. 2008. Measuring Factor Income Shares at the Sectoral Level. *Review of Economic Dynamics* 11, no. 4: 820–35.

9

Are Slower Productivity and Higher Inequality Related?

JASON FURMAN AND PETER ORSZAG

The most important development in the US economy over the past 40 years has been the deceleration in the typical household's income, a trend also experienced by many other advanced economies. From 1948 to 1973, real median family income in the United States rose 3.0 percent a year. At this rate, incomes doubled once a generation and there was a 96 percent chance that a child would have a higher income than his or her parents. Since 1973 the median family has seen its real income grow by only 0.4 percent a year, a rate at which it would take more than a century to double. As a result, 28 percent of children have lower income than their parents did.

The slowdown in income growth can be traced to two simultaneous developments (see also chapter 8 in this volume by Anna Stansbury and Lawrence Summers). The first is the decline in productivity growth. Output per hour grew by 2.8 percent a year between 1948 and 1973 but by just 1.7 percent a year since 1973. The performance in the past decade has been even worse, with productivity increasing at an annual rate of only 1.2 percent.

Jason Furman, nonresident senior fellow at the Peterson Institute for International Economics and professor of practice at the Harvard Kennedy School, served as a top economic adviser to President Barack Obama during the eight years of his presidency, including as chair of the Council of Economic Advisers. Peter Orszag is vice chairman of investment banking and managing director at Lazard Freres & Co. and member of the Board of Directors of the Peterson Institute for International Economics. He previously served as director of the Office of Management and Budget in the Obama administration and also as director of the Congressional Budget Office. The authors thank Wilson Powell III for outstanding research assistance, Madona Devasahayam and Barbara Karni for excellent copyediting, and Jaana Remes, Lawrence Summers, and Jeromin Zettlmeyer for helpful comments and discussions.

The second development is the rise in inequality. From 1948 to 1973, the share of income going to the bottom 90 percent of Americans held roughly steady, at about two-thirds. This share has fallen steadily since then, to just over half today. The combination of slower income growth and more unequal division of income has dealt a double blow to typical families.

This chapter explores whether the fall in productivity growth and the rise in inequality are related. One possibility is that slower productivity growth is causing rising inequality. In the traditional competitive explanation for rising inequality, increased demand for skills in the form of skill-biased technological change was met by a deceleration in the supply of skills, as a result of a slowdown in the rate of increase of educational attainment, increasing the relative wages of skilled workers (Goldin and Katz 2008). This model explains much of the increase in earnings inequality through about 2000 but leaves important aspects of earnings inequality, especially more recent trends and inequality at the very top of the income distribution, unexplained. Moreover, it would predict that slower productivity growth would result in less skill-biased technological change and thus a reduction in inequality. The traditional competitive theories of inequality can thus not fully account for the dual changes in productivity and inequality.

Another potential explanation is that rising inequality could be harming growth. There is some macroeconomic evidence for this view as well as plausible microeconomic channels, such as the impact of inequality on the ability to harness the talents of potential innovators across the income spectrum (Cingano 2014; Ostry, Berg, and Tsangarides 2014; Bell et al. 2017). Furman (2019) expresses some skepticism about a general empirical link between inequality and economic growth. But regardless of one's view on the existence and sign of such a link, any plausible magnitude for such an effect would fall well short of explaining the 1 to 1.5 percentage point drop in productivity growth.

A third possibility, the one this chapter explores, is that the slowdown of productivity growth and the rise of inequality have a common cause: Reduced competition and reduced dynamism—in part caused by specific policy changes—have contributed to both phenomena.

This chapter does not advance a simple monocausal explanation; many factors, some common and some unrelated, have affected productivity growth and inequality. Instead, it tries to explore whether this hypothesis is consistent with empirical observations. The question of whether the hypothesis explains a part, potentially even a key part, of both phenomena is important both for academics and for policymakers, because it opens up the opportunity to craft a whole new set of policies. New policies, in areas such as product and labor markets, have the potential to yield benefits for both productivity and inequality.

This chapter builds on a paper the authors originally released in 2015 that speculated on some aspects of these links (Furman and Orszag 2018). That paper drew on new research that found that much of the increase in earnings inequality was between, not within, firms (Barth et al. 2016, Song et al. 2015). Since 2015, research has corroborated and advanced the paper's broader thesis. Gutiérrez and Philippon (2017a, 2017b) link the slowdown in investment at the industry level to reduced competition. Barkai (2016) finds evidence that reduced competition and higher markups reduced the labor share of income. Autor et al. (2017) link increased concentration to larger declines in the labor share of income (although they view the increased concentration as the result of more not less competition).

This chapter is organized as follows. The first section reviews some of the key stylized facts about the slowdown of productivity growth and the rise of inequality that require explanation. The second section discusses reduced dynamism and competition and the roles they may play in both phenomena. The third section examines some of the potential causes of this reduced dynamism and competition. The last section summarizes the chapter and draws policy implications.

Stylized Facts about Productivity Growth and Inequality

Productivity

The most important fact about productivity growth in the United States is that it started slowing in 1973 and, after an upswing between 1995 and 2005, has been growing even more slowly since 2005 than during the initial slowdown (figure 9.1).

The productivity slowdown has not been universal. Some firms are performing very well—in fact, increasingly well compared with other firms. Rates of return on equity across the S&P 500 have become increasingly skewed, with more firms earning very high returns (figure 9.2).

Measures of the return on capital have also become much more skewed. This trend is particularly evident when goodwill is excluded from the definition of capital, but it holds even when goodwill is included (figure 9.3).[1] The growth in the magnitude of rents in the economy lies somewhere between these two measures, as at least some of what is considered rent gets counted as goodwill, making the return to that type of capital seem more normal than it really is.

---

1. Goodwill refers to the excess of purchase price over the book value of a company. For the purposes of computing return on invested capital, it may or may not be considered part of the definition of a company's capital.

Figure 9.1 Productivity growth in the United States, 1948–2016

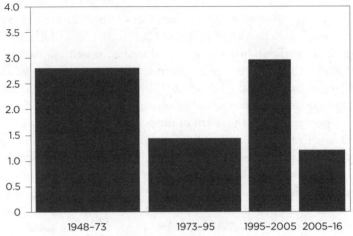

percent change, annual rate

Note: Productivity growth is for the nonfarm business sector.
Source: Bureau of Labor Statistics; authors' calculations.

Figure 9.2 Distribution of annual returns on equity across S&P 500, 1996 and 2004

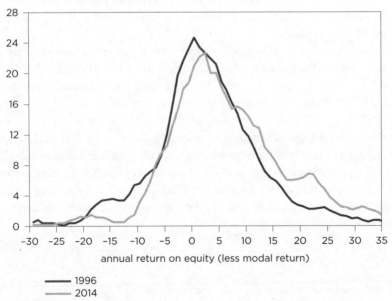

number of firms with given return on equity

annual return on equity (less modal return)

— 1996
···· 2014

Source: Furman and Orszag (2018).

Figure 9.3   Annual return on invested capital at publicly traded nonfinancial firms in the United States, 1965–2014

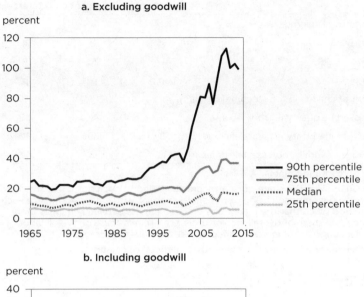

a. Excluding goodwill

percent

90th percentile
75th percentile
Median
25th percentile

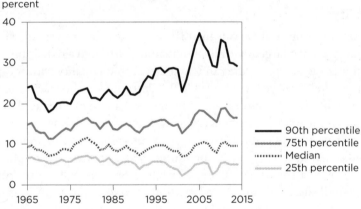

b. Including goodwill

percent

90th percentile
75th percentile
Median
25th percentile

Source: Furman and Orszag (2018).

Research by the Organization for Economic Cooperation and Development (OECD) finds that frontier firms have continued to make rapid progress in productivity while laggard firms have not—an indication that productivity growth at the frontier remains strong but is not being diffused throughout the economy (Andrews, Criscuolo, and Gal 2015). The OECD study is limited by the fact that it goes back only to 2001; it cannot therefore answer the question of how typical or atypical this disconnect is. Nevertheless, its findings are part of a consistent story.

Table 9.1 Decomposition of increases in shares of total income in the United States, 1979–2013 (percent, unless otherwise noted)

Item	Top 10 percent	Top 1 percent	Top 0.1 percent
Share of total income			
1979	35	11	4
2013	47	20	9
Change	12 p.p.	9 p.p.	6 p.p.
Percent of change in total income due to:			
Increased inequality in labor income	76	47	38
Increased inequality in capital income	8	39	50
Change in overall labor/capital shares	16	14	12

p.p. = percentage points

Note: Changes in the share of total income accruing to each portion of the distribution are decomposed using a shift-share analysis, with equal weights for each time period (such that there are no interaction effects between changes in the labor/capital share of overall income and each group's share of overall labor/capital income). Income shares are centered three-year averages.

Source: Piketty, Saez, and Zucman (2017); authors' calculations.

Inequality

The most important fact about inequality is that it has increased. The increase has occurred largely within labor income, although a reduction in the share of income going to labor and an increase in inequality within capital income have also played a role. Table 9.1 decomposes the fraction of the increase in different forms of inequality that are caused by increased dispersion of labor earnings (e.g., managers being paid more than line workers); increasing dispersion of capital income (e.g., some people getting more of the dividends than others); and a reduction in the labor share (corresponding to an increase in the capital share, which is more unequally distributed). Further up the income scale, the relative importance of increased inequality within capital income grows and increased inequality within labor income falls, but the change in the labor share remains a relatively less important factor.

Within labor income, the rise in inequality largely reflects changes between the average worker at different firms or establishments rather than between workers within firms, according to research by Barth et al. (2016) and Song et al. (2015). CEO pay did not rise relative to median worker pay in the past 20 years (figure 9.4). Instead, workers at highly profitable companies (like Google and Goldman Sachs) are being paid more relative to workers at less successful companies. Decomposition of the increase in earnings inequality reveals that most of the growth in inequality is across not within firms.

Figure 9.4 Ratio of CEO to worker compensation in the United States, 1965–2016

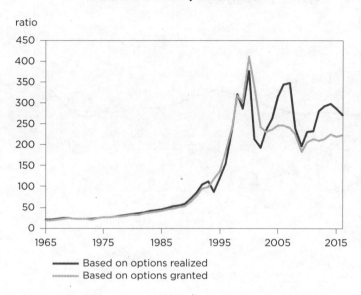

ratio

Based on options realized
Based on options granted

Source: Mishel and Schieder (2017).

In part, the variations across firms seem to be the result of sorting—for example, businesses contracting out janitorial services to a new, lower-paid janitorial services firm. But a longstanding body of labor economics research on interindustry wage differentials also finds that companies that are more successful tend to share some of that success with their workers—that is, that janitors are paid more by successful firms than by unsuccessful ones (Krueger and Summers 1988, Abowd et al. 2012). Although this version of rent-sharing has weakened somewhat over time, it continues to play a role (Krueger 2013).

Another possibility is that firm boundaries are evolving in ways that affect the decomposition of between- and within-firm components. Bloom et al. (2018) find that large-firm wage premiums (the difference between the amount paid to a worker at a large firm and the amount paid to a similar worker at a small firm) are declining and speculate that a key reason may be outsourcing. It seems unlikely, however, that this phenomenon is large enough to explain why the bulk of the rise in wage inequality is between firms.

In sum, the persistence of large dispersions in rates of return and also interindustry wage differentials would be puzzling in a world with perfect competition and free mobility of labor. The next section documents the ways in which the real world is falling increasingly short of these ideals.

Figure 9.5   Return to capital versus safe rate of return in the United States, 1985–2015

percent

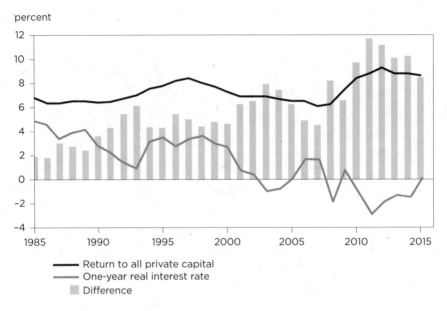

—— Return to all private capital
········ One-year real interest rate
▨ Difference

Note: The rate of return to all private capital was calculated by dividing private capital income in current dollars by the private capital stock in current dollars. Private capital income is defined as the sum of (1) corporate profits excluding federal government tax receipts on corporate income, (2) net interest and miscellaneous payments, (3) rental income of all persons, (4) business current transfer payments, (5) current surpluses of government enterprises, (6) property and severance taxes, and (7) the capital share of proprietors' income, where the capital share was assumed to match the capital share of aggregate income. Private capital stock is defined as the sum of (1) the net stock of produced private assets for all private enterprises, (2) the value of total private land inferred from the Financial Accounts of the United States, and (3) the value of US capital deployed abroad less foreign capital deployed in the United States. The return to nonfinancial corporate capital is that reported by the Bureau of Economic Analysis.

Sources: Bureau of Economic Analysis; Federal Reserve Board of Governors; authors' calculations.

Increases in Concentration and Reductions in Dynamism

Evidence is mounting that competitive market pressures are declining. One indication is the fact that, although the rate of return on safe assets has fallen, the rate of return on overall capital has held steady or even risen somewhat (figure 9.5). As a result, the premium on capital over safe assets has risen from about 200 basis points to more than 800 basis points. Theoretically, this increase could reflect the fact that capital is riskier than before, "safe" assets are safer than before, or rents have risen. At a macroeconomic level, the third hypothesis is most consistent with the fact that although prices (the premium on capital) have risen, quantities (the rate of investment) have fallen. (The exact relationship between competition and invest-

Table 9.2 Changes in market concentration in the United States between 1997 and 2012, by industry

Industry	Revenue earned by 50 largest firms, 2012 (billions of dollars)	Revenue share earned by 50 largest firms, 2012 (percent)	Percentage point change in revenue share earned by 50 largest firms, 1997–2012
Transportation and warehousing	307.9	42.1	11.4
Retail trade	1,555.8	36.9	11.2
Finance and insurance	1,762.7	48.5	9.9
Wholesale trade	2,183.1	27.6	7.3
Real estate rental and leasing	121.6	24.9	5.4
Utilities	367.7	69.1	4.6
Educational services	12.1	22.7	4.2[a]
Professional, scientific, and technical services	278.2	18.8	2.8[a]
Arts, entertainment, and recreation	39.5	19.6	2.5[a]
Administrative/support	159.2	23.7	1.6
Health care and assistance	350.2	17.2	0.8[a]
Accommodation and food services	149.8	21.2	0.1
Other services, nonpublic administration	46.7	10.9	–0.2[a]

a. The percentage point change is calculated using only taxable firms in that industry, as its 1997 revenue share data are available only for the 50 largest taxable firms and the 50 largest tax-exempt firms as separate categories, rather than for all firms combined.

Source: Council of Economic Advisers (2016).

ment depends on the specifics, but in a standard neoclassical model, firms facing less competition will raise their markups, reduce output, and reduce factor inputs of both labor and capital.)

The microeconomic evidence is consistent with this view. At a high level of aggregation, most industries have seen a few large players account for an increasing share of the market (table 9.2) (Council of Economic Advisers 2016; Grullon, Larkin, and Michaely 2017). This pattern is also found in more disaggregated data. Autor et al. (2017) show a consistent increase in concentration in both sales and employment and a negative relationship between concentration and the labor share at the industry level. Gutiérrez and Philippon (2017a, 2017b) show that governance, including common ownership, and reduced competition can account for the majority of underinvestment since the early 2000s and that most of the decline in investment comes from the leading firms in an industry. The microdata match the macroeconomic observation: Reductions in investment growth, including

Figure 9.6 Firm dynamism in the United States, 1978–2015

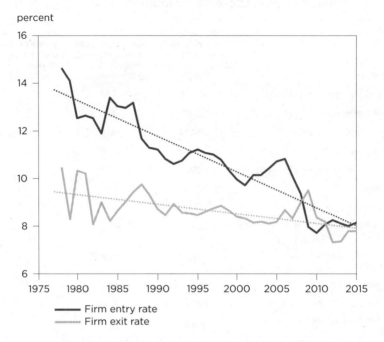

percent

Source: US Census Bureau, *Business Dynamics Statistics*; authors' calculations.

in research and development (R&D), are larger in industries that have seen larger increases in concentration.

Case studies in a wide range of industries confirm these results. Corbae and D'Erasmo (2013) find increased concentration in the loan shares of major financial institutions. Shields (2010) finds an increased share of revenue in the top firms in eight of nine agricultural industries. Gaynor, Ho, and Town (2015) find a 50 percent increase in the average Herfindahl-Hirschman index in the hospital sector. Researchers also find increases in concentration in railroads (Prater et al. 2012) and wireless services (FCC 2015).

These findings may understate the degree of consolidation, because they measure only the market shares of individual firms. Looking at the market shares of owners of firms reveals even more consolidation, as documented in a series of papers by Martin Schmalz and others (Azar, Raina, and Schmalz 2016; Anton et al. 2017; Azar, Schmalz, and Tecu 2018). In particular, common ownership has grown, as a small number of large asset managers increasingly own large stakes in all of the major players in an industry, potentially leading them to favor uncompetitive behavior.

At the same time, almost throughout the economy there is less dynamism, fluidity, and churn. A one-third reduction in the rate of new business

Figure 9.7 Young firms as a share of total firms and total employment in the United States, 1982–2015

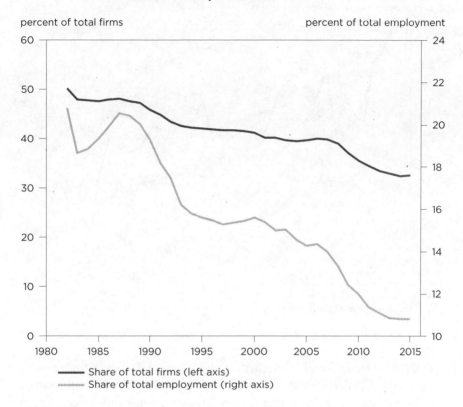

percent of total firms   percent of total employment

——— Share of total firms (left axis)
·········· Share of total employment (right axis)

Source: US Census Bureau, *Business Dynamics Statistics*; authors' calculations.

formation, together with a steady exit rate, means that, on average, firms are larger and older today and account for a larger share of employment than they used to (figures 9.6 and 9.7). Since the early 1980s, the share of firms that are less than five years old has fallen by about a third, and the share of employment accounted for by these firms has fallen by nearly half.

Reduced fluidity has also been observed in almost every labor market series. From the perspective of employers, the rates of job creation and job destruction have fallen steadily (figure 9.8). Hyatt and Spletzer (2013), Davis and Haltiwanger (2014), and Decker et al. (2014, 2018) find that the shift toward older firms is at least one factor related to the decline in labor market fluidity, though the changing age structure of firms appears to account for a small share of the drop.

From the perspective of employees, the rates of shifting between different places, industries, and occupations and even employment-to-employment transitions have all fallen steadily. Across a range of measures, Molloy

Figure 9.8   Labor market dynamism in the United States, 1977–2015

percent of jobs created or destroyed

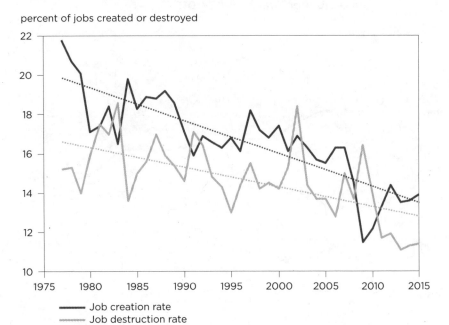

Job creation rate
Job destruction rate

Source: US Census Bureau, *Business Dynamics Statistics*; authors' calculations.

et al. (2016) find that labor market fluidity has been declining since at least the 1980s. The decline has averaged about 10 to 15 percent, with nearly a 25 percent drop in employment-to-employment transitions. Over a longer period, declines in geographic mobility have been even more dramatic. By 2013 the interstate migration rate was half what it was in 1948–71, and intrastate migrations rates had fallen by about a third (Molloy, Smith, and Wozniak 2014).

Why Has Concentration Risen While Dynamism Has Fallen?

Two stories explain rising concentration and falling dynamism. The first—that both phenomena reflect improvements in efficiency—is benign. According to it, large firms may be the ones that drive improvements in efficiency. Telecommunications companies, for example, have increasing returns to scale that make it inefficient and difficult for many wireless providers to coexist. Network externalities represent a genuine benefit: A single social network on which users can find all their friends is more useful than fragmented networks that include only some of them. Increased price sensitivity on the part of consumers can lead to greater concentration in more efficient firms. Global competition may drive the consolidation of national capacity to reach the larger scale necessary to compete in the international market (this factor is particularly relevant only for the 13 percent of the US economy that is exposed to trade). Reductions in fluidity may also have a benign explanation if matching technologies have improved so that workers are able to more efficiently sort themselves into jobs.

All of these explanations have some merit, and in certain cases or sectors that merit may be substantial. To the degree that concentration has risen for these reasons, there may be a role for policy to address certain undesirable side effects—natural monopolies, for example, may need various forms of regulated prices—in ways that are distinct from just increasing competition or reducing policy-erected barriers to entry.

All of these explanations are consistent with increasing productivity growth, which is indeed evident in some sectors, such as retail (Crouzet and Eberly 2018), or earlier time periods (Gutiérrez and Philippon 2017a). It does not match recent economy-wide data, however, motivating the search for other explanations.

A less benign explanation is a reduction in antitrust enforcement. The United States experienced a shift in prevailing attitudes toward antitrust beginning in the early 1980s, with the growth of Chicago School views that competition is more extensive than previously thought, that consolidation is less harmful than previously thought, and that remedies to promote more competition can bring more costs than benefits (Easterbrook 1984, Bork 1993, Posner 2009).

This intellectual development has affected both enforcement agencies and the courts. The result has been a near end to actions preventing vertical mergers and a curtailment of actions preventing horizontal mergers. The Federal Trade Commission (FTC) has effectively stopped enforcement actions on mergers that reduce the number of competitors to five, six, or seven and reduced enforcement actions on other mergers (Kwoka 2017). Recently, parts of the antitrust community have started to revisit whether the pendulum has shifted too far toward the Chicago view.[2]

More evidence that the increase in concentration is not the natural result of efficiency but instead reflects deliberate policy choices comes from the fact that although concentration has risen in the United States, it has fallen in the eurozone and some European Union members, including the United Kingdom. Döttling, Gutiérrez, and Philippon (2017) suggest that divergent paths in antitrust efforts, which have weakened in the United States

---

2. Pitofsky (2008) and "The University of Chicago Worries about a Lack of Competition, *Economist*, April 12, 2017, www.economist.com/business/2017/04/12/the-university-of-chicago-worries-about-a-lack-of-competition.

and become stronger in Europe, may be one factor contributing to the observed trends in competition.

Other policy developments affecting this dynamic have been the increased importance of intellectual property protections, which create a legal form of monopoly, and policies that hamper geographic mobility, such as the expansion of occupational licensing and land use restrictions. The extent of occupational licensing has grown substantially, rising from 5 percent of the workforce in the 1950s to 25 percent of the workforce by 2008. The growth of previously licensed occupations, such as education and medicine, does not explain most of the rise (Department of the Treasury Office of Economic Policy et al. 2015). The expanded prevalence of licensing, combined with state-specific licensing requirements, creates a burden for licensed workers seeking to move across state lines. By increasing the cost of housing, the growth of land use restrictions has curtailed mobility to higher-wage areas (Furman 2015). Decker et al. (2018) highlight the role of adjustment frictions, as opposed to idiosyncratic firm-level productivity shocks, in driving both wider firm-level variance and a decline in productivity growth since 2000.

Summary and Policy Implications

There is mounting evidence that the reduction in competition and dynamism has contributed to both the slowdown in productivity growth and the increase in inequality. This reduction is partly a natural reflection of trends such as the increased importance of network externalities and partly a manmade reflection of policy choices, such as increased regulatory barriers to entry. These increased rigidities have contributed to the rise in concentration and increased dispersion of firm-level profitability. The result is less innovation, either through a straightforward channel of less investment or through broader factors, such as firms not wanting to cannibalize their own market shares (Arrow 1962).

These channels have also contributed to rising inequality, in a number of ways. One is through a "rent-sharing" channel, as increasingly disparate firm-level success translates into increasingly disparate wages for workers at these firms. A second mechanism is through increased leverage by employers, which reduces wages and raises profits, in part because workers with fewer choices and less mobility may have less ability to bargain for wage increases.

Three policy conclusions emerge from this analysis:

- To the degree that concentration or reduced fluidity is the result of improvements in efficiency, there is no market failure and no need for product market policies. Should efficiency improvements result in higher-than-desired levels of inequality, the appropriate remedy is through the tax and transfer system, not through interference with the functioning of markets themselves.

- To the degree that concentration or reduced fluidity is the result of policy, the offending policies should be changed. Doing so could entail more vigorously enforcing antitrust policies, limiting the ever-expanding scope of intellectual property protections, and reducing regulations (such as occupational licensing and land use restrictions) that create barriers to entry and mobility for both workers and firms. Addressing these policy-induced market failures holds out the prospect of both increasing productivity growth and reducing inequality, bringing a wider range of instruments to bear on these questions than has often been the case.

- To the degree that both efficiency and policy contribute to increased concentration, the policy implications are less clear. In the technology sector, for example, there are tremendous efficiencies from the innovation associated with leading companies and their scale—but network effects also create tremendous barriers to entry in areas such as online advertising, search, and operating systems for mobile phones and computers. Traditional antitrust remedies would jeopardize these efficiencies, but doing nothing risks slowing innovation accompanied by increased inequality. At a minimum, encouraging greater competition through more individual ownership of data and encouragement of common standards could help achieve the right balance.

References

Abowd, John M., Francis Kramarz, Paul Lengermann, Kevin L. McKinney, and Sébastien Roux. 2012. Persistent Inter-industry Wage Differences: Rent Sharing and Opportunity Costs. *IZA Journal of Labor Economics* 1, no. 7: 1–25.

Andrews, Dan, Chiara Criscuolo, and Peter N. Gal. 2015. *Frontier Firms, Technology Diffusion and Public Policy: Micro Evidence from OECD Countries*. Future of Productivity Background Paper. Paris: Organization for Economic Cooperation and Development.

Anton, Miguel, Florian Ederer, Mireia Gine, and Martin C. Schmalz. 2017. *Common Ownership, Competition, and Top Management Incentives*. Ross School of Business Paper 1328. Ann Arbor, MI: University of Michigan

Arrow, Kenneth. 1962. Economic Welfare and the Allocation of Resources for Inventions. In *The Rate and Direction of Inventive Activity*, ed. R. Nelson. Princeton, NJ: Princeton University Press.

Autor, David, David Dorn, Lawrence F. Katz, Christina Patterson, and John Van Reenan. 2017. *The Fall of the Labor Share and the Rise of Superstar Firms*. NBER Working Paper 23396. Cambridge, MA: National Bureau of Economic Research.

Azar, José, Sahil Raina, and Martin C. Schmalz. 2016. *Ultimate Ownership and Bank Competition*. Working Paper. Available at https://ssrn.com/abstract=2710252 (accessed on July 5, 2018).

Azar, José, Martin C. Schmalz, and Isabel Tecu. 2018. Anti-Competitive Effects of Common Ownership. *Journal of Finance* 7, no. 3.

Barkai, Simcha. 2016. *Declining Labor and Capital Shares*. Working Paper. Chicago: Department of Economics and Booth School of Business, University of Chicago.

Barth, Erling, Alex Bryson, James C. Davis, and Richard Freeman. 2016. It's Where You Work: Increases in Earnings Dispersion across Establishments and Individuals in the United States. *Journal of Labor Economics* 34, no. S2: S67–S97.

Bell, Alexander M., Raj Chetty, Xavier Jaravel, Neviana Petkova, and John Van Reenan. 2017. *Who Becomes an Inventor in America? The Importance of Exposure to Innovation*. NBER Working Paper 24062. Cambridge, MA: National Bureau of Economic Research.

Bloom, Nicholas, Fatih Guvenen, Benjamin S. Smith, Jae Song, and Till von Wachter. 2018. Inequality and the Disappearing Large Firm Wage Premium. Paper presented at the 2018 American Economic Association Annual Meeting, Philadelphia, January 5–7.

Bork, Robert H. 1993. *The Antitrust Paradox*, 2nd edition. New York: Free Press.

Cingano, Federico. 2014. *Trends in Income Inequality and Its Impact on Economic Growth*. OECD Social, Employment and Migration Working Paper 163. Paris: OECD Publishing.

Corbae, Dean, and Pablo D'Erasmo. 2013. *A Quantitative Model of Banking Industry Dynamics*. Working Paper. Available at https://docs.google.com/viewer?a=v&pid=sites&srcid=ZG VmYXVsdGRvbWFpbnxwYWJsb2RlcmFzbW98Z3g6NzZiZjgyYmNiNTAzYmRlZA (accessed on July 5, 2018).

Council of Economic Advisers. 2016. *Benefits of Competition and Indicators of Market Power*. Issue Brief (May). Washington.

Crouzet, Nicolas, and Janice Eberly. 2018. Intangibles, Investment, and Efficiency. *American Economic Association Papers and Proceedings* 108: 426–31.

Davis, Steven, and John Haltiwanger. 2014. *Labor Market Fluidity and Economic Performance*. NBER Working Paper 20479. Cambridge, MA: National Bureau of Economic Research.

Decker, Ryan, John Haltiwanger, Ron Jarmin, and Javier Miranda. 2014. The Role of Entrepreneurship in U.S. Job Creation and Economic Dynamism. *Journal of Economic Perspectives* 28, no. 3: 3–24.

Decker, Ryan, John Haltiwanger, Ron Jarmin, and Javier Miranda. 2018. *Changing Business Dynamism and Productivity: Shocks vs. Responsiveness*. NBER Working Paper 24236. Cambridge, MA: National Bureau of Economic Research.

Department of the Treasury Office of Economic Policy, Council of Economic Advisers, and Department of Labor. 2015. *Occupational Licensing: A Framework for Policy Makers* (July). Washington: White House.

Döttling, Robin, Germán Gutiérrez, and Thomas Philippon. 2017. *Is There an Investment Gap in Advanced Economies? If So, Why?* Working Paper. Sintra, Portugal: ECB Forum on Central Banking.

Easterbrook, Frank H. 1984. The Limits of Antitrust. *Texas Law Review* 63, no. 1: 1–40.

FCC (Federal Communications Commission). 2015. *Eighteenth Mobile Wireless Competition Report*. Washington. Available at https://apps.fcc.gov/edocs_public/attachmatch/DA-15-1487A1.pdf.

Furman, Jason. 2015. Barriers to Shared Growth: The Case of Land Use Regulation and Economic Rents. Remarks at the Urban Institute, Washington, November 20.

Furman, Jason. 2019 (forthcoming). Should Policy Makers Care Whether Inequality is Helpful or Harmful for Growth? In *Evolution or Revolution? Rethinking Macroeconomics after the Great Recession*, ed. Olivier Blanchard and Lawrence H. Summers. Cambridge, MA: MIT Press.

Furman, Jason, and Peter Orszag. 2018. A Firm-Level Perspective on the Role of Rents in the Rise in Inequality. In *Toward a Just Society: Joseph Stiglitz and Twenty-First Century Economics*, ed. M. Guzman. New York: Columbia University Press.

Gaynor, Martin, Kate Ho, and Robert J. Town. 2015. The Industrial Organization of Health-Care Markets. *Journal of Economic Literature* 53, no. 2: 235–84.

Goldin, Claudia, and Lawrence F. Katz. 2008. *The Race Between Education and Technology*. Cambridge, MA: Belknap Press of Harvard University Press.

Grullon, Gustavo, Yelena Larkin, and Roni Michaely. 2017. *Are U.S. Industries Becoming More Concentrated?* Working Paper (August 31). Available at SSRN: https://ssrn.com/abstract= 2612047 (accessed on July 5, 2018).

Gutiérrez, Germán, and Thomas Philippon. 2017a. *Declining Competition and Investment in the U.S.* NBER Working Paper 23583. Cambridge, MA: National Bureau of Economic Research.

Gutiérrez, Germán, and Thomas Philippon. 2017b. Investment-less Growth: An Empirical Investigation. *Brookings Papers on Economic Activity* (Fall): 89–169. Available at www.brookings.edu/bpea-articles/investment-less-growth-an-empirical-investigation/.

Hyatt, Henry R., and James R. Spletzer. 2013. The Recent Decline in Employment Dynamics. *IZA Journal of Labor Economics* 2, no. 1: 1–21.

Krueger, Alan B. 2013. Land of Hope and Dreams: Rock and Roll, Economics, and Rebuilding the Middle Class. Remarks at the Rock and Roll Hall of Fame, Cleveland, OH, June 12.

Krueger, Alan B., and Lawrence H. Summers. 1988. Efficiency Wages and the Inter-Industry Wage Structure. *Econometrica* 56, no. 2: 259–93.

Kwoka, John E. 2017. *U.S. Antitrust and Competition Policy Amid the New Merger Wave*. Issue Brief. Washington: Center for Equitable Growth.

Mishel, Lawrence, and Jessica Schieder. 2017. *CEO Pay Remains High Relative to the Pay of Typical Workers and High-Wage Earners*. Washington: Economic Policy Institute.

Molloy, Raven, Christopher Smith, Riccardo Trezzi, and Abigail Wozniak. 2016. Understanding Declining Fluidity in the U.S. Labor Market. *Brookings Papers on Economic Activity* (Spring): 183–259. Washington: Brookings Institution.

Molloy, Raven, Christopher Smith, and Abigail Wozniak. 2014. *Declining Migration within the U.S.: The Role of the Labor Market*. NBER Working Paper 20065. Cambridge, MA: National Bureau of Economic Research.

Ostry, Jonathan D, Andrew Berg, and Charalambos G. Tsangarides. 2014. *Redistribution, Inequality, and Growth*. Staff Discussion Note 14/02. Washington: International Monetary Fund.

Piketty, Thomas, Emmanuel Saez, and Gabriel Zucman. 2017. Data Appendix to Distributional National Accounts: Methods and Estimates for the United States (November). Available at gabriel-zucman.eu/files/PSZ2017AppendixTablesII(Distrib).xlsx.

Pitofsky, Robert, ed. 2008. *How the Chicago School Overshot the Mark: The Effect of Conservative Economic Analysis on U.S. Antitrust.* Oxford: Oxford University Press.

Posner, Richard A. 2009. *Antitrust Law.* Chicago: University of Chicago Press.

Prater, Marvin E., Ken Casavant, Eric Jessup, Bruce Blanton, Pierre Bahizi, Daniel Nibarger, and Isaac Weingram. 2012. Rail Competition Changes since the Staggers Act. *Journal of the Transportation Research Forum* 49, no. 3: 111–32.

Shields, Dennis A. 2010. *Consolidation and Concentration in the U.S. Dairy Industry* (April 27). Washington: Congressional Research Service. Available at http://nationalaglawcenter.org/wpcontent/uploads/assets/crs/R41224.pdf.

Song, Jae, David J. Price, Fatih Guvenen, Nicholas Bloom, and Till von Wachter. 2016. *Firming Up Inequality.* NBER Working Paper 21199. Cambridge, MA: National Bureau of Economic Research.

10

Political Economy of Secular Stagnation: Why Capital in the United States Swipes Right

DANIEL W. DREZNER

A key element of America's political creed is that liberal democracies rarely get stuck in a rut. "Liberal democracy is also strong because, to a greater extent than any other political form, it harbors the power of self-correction," notes Galston (2018, 18). According to this narrative, democratic institutions incentivize against persistently bad policy equilibria. Businesses cease supporting political parties that fail to deliver economic growth over sustained periods of time. Voters oust leaders presiding over a weak economy, particularly if large corporations and small businesses defect from the party in power. Overall, inclusive institutions will outperform extractive institutions in generating economic growth (North and Weingast 1989; Mansfield, Milner, and Rosendorff 2000; Acemoglu and Robinson 2012).

As concerns about secular stagnation persist, it is worth considering whether this creed remains valid. The prolonged period of low productivity growth threatens to generate path-dependent effects on the US political economy.

Secular stagnation has exacerbated two trends in the United States: rising levels of economic inequality and rising levels of political polarization. The latter phenomenon introduces a potent challenge to the former. Survey evidence suggests that people at the top end of the income spectrum have libertarian policy preferences (Page, Bartels, and Seawright 2013). They

Daniel Drezner is professor of international politics at the Fletcher School of Law and Diplomacy, Tufts University. He is grateful to Caroline Atkinson, Kim Elliott, Neil Mehrotra, Adam Posen, Jeromin Zettelmeyer, and especially Anna Greenberg for their feedback.

also exercise more influence over political outcomes than ordinary citizens. At the same time, populism has come to dominate both sides of the political spectrum, shifting mass public attitudes away from high-net-worth individuals. These changes should make the economic elite a ripe target for populist anger. In a world of secular stagnation, how do plutocrats continue to exercise influence without triggering political blowback?

This chapter argues that in a polarized political climate, secular stagnation will encourage America's economic elite to tilt further rightward in the coming decade, even though the Republican Party will continue to drift in a populist direction, supporting new barriers to international trade and migration. In the past, economic elites might have been comfortable with a market-friendly approach from left-leaning parties. In the future, that comfort will fade, because both the political space for a moderate left approach to governing and the economic growth generated by such an approach appear to be shrinking. Between accommodating economic populism from the left and nationalist populism from the right, plutocrats will opt for the latter. Populist nationalism will not generate greater economic growth, but it does lead to redistribution that favors owners of capital. Preliminary evidence for this redistribution can already be seen from the reactions of plutocrats to the Trump administration's first year in office.

Two caveats are in order. First, the empirical scope of this chapter is constrained to "liberal market economies" such as the United States and United Kingdom (Soskice and Hall 2001). Its finding applies with far less force to the coordinated market economies of continental Europe or Japan. Second, the political economy equilibrium described here may not be stable in the long run. There is every reason to believe, however, that it is sustainable over the time horizon discussed in this volume.

The chapter is organized as follows. The first section describes the trends in political polarization and economic inequality that predate secular stagnation. The second section looks at the policy preferences of corporations and high-net-worth individuals and examines why those preferences are increasingly out of sync with the American body politic. The third and fourth sections explain why capital will not ally with left-wing economic populists but can live with right-wing populist nationalism as a second-best outcome. Both sections examine the behavior of high-net-worth individuals in the first year of the Trump administration. The last section discusses the longer-term effects of capital persistently swiping right.

Key Political Trends beyond Secular Stagnation

Understanding the effects of secular stagnation on the US political economy requires an understanding of the growth of economic inequality and the rise of political polarization (Drezner 2017b). Whether one looks at wages, income, or wealth, the data in the United States are clear-cut: Over the past 30–40 years, the wealthiest Americans have done much better for themselves than everyone else. Indeed, economic inequality in the United States is the highest it has been since before World War II.

Piketty (2014) documents the rise in income inequality over the past few decades. In 1975 the top 10 percent of Americans earned less than 30 percent of national income; by 2010 that figure had climbed to more than 45 percent. The top 1 percent did particularly well during this period, more than doubling its share of national income over the past 40 years, from less than 10 percent to more than 20 percent. The 1 percent captured 52 percent of the gains in national income between 1993 and 2008; between 2009 and 2012, that share climbed to 95 percent.[1] And just as the top 1 percent did better than the top 10 percent, the top 1/10th of 1 percent did even better than that. Over the same time period, the richest of the rich more than quintupled their share of national income, from approximately 2 percent to 11 percent.[2] Similarly, between 1974 and 2014, the top 1/100th of 1 percent increased its share of national income sixfold, to approximately 5 percent.

Wealth inequality increased even more. According to Saez and Zucman (2016), the top 1/100th of 1 percent increased their share of national wealth from approximately 2 percent in the mid-1970s to more than 10 percent in 2012. The current distribution of wealth in the United States has returned to the Gilded Age levels of 1910 (Shorrocks, Davies, and Lluberas 2014). Whether the cause has been globalization, the rise of finance, the economics of superstars, or the ineluctable laws of capitalism, both wealth and income inequality are on the rise—and there are excellent reasons to project that the concentration of wealth at the top could increase (Piketty 2014, 2015).

As the inequality of wealth has increased in the United States, so has the inequality of contributions to political life. Survey data show that the wealthy are far better informed about politics and more politically active than the rest of the public. Political scientists Cook, Page, and Moskowitz (2014, 396) conclude that it is "the wealthy who are the real Über-citizens of the American polity. Their participation levels far exceed any others that scholars have found." A parallel study by Page, Bartels, and Seawright (2013) that polled very affluent Americans finds that 84 percent paid attention to politics most of the time, 99 percent had voted in the previous presidential election, and 40 percent had been in personal contact with a US senator.

---

1. Brenda Cronin, "Some 95% of 2009–2012 Income Gains Went to Wealthiest 1%," *Wall Street Journal*, September 10, 2013.

2. Derek Thompson, "How You, I, and Everyone Got the Top 1 Percent All Wrong," *The Atlantic*, March 30, 2014.

The gap in political participation is reflected in the ultra-rich being responsible for an ever-greater share of contributions to political campaigns. The share of campaign contributions from the top 1/100th of 1 percent of Americans increased from less than 10 percent in 1982 to more than 40 percent in 2012 (Bonica et al. 2013). Particularly since the *Citizens United* decision in 2010, multinational corporations and high-net-worth individuals have been responsible for a growing share of campaign contributions (Page, Seawright, and LaCombe 2015). According to the *New York Times*, fewer than 160 families were responsible for almost half the campaign contributions made during the first phase of the 2016 election cycle, "a concentration of political donors that is unprecedented in the modern era."[3] According to the *Washington Post*, just 50 families were responsible for more than 40 percent of all super PAC funding in the primary phase of the presidential campaign.[4]

Through the channel of campaign finance, high-net-worth individuals and multinational corporations can exert outsized influence on policy outputs. They must cope, however, with a countervailing trend: the rise of political polarization. A plethora of political science research demonstrates that polarization in the United States is greater than ever before. The best evidence for polarization comes from measures of congressional voting. From the mid-1970s onward, partisan splits can explain an increasing fraction of roll call votes in Congress. Political science measures of ideology show that over the past four decades, the average Democrat moved leftward and the average Republican moved rightward. Congress is more polarized now than at any time in the past 125 years.

Some commentators like to claim a "both sides" perspective on this trend.[5] And it is true that both parties migrated away from the center in recent decades. The data, however, are incontrovertible on the asymmetry of party polarization. Republicans in Congress have moved much farther to the right than Democrats have to the left. Barber and McCarty (2013, 21) conclude that "the most discernible trend has been the marked movement of the Republican Party to the right." Keith Poole, one of the fathers of the

---

3. Nicholas Confessore, "The Families Funding the 2016 Election," *New York Times*, October 10, 2015.

4. Matea Gold and Anu Narayanswamy, "The New Gilded Age: Close to Half of All Super-PAC Money Comes from 50 Donors," *Washington Post*, April 15, 2016.

5. See, for example, Peter Wehner, "Have Democrats Pulled Too Far Left?" *New York Times*, May 27, 2015.

polarization literature, concludes that Republicans are now farther to the right than they have been in 100 years.[6]

The evidence for rising levels of partisanship goes well beyond Congress. Other measures of partisan conflict show a similar increase in political polarization (Azzimonti 2014). According to a 2014 Pew survey, the number of citizens who demonstrate consistently liberal or conservative viewpoints has doubled in the past generation (Dimock et al. 2014). For both Democrats and Republicans, party elites have become more ideologically extreme than the broader party membership (Hetherington 2001, Bafumi and Herron 2010). Political elites are now more ideologically extreme than at any time in postwar history. As one Pew survey (Dimock et al. 2014, 6) concludes, "divisions are greatest among those who are the most engaged and active in the political process."

The ideological composition of both political parties has also become much more homogeneous in recent decades. Democratic voters are more likely to identify with the Democratic Party's positions on different policies, and Republican voters feel similarly about the GOP platform. Political scientists label this phenomenon *partisan sorting*.

Some political scientists argue that greater partisan sorting does not mean that the public is increasingly polarized. But even the data produced by skeptics show that political polarization among the mass public has increased since the turn of this century (Garner and Palmer 2011, Hill and Tausanovitch 2015). Furthermore, partisan sorting generates psychological effects that impinge on politics (Mason 2015). Having one's identity defined by ideology makes it much easier to stigmatize people who hold contrary views. One recent public opinion analysis (Iyengar, Sood, and Lelkes 2012, 428) concludes that "the sense of partisan identity is increasingly associated with a Manichean, 'us against them' view of the political world."

Identification with one partisan group makes it easier for individuals to demonize members of the other partisan group. An abundance of evidence shows that partisans on one side increasingly dislike and distrust partisans on the other side. Party activists now report that they dislike the other party's activists more than they did a generation ago (Shaw 2012). Between 1994 and 2014, the share of Republicans and Democrats that believed that the other party is "a threat to the nation's well-being" more than doubled (Dimock et al. 2014). Americans are also more likely to believe that the other party's members are less intelligent than they were 30 years ago. One recent experimental study concluded that Americans discriminated more based on political partisanship than on either race or gender (Iyengar

6. Quoted in Frank James, "Political Scientist: Republicans Most Conservative They've Been in 100 Years," NPR, April 13, 2012.

and Westwood 2015). As David Brooks put it, "Becoming a Republican or becoming a Democrat has become an ethnic category."[7] This effect reduces the likelihood of centrist, bipartisan cooperation on policy.

Choice of the Second-Best for Plutocrats

West (2014, 9) notes that "the super rich, as a group, hold policy views that are significantly different from those of ordinary citizens." The plutocratic class tilts in a libertarian direction. This tendency emerges in both surveys of wealthy Americans and impressionistic accounts of their worldviews. The economic elite possess divergent policy preferences on social or environmental issues; they are much more homogeneous on matters of economic policy.

Ferenstein surveyed more than 100 Silicon Valley founders.[8] He observed a distinct gap between their political attitudes and those of the mass public. According to Page, Bartels, and Seawright (2013), wealthy Americans strongly prefer cutting government spending on social insurance programs like Social Security or Medicaid as well as spending on national defense. Only 35 percent of wealthy Americans support spending what is necessary to ensure good public schools, a sharp contrast to the 87 percent of the general public that holds that view.

The caricature of the 1 percent as Randian is flatly false. Wealthy Americans more strongly favor public spending on infrastructure and scientific research than other Americans, for example. On all social insurance programs, however, plutocrats are far more libertarian than the mass public. All surveys of high-net-worth Americans show that they are far less supportive of unemployment insurance, worker retraining, labor unions, economic regulation, or government redistribution of income than the general public (Freeland 2012; Page, Bartels, and Seawright 2013; Cook, Page, and Moskowitz 2014; Drezner 2017b).

The lived experiences of high-net-worth individuals and corporate CEOs alters their perspective on public policy. Today's plutocrats attend glamorous intellectual gatherings and sponsor other high-profile confabs. Many of them participate in the same circuit of events, mingling with one another to the exclusion of people from different economic strata (Drezner 2017b). The number of "big idea" events has mushroomed, from PopTech to the Aspen Ideas Festival to TED to the World Economic Forum. As Free-

---

7. Quoted in Marc Fisher, "The Evolution of David Brooks," *Moment*, January/February 2016.

8. Greg Ferenstein, "What Silicon Valley Really Thinks About Politics," *Medium*, November 6, 2015, https://medium.com/the-ferenstein-wire/what-silicon-valley-really-thinks-about-politics-an-attempted-measurement-d37ed96a9251#.yvzcssoo2.

land (2012, 67) notes, "the real community life of the twenty-first century plutocracy occurs on the international conference circuit."

After a steady diet of global confabs, a certain mindset begins to calcify. As Freeland (2012, 238) observes, "For the super-elite, a sense of meritocratic achievement can inspire self-regard, and that self-regard—especially when compounded by their isolation among like-mined peers—can lead to obliviousness and indifference to the suffering of others."

Psychology research confirms that because they are surrounded primarily by other wealthy people, wealthy people overestimate the wealth of others and undervalue the benefits of social insurance policies (Dawtry, Sutton, and Sibley 2015). This problem becomes even more acute as inequality increases (Côté, Hose, and Willer 2015). Such insulation can lead to an atrophying of political antennae, as exemplified by entrepreneur Elon Musk telling dinner companions that poverty is not that big of a problem in South Africa[9] or billionaires writing letters to the *Wall Street Journal* comparing political antipathy toward the wealthy to Kristallnacht.[10]

While plutocrats prefer a more limited role for the state in the economy, the polarization of American society is complicating converting that preference into policy. Socially liberal, fiscally conservative policy positions represent a centrist position in the United States, but polarization is forcing both major parties to deviate away from the median voter. Paradoxically, this polarization enables both parties to advocate for even greater shifts away from the center. Romer and Rosenthal (1978) point out that agenda-setters could exploit the differences between the median voter's policy preferences and the actual status quo to articulate a new policy that comes as close as possible to their preferences. The farther away the status quo is from the median voter, the more a partisan agenda-setter can propose an alternative that also deviates from the center while still attracting a majority of support. This dynamic played out during the era of secular stagnation. In this century, George W. Bush was more conservative than his father, Barack Obama was more liberal than Bill Clinton, and Donald Trump has been more conservative than either Bush. This polarization of presidential politics has eroded the hold of the median voter theorem over American politics.

Elements of the GOP's rightward shift, such as the Tea Party movement, are thoroughly consistent with plutocratic policy preferences. Indeed, lib-

---

9. Leila Janah, "Shouldn't We Fix Poverty before Migrating to Mars?," *Medium*, May 27, 2015, https://medium.com/@leilajanah/migration-is-the-story-of-my-life-my-parents-and-grand-parents-journeyed-across-four-continents-to-2ef2ced74bf#.yx7wtrxyq.

10. Thomas Perkins, "Progressive Kristallnacht Coming?," letter to the *Wall Street Journal*, January 24, 2014. For a related example, see Monica Langley, "Texas Billionaire Doles Out Election's Biggest Checks," *Wall Street Journal*, January 22, 2013.

ertarian plutocrats helped design state-level policies in Wisconsin, Kansas, and Louisiana.

At the national level, however, the GOP's rightward shift has taken on a populist cast. Populism is defined in part by what it opposes—namely, elitism and pluralism (Mudde 2004, Müller 2016). Pluralists recognize that modern societies possess a plethora of different, cross-cutting political cleavages and variegated interests that make it difficult to divine a singular general will of the people. Populists argue that what ails society are corrupt elites that have squashed or ignored the people's true preferences. As Müller (2016, 3) notes, "When running for office, populists portray their political competitors as part of the immoral, corrupt elite." The best-articulated version of right-wing populism (Lind 2017, 47) in the United States rails against "managerial minorities" who have "run amok, using their near-monopoly of power and influence in all sectors—private, public, and nonprofit—to erect policies that advantage their members to the detriment of their fellow citizens."

Right-wing populism is nationalist, not internationalist. On foreign economic policy issues, this populist tilt is expressed as a rejection of economic globalization and the multilateral institutions that undergird it (Drezner 2017a, Mead 2017). The Brexit referendum represents the apotheosis of this populist sentiment in the United Kingdom. In the United States, Donald Trump stressed this "America First" theme in his inaugural address, arguing that, "We must protect our borders from the ravages of other countries making our products, stealing our companies, and destroying our jobs. Protection will lead to great prosperity and strength."[11]

Ineluctably, populists stress an anti-elite form of identity politics to attract voters. An exclusionary form of identity politics better explains recent voting patterns than the "economic anxiety" argument that many commentators have put forward. There is no denying that financial crises can trigger the rise of populist nationalism (Funke, Schularick, and Trebesh 2016). Nonetheless, analyses of polling data in both the Brexit referendum and the 2016 US presidential election reveal similar findings (Inglehart and Norris 2016, Rothwell 2016). Although economic distress did play a supporting role in driving support for the pro-Brexit campaign in the United Kingdom and for Trump in the United States, a more significant causal factor was at play. In both countries, the bigger driver for voters to support the populist position was whether they felt that the racial and ethnic composition of the country was changing too quickly. Pew surveys reveal that Europeans who support populist parties are far more likely to believe that

---

11. The text of the inaugural address can be accessed at www.whitehouse.gov/briefings-statements/the-inaugural-address/.

cultural factors, rather than civic values, are an important component of national identity.[12]

Polarization and populism produced a 2016 electorate that was genuinely antithetical to high-net-worth individuals. Drutman (2017) used the 2016 VOTER survey to map how US voters thought about economic policy and political identity. Unsurprisingly, Hillary Clinton's voters gravitated toward most left-leaning economic policies and cosmopolitan social policies and Donald Trump's voters clustered around a nationalist political identity and somewhat more conservative economic policies. Polling by both VOTER and the Chicago Council on Global Affairs (Smeltz et al. 2017) reveals that Republicans are now far more protectionist on trade and immigration.

These findings present a conundrum for high-net-worth individuals and corporate CEOs. They have fewer legal constraints and more resources to throw at influencing political life than ever before, but the polarization of the American public has left plutocrats with an unappetizing choice. They can certainly attempt to influence the marketplace of ideas to shift public attitudes in a more pro-globalization direction. Structural forces, however, limit the ability of even wealthy elites to shift public opinion on polarized issues. When an issue has moved to the political forefront, partisanship inhibits any expert consensus or public relations efforts from having an appreciable effect on public opinion (Drezner 2017b, Guisinger and Saunders 2017).

Plutocrats must thus search for the second-best outcome. They can ally with economic populists or support populist nationalism. In a world of secular stagnation, there are excellent reasons to believe that capital will always swipe right.

Why Capital Will Not Swipe Left

In the 20th century, it would have been possible to conceive of an alliance between the Democratic Party and a healthy fraction of the plutocratic class. The political compact that Democrats offered owners of capital was simple. Corporations and the wealthy would take a hit from higher taxes and more stringent regulation. In return, Democrats would support large investments in public goods and more active Keynesian macroeconomic policy, which would generate higher rates of economic growth. The acceleration of economic globalization made it even easier for left-leaning parties to sell this policy agenda. A commitment to freer trade signaled to capital a more

---

12. Bruce Stokes, "What It Takes to Truly Be 'One of Us,'" Pew Research Center, February 2017.

market-friendly left party (Mansfield and Milner 2017). Political economy research in the 1990s suggested that high-tax, high-spending states could maintain viable rates of economic growth (Garrett and Lange 1991). The literature on varieties of capitalism is predicated on the idea that coordinated market economies that rely on greater state intervention into the economy could be competitive in the global marketplace (Soskice and Hall 2001).

In the 1990s, even the Anglo-American economies seemed beguiled by this approach. Bill Clinton raised taxes in his first year in office and presided over an unparalleled economic boom. In the United Kingdom, Tony Blair offered a "Third Way" approach, in which robust government activism could be a handmaiden, not a hindrance, to the private sector. It was possible for left parties to make the case that even if their policies imposed greater costs on plutocrats, they yielded greater rewards.

Two trends have made it much more difficult for left parties to make a similar proffer to the plutocratic class in the 21st century. The first is that left parties have moved farther to the left. The Labor Party of Jeremy Corbyn looks radically different from the party of Tony Blair or Gordon Brown. Indeed, Blair's fall from grace implies that the Third Way is not politically viable in the United Kingdom in the medium term.

A similar trend toward economic populism is observable in the United States. Just as Barack Obama was to the left of Bill Clinton, the 2016 presidential candidates campaigned to the left of Obama. Bernie Sanders, a self-proclaimed democratic socialist, forced Hillary Clinton to tack left on economic issues (like the Trans-Pacific Partnership) in the 2016 Democratic primary. This leftward shift of the Democratic Party in the United States and social democratic parties in Europe reinforced private sector beliefs that right-wing parties are more business friendly (Weymouth and Broz 2013, Barta and Johnston 2018).

Even if the next Democratic standard-bearer tacked back to the center in a presidential campaign, high-net-worth individuals and multinational corporations would be unlikely to do so. The brute fact of secular stagnation sabotages the bargain that left parties can offer the plutocratic class. In return for higher taxes and greater regulation, left governments have to be able to deliver on higher rates of economic growth. The 21st century productivity slowdown vitiates the likelihood of fulfilling that promise. For a skeptical plutocratic class, the reduced probability of growth makes it easier to reject any compact proffered by left parties.

Of course, even in 2017 some high-net-worth individuals, such as Tom Steyer and George Soros, preferred left parties. And the Trump administration's myriad policy gaffes helped burn bridges with some Silicon Valley plutocrats, such as Sergey Brin and Elon Musk. Corporate campaign contributions still tilt toward the GOP, however, by a 2:1 ratio.[13]

Why Capital Will Swipe Right

If secular stagnation is a fact of economic life regardless of the party in power, why would capital still prefer populist nationalism? Populists like Donald Trump prefer trade protectionism and restrictions on legal immigration. Such policies could be just as problematic for corporations and plutocrats as the less business-friendly legislation of economic populists. Why will capital continue to swipe right?

The answer is that in a world of slow economic growth, redistribution policies matter far more than pro-growth policies, and populists on the right will pursue initiatives that redistribute wealth toward owners of capital. Populists on the right prefer tax cuts, deregulation, and consultation with business far more than do populists on the left. Wolf describes this mélange of policies as "pluto-populism"; others refer to it as a "messy mix of free market fundamentalism and hyper-nationalistic populism."[14] Although the growth-generating effects of these policies are open to debate, they undeniably confer greater benefits on people who earn income from interest and profits rather than wages.

The Trump administration's economic policy performance in its first year of office justifies this perception by high-net-worth individuals. A key undercurrent of the GOP's various healthcare bills was that they included an estimated $600 billion in tax cuts for the wealthiest Americans.[15] Despite public proclamations that the administration's tax plan would not benefit the wealthy,[16] most independent assessments conclude that they do so. The president himself indicated as much on December 23, 2017, when, following passage of the tax bill, he told friends at Mar-a-Lago, "You all just got a lot richer." The *New York Times* reported that "the tax plan that the Trump ad-

---

13. Andrew Prokop, "40 charts that explain money in politics," *Vox*, www.vox.com/2014/7/30/5949581/money-in-politics-charts-explain, July 30, 2014; Philip Bump, "The massive difference in how Democrats and Republicans raise money," *Washington Post*, July 16, 2014.

14. Martin Wolf, "Donald Trump's Pluto-Populism Laid Bare," *Financial Times*, May 2, 2017; Daniel Bessner and Matthew Sparke, "Don't Let His Trade Policy Fool You: Trump Is a Neoliberal," *Washington Post*, March 22, 2017. See also Greg Sargent, "The Trump Pivot: Make the Plutocrats Happy. Keep Feeding His Voters Nativism," *Washington Post*, April 14, 2017.

15. Derek Thompson, "The GOP's Plan Is Basically a $600 Billion Tax Cut for Rich Americans," *The Atlantic*, March 7, 2017.

16. Rachael Bade and Aaron Lorenzo, "Trump Defies GOP over Tax Cuts for the Rich," *Politico*, September 26, 2017.

ministration outlined…is a potentially huge windfall for the wealthiest Americans. It would not directly benefit the bottom third of the population."[17] The Tax Policy Center concluded that "taxpayers in the top 1 percent (incomes above $730,000) would receive about 50 percent of the total tax benefit; their after-tax income would increase an average of 8.5 percent."[18] The two biggest items of the administration's 2017 legislative agenda amount to a redistribution of wealth to the top of the income spectrum.

The Trump administration has had only mixed success in passing its broader legislative agenda. It has made strides in deregulation, however. Congress overturned a rule that would have made it easier for groups of consumers to sue banks.[19] Through its use of the Congressional Review Act, the GOP has eliminated many of the Obama administration's 2016 regulatory initiatives. Under the leadership of Scott Pruitt, the Environmental Protection Agency (EPA) has rolled back environmental regulation. In his first few months in office, Pruitt scaled back more than 30 environmental rules, "a regulatory rollback larger in scope than any other over so short a time in the agency's 47-year history."[20] EPA appointees come primarily from the industries the agency is supposed to regulate. Multiple reports suggest that Pruitt's primary sources of information in making regulatory decisions are industry lobbyists.[21]

The Trump administration is open to business requests for deregulation. The White House took great pains in its early months to consult with CEOs on the most important areas to deregulate. It has shielded business executives from public scrutiny when consultation does take place.[22] The

---

17. Binyamin Appelbaum, "Trump Tax Plan Benefits Wealthy, Including Trump," *New York Times*, September 27, 2017.

18. Tax Policy Center, "A Preliminary Analysis of the Unified Framework," September 29, 2017, www.taxpolicycenter.org/publications/preliminary-analysis-unified-framework/full.

19. Andrew Ackerman and Yuka Hayashi, "Congress Makes It Harder to Sue the Financial Industry," *Wall Street Journal*, October 24, 2017.

20. Coral Davenport, "Counseled by Industry, Not Staff, E.P.A. Chief Is off to a Blazing Start," *New York Times*, July 1, 2017.

21. Coral Davenport, "Counseled by Industry, Not Staff, E.P.A. Chief Is off to a Blazing Start," *New York Times*, July 1, 2017; Sheila Kaplan and Eric Lipton, "Chemical Industry Ally Faces Critics in Bid for Top E.P.A. Post," *New York Times*, September 19, 2017; Eric Lipton, "Why Has the E.P.A. Shifted on Toxic Chemicals? An Industry Insider Helps Call the Shots," *New York Times*, October 22, 2017; Steven Mufson and Juliet Elperin, "EPA Chief Pruitt Met with Many Corporate Execs. Then He Made Decisions in their Favor," *Washington Post*, September 23, 2017.

22. Andrew Restuccia, "CEOs Take Front-Seat Role Driving Policy," *Politico*, March 28, 2017; Philip Rucker and Ed O'Keefe, "In Trump's Washington, Public Business Increasingly Handled behind Closed Doors," *Washington Post*, June 19, 2017.

Trump administration has appointed a raft of corporate-friendly judges to the federal bench, in close consultation with the conservative Federalist Society. The Heritage Foundation announced that the Trump White House had embraced nearly two-thirds of its proposed policy agenda.[23]

This cluster of policy preferences helps explain the acceleration of the boom in asset market prices since Trump's election. For most of 2017, there was a gap between the "hard data" that measure economic output, employment, home sales, and commercial lending and the "soft data" of business expectations and consumer confidence. The hard data pointed to an economy that had changed little between 2016 and 2017. The soft data showed a massive surge in confidence, based in part on expectations that the Trump administration would be friendly to capital, which led to a surge in stock market prices. The result is a US economy in which the primary means of wealth creation comes from capital gains rather than the creation of new wealth (Beardsley et al. 2017).

For high-net-worth individuals, the political choice is simple. Wealth maximizers will opt for the positive redistributive effects of right-leaning populists. The boost in the returns to capital far outweighs any material downsides that might arise from protectionism and restrictions on immigration.

This logic holds for multinational corporations as well. Large firms may be more vulnerable to the disruption of global supply chains and limitations on the importation of labor. In a first-best world, most multinationals would prefer unfettered global access to the factors of production. Multinational corporations are sophisticated enough to develop policies that circumvent government barriers, however. In the face of restrictions on migrant labor, for example, firms can rely on offshore outsourcing or foreign direct investment as second-best alternatives (Peters 2017). They can also lobby the administration to preserve agreements perceived as vital to US business.[24] Their efforts appear to have helped convince President Trump to reverse course on a number of populist policy proposals he made during the campaign, such as labelling China a currency manipulator and withdrawing from the North American Free Trade Agreement (NAFTA).[25]

The failure of a right-wing populist government to follow through on all of its economic promises has the potential to trigger political blowback.

---

23. Jeremy Peters, "Heritage Foundation Says Trump Has Embraced Two-Thirds of Its Agenda," *New York Times*, January 22, 2018.

24. Betsy Woodruff and Lachlan Markay, "Trump's Turbulent Tariff Policy Has Been Nirvana for K Street," *Daily Beast*, May 2, 2018.

25. Peter Nicholas, Paul Vieira, and José de Córdoba, "Why Donald Trump Decided to Back off NAFTA Threat," *Wall Street Journal*, April 27, 2017.

Indeed, elite conservatives in the United States have begun to observe and complain about the pluto-populism of the current administration. Surveying the first few months of the administration, Ramesh Ponnuru and Rich Lowry lamented in *National Review* that "the Trump administration hasn't created a new populist departure in American politics; it hasn't even— as some of us hoped—nudged Republican policymaking in a more populist direction to better account for the interests of working-class voters. The early months of the Trump administration have proven to be populism's false start." And the founder of the populist journal *American Affairs* characterized the first half-year of the Trump administration as "mediocre conventional Republicanism with a lot more noise."[26] Lind's (2017, 53) critique of the pre-2016 status quo, in which policies were designed to "boost profits without increasing productivity," perfectly captures the Trump administration's policy outputs.

Conservative political elites may be disenchanted with the current administration's policies. If capital is fine with pluto-populism, however, so are conservative voters. Trump's mix of identity politics and populist nationalism resonates far better with GOP voters than the more traditional GOP message.

Polling by the Chicago Council on Global Affairs (Smeltz et al. 2017) demonstrates that for decades, elites on both sides of the aisle were more enthusiastic about globalization than voters. That gap has been far wider on the GOP side than the Democratic side (figures 10.1 and 10.2). On trade, GOP elites were more than 30 percentage points more positive than GOP voters on globalization. On immigration, the gap was almost 50 percentage points. Trump's populist rhetoric on these issues is closer to the sympathies of the median GOP voter than it is to the views of Paul Ryan or John McCain. The cooptation of key social conservative groups also acts as backlash insurance for the administration's policies that favor plutocrats.[27] In 2017 wealthy donors backed Trump more than the congressional wing of the GOP did.[28]

---

26. Ramesh Ponnuru and Rich Lowry, "Populism's False Start," *National Review*, May 25, 2017; Eliana Johnson and Josh Dawsey, "GOP Despairs at Inability to Deliver," *Politico*, July 23, 2017.

27. Thomas Edsall, "Donald Trump's Identity Politics," *New York Times*, August 24, 2017; Peter Montgomery, "The Religious Right Moves to Cement Political Power under President Trump," *American Prospect*, September 1, 2017; Noah Rothman, "Trump Supporters' Lowered Expectations," *Commentary*, October 9, 2017; Tim Alberta, "Donald Trump and the Dawn of the Evangelical-Nationalist Alliance," *Politico*, October 14, 2017.

28. Alex Isenstadt and Gabriel Debenedetti, "Angry GOP Donors Close Their Wallets," *Politico*, October 5, 2017.

Figure 10.1 Globalization

Do you believe that globalization, especially the increasing connections of our economy with others around the world, is mostly good or mostly bad for the United States? (percent mostly good)

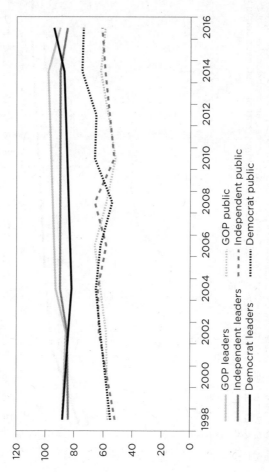

GOP leaders
Independent leaders
Democrat leaders

GOP public
Independent public
Democrat public

Source: Smeltz et al. (2017). Reprinted with permission.

Figure 10.2 Large numbers of immigrants and refugees

Below is a list of possible threats to the vital interest of the United States in the next 10 years. For each one, please select whether you see this as a critical threat, an important but not critical threat, or not an important threat at all: Large numbers of immigrants and refugees coming to the US (percent critical threat)

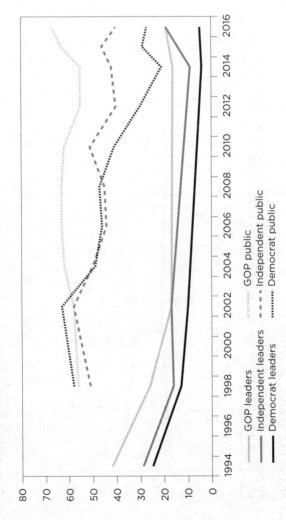

GOP leaders — GOP public
Independent leaders — Independent public
Democrat leaders — Democrat public

Source: Smeltz et al. (2017). Reprinted with permission.

Conclusion

The political preferences of high-net-worth individuals and large corporations are relatively homogeneous on economic policy issues. Capital prefers a light touch from the state: low taxes, accommodating regulation, and minimal protectionism. The increase in political polarization, however, has made it more difficult for capital to convert its preferences into policy. Plutocrats face an unappetizing choice between left-wing economic populists in the mold of Bernie Sanders and right-wing nationalist populists in the mold of Donald Trump.

Secular stagnation has caused capital to side with the right wing. The productivity slowdown has rendered the left-wing compact of higher taxes and regulation in return for more public goods investment and higher rates of economic growth less credible. Plutocrats do not believe that economic populists can deliver on that bargain, and political leaders on the left are wary of seeming too friendly to capital. Right-wing policy proposals will not yield more growth, but they will produce a redistribution of income toward owners of capital. In a steady state of low growth, it is unsurprising that plutocrats will opt to increase their income through a redistribution of existing gains.

The more capital allies exclusively with a conservative view of redistribution, the more corrosive its effects on the political economy. Historical institutionalists argue that once a policy framework is erected, interests will emerge with asset-specific investments in that framework (Thelen 1999, Pierson 2000). Applying this logic to the current moment, owners of capital will increasingly depend on Republican control over the levers of power to ensure the maintenance of business-friendly taxes, regulation, and procurement policies, accelerating the trend toward rent-seeking in the United States (Bessen 2016, Litan and Hathaway 2017). This rent-seeking will be tied more closely to conservatives staying in power. Firms with close ties to the Obama administration suffered lower rates of returns after the 2016 election (Brown and Huang 2017). This dynamic incentivizes firms allied with the current administration to invest even more in supporting the GOP, in order to avoid a similar negative shock.

This pattern is already on display in the run-up to the 2018 midterms.[29] The growing concentration of US businesses could cause even left-leaning sectors—such as Silicon Valley or Hollywood—to support the GOP, in

---

29. James Hohmann and Michelle Ye Hee Lee, "How the Koch Network Learned to Thrive in the Trump Era," *Washington Post*, January 29, 2018; Haley Byrd, "Koch Network Gears Up for 'Challenging Environment' in 2018," *Weekly Standard*, January 28, 2018.

order to avoid antitrust actions.[30] Indeed, plutocrats could go so far as to encourage institutional changes that stack the deck against left-leaning voters. Plutocratic support for weakening public sector unions, gerrymandering, and stringent voter ID laws are all examples of this kind of behavior (Hacker and Pierson 2006).

The medium-run consequences of capital swiping right are significant. The evidence suggests that Trump's tax cuts and deregulation will have minimal effects on economic growth.[31] But lax antitrust policies will accelerate the transformation of the US economy into sectors dominated by monopolies. The cumulative macroeconomic effect of this concentration is to drag down economic growth (De Loecker and Eeckhout 2017). Large firms' reliance on support from the state will cause a diversion of entrepreneurial talent from productive to unproductive uses (Baumol 1990, Litan and Hathaway 2017).

Allowing these path-dependent effects to extend into the long run will create a doom loop of dysfunction. When it comes to public policy, economic growth is a political palliative: It is much easier to cut taxes, invest in public goods, reduce budget deficits, or enact sweeping policy reforms when growth rates are high. When growth is robust, policymaking looks more like a non-zero-sum game. Secular stagnation and political polarization eliminate the ability of parties in power to institute ambitious policies.

This new constraint has an asymmetric effect that benefits Republicans at the expense of Democrats. Since the Reagan era, the GOP has run for office on the ideology that government solutions to policy problems do not work. The "pluto-populism" that they implement, however, will reduce economic growth even farther while redistributing income toward owners of capital. The continued poor performance of the US economy will simply encourage Republicans to double down on their message that government is not the answer. This message may resonate with voters who recognize hard times but refuse to believe that government can provide any answers (Cramer 2016).

It is rare but not unprecedented for advanced industrial democracies to fall into a steady state of political decline. Argentina achieved this outcome after the Belle Époque era (Taylor 1994). More recently, some democracies in Eastern Europe devolved into a state of liberal rent-seeking (Levitsky and Ziblatt 2018). It is possible that pluto-populism will have the same effect on the United States.

---

30. See, for example, Jeff Nicas, "Silicon Valley Warms to Trump After a Chilly Start," *New York Times*, March 30, 2018.

31. Hilary Schmidt, "The Economic Impact of the Trump Tax Cuts," *International Banker*, April 25, 2018.

References

Acemoglu, Daron, and James Robinson. 2012. *Why Nations Fail: The Origins of Power, Prosperity and Poverty*. New York: Crown Books.

Azzimonti, Marina. 2014. *Partisan Conflict*. Federal Reserve Bank of Philadelphia Working Paper 14-19.

Bafumi, Joseph, and Michael C. Herron. 2010. Leapfrog Representation and Extremism: A Study of American Voters and Their Members in Congress. *American Political Science Review* 104, no. 3: 519–42.

Barber, Michael, and Nolan McCarty. 2013. Causes and Consequences of Polarization. In *Negotiating Agreement in Politics*, ed. Jane Mansbridge and Cathie Jo Martin. Washington: American Political Science Association.

Barta, Zsófia, and Alison Johnston. 2018. Rating Politics? Partisan Discrimination in Credit Ratings in Developed Economies. *Comparative Political Studies* 51, no. 5: 587–620.

Baumol, William. 1990. Entrepreneurship: Productive, Unproductive, and Destructive. *Journal of Political Economy* 98, no. 5: 893–921.

Beardsley, Brent, Bruce Holley, Mariam Jaafar, Daniel Kessler, Federico Muxí, Matthias Naumann, Jürgen Rogg, Tjun Tang, André Xavier, and Anna Zakrzewski. 2017. *Global Wealth 2017*. Boston: Boston Consulting Group.

Bessen, James E. 2016. *Accounting for Rising Corporate Profits: Intangibles or Regulatory Rents?* Boston University School of Law, Law and Economics Research Paper 16-18.

Bonica, Adam, Nolan McCarty, Keith Poole, and Howard Rosenthal. 2013. Why Hasn't Democracy Slowed Rising Inequality? *Journal of Economic Perspectives* 27, no. 3: 103–23.

Brown, Jeffrey, and Jiekun Huang. 2017. *All the President's Friends: Political Access and Firm Value*. NBER Working Paper 23356. Cambridge, MA: National Bureau of Economic Research.

Cook, Fay Lomax, Benjamin I. Page, and Rachel Moskowitz. 2014. Political Engagement by Wealthy Americans. *Political Science Quarterly* 129, no. 3: 381–98.

Côté, Stéphane, Julian Hose, and Robb Willer. 2015. High Economic Inequality Leads Higher-Income Individuals to be Less Generous. *Proceedings of the National Academy of Sciences* 112, no. 52: 15838–43.

Cramer, Katherine. 2016. *The Politics of Resentment: Rural Consciousness in Wisconsin and the Rise of Scott Walker*. Chicago: University of Chicago Press.

Dawtry, Rael J., Robbie M. Sutton, and Chris G. Sibley. 2015. Why Wealthier People Think People Are Wealthier, and Why It Matters: From Social Sampling to Redistributive Attitudes. *Psychological Science* 26, no. 9: 1389–1400.

De Loecker, Jan, and Jan Eeckhout. 2017. *The Rise of Market Power and the Macroeconomic Implications*. NBER Working Paper 23687. Cambridge, MA: National Bureau of Economic Research.

Dimock, Michael, Jocelyn Kiley, Scott Keeter, and Carroll Doherty. 2014. *Political Polarization and the American Public*. Washington: Pew Research Center.

Drezner, Daniel W. 2017a. The Angry Populist as Foreign Policy Leader: Real Change or Just Hot Air? *Fletcher Forum of World Affairs* 41, no. 1 (Summer): 23–43.

Drezner, Daniel W. 2017b. *The Ideas Industry: How Pessimists, Partisans, and Plutocrats Are Transforming the Marketplace of Ideas*. New York: Oxford University Press.

Drutman, Lee. 2017. *Political Divisions in 2016 and Beyond*. Voter Study Group (June). Available at https://www.voterstudygroup.org/publications/2016-elections/political-divisions-in-2016-and-beyond.

Freeland, Chrystia. 2012. *Plutocrats: The Rise of the New Global Super-Rich and the Fall of Everyone Else*. New York: Penguin.

Funke, Manuel, Moritz Schularick, and Christoph Trebesh. 2016. Going to Extremes: Politics after Financial Crises, 1870–2014. *European Economic Review* 88 (September): 227-60.

Galston, William. 2018. The Populist Challenge to Liberal Democracy. *Journal of Democracy* 29, no. 2: 5–19.

Garner, Andrew, and Harvey Palmer. 2011. Polarization and Issue Consistency over Time. *Political Behavior* 33, no. 2: 225–46.

Garrett, Geoffrey, and Peter Lange. 1991. Political Responses to Interdependence: What's "Left" for the Left? *International Organization* 45, no. 4: 539-64.

Guisinger, Alexandra, and Elizabeth N. Saunders. 2017. Mapping the Boundaries of Elite Cues: How Elites Shape Mass Opinion across International Issues. *International Studies Quarterly* 61, no. 3: 425–41.

Hacker, Jacob S., and Paul Pierson. 2006. *Off Center: The Republican Revolution and the Erosion of American Democracy*. New Haven, CT: Yale University Press.

Hetherington, Marc J. 2001. Resurgent Mass Partisanship: The Role of Elite Polarization. *American Political Science Review* 95, no. 3: 619-31.

Hill, Seth J., and Chris Tausanovitch. 2015. A Disconnect in Representation? Comparison of Trends in Congressional and Public Polarization. *Journal of Politics* 77, no. 4: 1058-75.

Inglehart, Ronald, and Pippa Norris. 2016. *Trump, Brexit, and the Rise of Populism: Economic Have-Nots and Cultural Backlash*. HKS Faculty Research Working Paper RWP16-026, Harvard Kennedy School, Cambridge, MA.

Iyengar, Shanto, Gaurav Sood, and Yphtach Lelkes. 2012. Affect, Not Ideology: A Social Identity Perspective on Polarization. *Public Opinion Quarterly* 76, no. 3: 405–31.

Iyengar, Shanto, and Sean Westwood. 2015. Fear and Loathing across Party Lines: New Evidence on Group Polarization. *American Journal of Political Science* 59, no. 3: 690–707.

Levitsky, Steven, and Daniel Ziblatt. 2018. *How Democracies Die*. New York: Crown Books.

Lind, Michael. 2017. The New Class War. *American Affairs* 1, no. 2: 40–60.

Litan, Robert, and Ian Hathaway. 2017. Is America Encouraging the Wrong Kind of Entrepreneurship? *Harvard Business Review*, June 13.

Mansfield, Edward, Helen Milner, and Peter Rosendorff. 2000. Free to Trade: Democracies, Autocracies, and International Trade. *American Political Science Review* 94, no. 2: 305–21.

Mansfield, Edward, and Helen Milner. 2017. The Domestic Politics of Preferential Trade Agreements in Hard Times. *World Trade Review*, September.

Mason, Lilliana. 2015. "I Disrespectfully Agree": The Differential Effects of Partisan Sorting on Social and Issue Polarization. *American Journal of Political Science* 59, no. 1: 128–45.

Mead, Walter Russell. 2017. The Jacksonian Revolt. *Foreign Affairs* 96, no. 1: 2–7.

Mudde, Cas. 2004. The Populist Zeitgeist. *Government and Opposition* 39, no. 4: 541–63.

Müller, Jan-Werner. 2016. *What Is Populism?* Philadelphia: University of Pennsylvania Press.

North, Douglass, and Barry Weingast. 1989. Constitutions and Commitment: The Evolution of Institutions Governing Public Choice in Seventeenth-Century England. *Journal of Economic History* 49, no. 4: 803–32.

Page, Benjamin I., Larry M. Bartels, and Jason Seawright. 2013. Democracy and the Policy Preferences of Wealthy Americans. *Perspectives on Politics* 11, no. 1: 51–73.

Page, Benjamin I., Jason Seawright, and Matthew LaCombe. 2015. Stealth Politics by U.S. Billionaires. Paper presented at the annual meeting of the American Political Science Association, San Francisco, CA.

Peters, Margaret. 2017. *Trading Barriers: Immigration and the Remaking of Globalization*. Princeton, NJ: Princeton University Press.

Pierson, Paul. 2000. Increasing Returns, Path Dependence, and the Study of Politics. *American Political Science Review* 94, no. 2: 251–67.

Piketty, Thomas. 2014. *Capital in the Twenty-First Century*. Cambridge, MA: Belknap Press.

Piketty, Thomas. 2015. Putting Distribution Back at the Center of Economics: Reflections on Capital in the Twenty-First Century. *Journal of Economic Perspectives* 29, no. 1: 67–88.

Romer, Thomas, and Howard Rosenthal. 1978. Political Resource Allocation, Controlled Agendas, and the Status Quo. *Public Choice* 33, no. 4: 27–43.

Rothwell, Jonathan. 2016. Explaining Nationalist Political Views: The Case of Donald Trump. Unpublished paper, Gallup, August.

Saez, Emmanuel, and Gabriel Zucman. 2016. Wealth Inequality in the United States since 1913: Evidence from Capitalized Income Tax Data. *Quarterly Journal of Economics* 131, no. 2: 519–78.

Shaw, Daron. 2012. If Everyone Votes Their Party, Why Do Presidential Election Outcomes Vary So Much? *The Forum* 10 (October).

Shorrocks, Anthony, Jim Davies, and Rodrigo Lluberas. 2014. *Global Wealth Report 2014*. Boston: Credit Suisse Research Institute.

Smeltz, Dina, Karl Friedhoff, Craig Kafura, Joshua Busby, Jonathan Monten, and Jordan Tama. 2017. *The Foreign Policy Establishment or Donald Trump: Which Better Reflects American Opinion?* Chicago: Chicago Council on Global Affairs. www.thechicagocouncil.org/sites/default/files/elite-report-foreign-policy-establishment-trump_170421_v2.pdf.

Soskice, David W., and Peter A. Hall. 2001. *Varieties of Capitalism: The Institutional Foundations of Comparative Advantage*. Oxford: Oxford University Press.

Taylor, Alan M. 1994. *Three Phases of Argentine Economic Growth*. NBER Working Paper 60. Cambridge, MA: National Bureau of Economic Research.

Thelen, Kathleen. 1999. Historical Institutionalism in Comparative Politics. *Annual Review of Political Science* 2, no. 1: 369–404.

West, Darrell. 2014. *Billionaires: Reflections on the Upper Crust*. Washington: Brookings Institution Press.

Weymouth, Stephen, and J. Lawrence Broz. 2013. Government Partisanship and Property Rights: Cross-Country Firm-Level Evidence. *Economics & Politics* 25, no. 2: 229–56.

About the Contributors

Axel Börsch-Supan is director of the Munich Center for the Economics of Aging (MEA) at the Max Planck Institute for Social Law and Social Policy, professor at the Technical University of Munich, and research associate at the National Bureau of Economic Research. He was assistant professor of public policy at Harvard University (1984–89). In 1989, he became professor of macroeconomics and public policy at Mannheim University. Börsch-Supan is member of the German National Academy of Sciences Leopoldina, the Berlin-Brandenburg, the Austrian Academy of Sciences, the Council of Advisors to the German Economics Ministry (chair 2004–08), and the German Pension Reform Commissions (2003 and 2018). He is a consultant to several governments, the European Commission, the Organization for Economic Cooperation and Development (OECD), and the World Bank. He holds a PhD in economics from MIT.

Daniel W. Drezner is professor of international politics at the Fletcher School of Law and Diplomacy at Tufts University, a nonresident senior fellow at the Brookings Institution, and the author of "Spoiler Alerts" for the *Washington Post*. Drezner has written six books, including *All Politics Is Global* and *The System Worked*, and edited two others, including *Avoiding Trivia*. He has published articles in numerous scholarly journals as well as in the *New York Times, Wall Street Journal*, and *Foreign Affairs*. His latest book, *The Ideas Industry: How Pessimists, Partisans, and Plutocrats Are Transforming the Marketplace of Ideas*, was published by Oxford University Press in the spring of 2017.

Elena Duggar is the chair of Moody's Macroeconomic Board, which develops the macroeconomic forecasts used in the rating process throughout the rating agency, facilitates analyst access to the forecasts, and presents Moody's views with external audiences. She also manages the research team in the Credit Strategy and Research group, which authors Moody's *Global Macroeconomic Outlooks*, *Global Credit Conditions Outlook*, and other thematic research, and helps form house views on macro and financial risk topics. Prior to 2016, Duggar served as Moody's Group Credit Officer for Sovereign Risk, covering the global sovereign ratings portfolio. She joined Moody's in 2007 and previously was an economist at the International Monetary Fund. She holds a BA in economics from Bates College and a PhD in economics from the University of California at Berkeley.

Karen Dynan, nonresident senior fellow at the Peterson Institute for International Economics since March 2017, is professor of the practice at the Harvard University Economics Department. She served as assistant secretary for economic policy and chief economist at the US Department of the Treasury from 2014 to 2017, where she led analysis of economic conditions and development of policies to address the nation's economic challenges. From 2009 to 2013, Dynan was vice president and codirector of the Economic Studies Program at the Brookings Institution. Before that, she was on the staff of the Federal Reserve Board, leading work in macroeconomic forecasting, household finances, and the Fed's response to the financial crisis. Dynan received her PhD in economics from Harvard University and her AB from Brown University.

Jason Furman, nonresident senior fellow at the Peterson Institute for International Economics since January 2017, served as a top economic adviser to President Barack Obama, including as the 28th chair of the Council of Economic Advisers from August 2013 to January 2017, acting as both Obama's chief economist and a member of the cabinet. Furman played an important role in most of the major economic policies of the Obama administration. He has authored numerous articles in scholarly journals and periodicals and is the editor of two books on economic policy. He holds a PhD in economics from Harvard University.

José De Gregorio, nonresident senior fellow at the Peterson Institute for International Economics since March 2014, is dean of the School of Economics and Business at the University of Chile. He was governor of the Central Bank of Chile and minister of the economy, mining, and energy of Chile. He is author of *How Latin America Weathered the Global Financial Crisis* (2014). De Gregorio has received a number of honors and awards, including Central Banker of the Year in Latin America for 2008, awarded by the *Banker*, a member of the *Financial Times* editorial group. He obtained his PhD in economics from MIT in 1990.

Filippo di Mauro is visiting professor at the Business School at the National University of Singapore and an external consultant of the Monetary Authority of Singapore and of the Singapore Economic Development Board. He is also chairman of CompNet, a large research network on competitiveness and productivity among EU institutions, and coordinator of the Productivity Research Network, a similar initiative based in Singapore and covering the Asia-Pacific region. He has been an economist at several central banks—Bank of Italy (1984–90, 1996–98), US Federal Reserve Board (May–September 2010), European Central Bank (1998–2016)—and international development organizations—Asian Development Bank (1990–94) and International Monetary Fund (1986–88, 1994–96). He joined the ECB when it started operating in 1998 and until 2010 directed international economic analysis and the global economy forecast in the ECB's economics department. An economics graduate of the University of Rome, di Mauro holds an MA and PhD in economics from the the University of Chicago and the American University, respectively.

Neil Mehrotra is an assistant professor in the Department of Economics at Brown University. He was a visiting scholar at the Federal Reserve Bank of Minneapolis from 2016 to 2017. He earned his PhD in economics from Columbia University in 2013 focusing on secular stagnation, monetary policy, and the role of financial frictions in recessions. His work has been published in *AEJ: Macroeconomics, IMF Economic Review,* and *International Journal of Central Banking.* He received an AB in economics from Princeton University in 2005. Prior to his graduate studies, he worked in the Global Investment Research division at Goldman Sachs in New York.

Bernardo Mottironi is an MRes/PhD student in economics at the London School of Economics. He was a research assistant at the European Central Bank. Before starting the doctoral program, he obtained his master's degree from Bocconi University, where he wrote a thesis on capital misallocation and international trade. His fields of interest include productivity growth, firms' competitiveness and the effects of globalization, with a focus on micro-macro linkages.

Peter R. Orszag is head of North American M&A and vice chairman of investment banking at Lazard Frères & Co. LLC in New York. He also serves as global co-head of healthcare at the firm and is a member of its Opinion Committee. Before joining Lazard in May 2016, he served as vice chairman of corporate and investment banking and chairman of the Financial Strategy and Solutions Group at Citigroup. He previously served as the director of the Office of Management and Budget in the Obama administration, a cabinet-level position, from January 2009 to July 2010. From January 2007 to December 2008, Orszag was the director of the Congressional Budget Office. He graduated summa cum laude in economics from Princeton University and obtained a PhD in economics from the London School of Economics, which he attended as a Marshall Scholar. He has coauthored or coedited a number of books. He is a member of the National Academy of Medicine and holds an honorary doctorate from Rensselaer Polytechnic Institute. He also serves on the Board of Directors of the Peterson Institute for International Economics, Mt. Sinai Medical Center, the Russell Sage Foundation, New Visions for Public Schools, and ideas42.

Gianmarco Ottaviano is full professor at the Department of Economics in Bocconi University. He was associate professor at Bocconi University, full professor at Bologna University, and professor at the London School of Economics. He is a research fellow at numerous international research centers, such as CEPR London (International Trade and Regional Economics Program), Bruegel Brussels, FEEM Milan, CReAM London, CSIC Barcelona, and GEP Nottingham. He is a member of the scientific committees of Centro di Alti Studi sulla Cina Contemporanea (CASCC) in Turin and Luiss Lab of European Economics in Rome and of the editorial boards of multiple journals, such as *Journal of Economic Geography* (Oxford University Press), *Journal of Urban Economics* (Elsevier), *Regional Science and Urban Economics* (Elsevier) and the *Economic Policy* panel (Blackwell). He graduated in economics from Bocconi University in Milan. He obtained a Master of Science degree in economics from the London School of Economics and Political Science and a PhD in economics from Université Catholique de Louvain.

Adam S. Posen has been the president of the Peterson Institute for International Economics since January 2013, after first joining in July 1997. Over his career, he has written about the financial and economic challenges faced by the European Union following the adoption of the euro, the lasting impact of Japan's economic crisis of the 1990s, and monetary and fiscal policies in the G-7. While at the Federal Reserve Bank of New York during 1994–97, he coauthored *Inflation Targeting: Lessons from the International Experience* with Ben Bernanke and Frederic Mishkin. From 2009 to 2012, Posen served a three-year term as an external voting member of the Bank of England's rate-setting Monetary Policy Committee (MPC). Posen received his BA and PhD from Harvard University. In addition to his leadership at the Institute, Posen advises the US Congressional Budget Office.

Louise Sheiner is the Robert S. Kerr Senior Fellow in Economic Studies and policy director at the Hutchins Center on Fiscal and Monetary Policy, Brookings Institution. She had served as an economist with the Board of Governors of the Federal Reserve System since 1993, most recently as the senior economist in the Fiscal Analysis Section of the Research and Statistics Division. During her time at the Fed, she was also appointed deputy assistant secretary for economic policy at the US Department of the Treasury (1996) and served as senior staff economist for the Council of Economic Advisers (1995–96). Before joining the Fed, Sheiner was an economist at the Joint Committee on Taxation. She pursues research on health spending and other fiscal issues. She received her PhD in economics from Harvard University, as well as an undergraduate degree in biology from Harvard.

Anna Stansbury is a PhD candidate in economics at Harvard University and a Stone PhD Scholar in Inequality and Wealth Concentration at Harvard's program on inequality and social policy. Her research is at the intersection of macroeconomics and labor economics, with a particular focus on income and wealth inequality, poverty, and unemployment. She has a master's in public policy from Harvard Kennedy School, where she was a Kennedy Scholar, and a BA in economics from Cambridge University.

Lawrence H. Summers is the Charles W. Eliot University Professor and president emeritus of Harvard University and the Weil Director of the Mossavar-Rahmani Center for Business & Government at Harvard Kennedy School. During the past two decades, he has served in a series of senior policy positions in Washington, DC, including the 71st Secretary of the Treasury for President Bill Clinton, director of the National Economic Council for President Barack Obama and vice president of development economics and chief economist of the World Bank. He received a Bachelor of Science degree from the Massachusetts Institute of Technology in 1975 and was awarded a PhD from Harvard in 1982. In 1983, he became one of the youngest individuals in recent history to be named as a tenured member of the Harvard University faculty. In 1987, Summers became the first social scientist ever to receive the annual Alan T. Waterman Award of the National Science Foundation, and in 1993 he was awarded the John Bates Clark Medal, given every two years to the outstanding American economist under the age of 40.

Jeromin Zettelmeyer has been senior fellow at the Peterson Institute for International Economics since September 2016 and was a nonresident senior fellow during 2013–14. From 2014 until September of 2016, he served as director-general for economic policy at the German Federal Ministry for Economic Affairs and Energy. He also represented Germany at the OECD Economic Policy Committee and served as a founding cochair of the OECD's Global Forum on Productivity. Before joining the German government, Zettelmeyer was director of research and deputy chief economist at the European Bank for Reconstruction and Development (August 2008–March 2014). He has published widely on topics including financial crises, sovereign debt, economic growth, and transition economies. Zettelmeyer holds a PhD in economics from MIT (1995) and an economics degree from the University of Bonn (1990).

Alessandro Zona-Mattioli is a trainee at the European Central Bank's Directorate General of Economic Development and a former CompNet trainee. He graduated in economics from Bocconi University and earned an MSc degree in economics also from Bocconi University. He spent an exchange semester at the Nanyang Technological University of Singapore and has been an IGIER visiting student at Bocconi University, mentored by Professor Jerome Adda.

Index

reliance on support from the state, 280
wage premiums declining, 251
Latin America
changes in five-year-ahead growth
forecasts, 150f
development accounting for, 159t, 179t
female participation in the labor force,
170–71
Latvia, 18f, 19f, 187f, 196f
left parties, moved farther to the left, 271
legislation, effects of recent tax-related,
88n–89n
liberal democracy, harboring the power of
self-correction, 263
"liberal market economies," 264
libertarian direction, plutocratic class
tilting in a, 268
licensing, 258, 259
lifecycle model, insights on effects of
productivity, 44–48
life expectancy, 125, 129
life-time earnings, calculating for the
simulation, 128
lifetime income paths, 74
lifetime income profiles, flattening of, 79,
83
linkage, between productivity and
compensation, 208, 219, 221, 223, 236
Lithuania, 154, 156f, 181t, 190t
living standards, lower expected future, 4
local productivity growth, deviation from
global productivity, 27–28
logarithm of exports of the median firm,
187f
log labor productivity, change in the US,
218f, 219f
long-term growth, for the world economy
declined, 149
long-term nominal interest rate, 29t
lower economic growth, leading to lower
income and consumption growth and
lower tax revenues, 56
lower GDP growth, meaning cashflow
adjustments, 62
lower incomes, putting downward pressure
on labor force participation rates, 83
lower mean compensation growth, 80
low fertility rate, components of, 129
low-growth scenario, 200

low-income families, programs supporting,
78
low productivity growth. See also
productivity, growth
affecting both the growth rate and the
real interest rate, 62
associated with less real bracket creep,
79–80
coinciding with lower real interest rates,
18–19
effect of lower labor force participation,
78
expected to lead to lower income and
consumption growth and lower tax
revenues, 56
as a fact in Western countries, 185
generating path-dependent effects on the
US political economy, 263
impact of, 57f
likely to increase government
expenditures as a share of GDP, 59
negative effect on sovereign debt
dynamics, 57f, 64
reducing inflation, 64n
reducing the incomes of working-age
population (and tax revenue), 75
Luxembourg, 18f, 19f

macroeconomic models, relationship
between real interest rates and
underlying productivity growth, 19–20
macroeconomic stabilization tool,
monetary policy as, 81
macroprudential policies, identifying and
containing emerging financial sector
risks, 7
Malaysia, 154, 156f, 157, 182t
managers, paid more than line workers, 250
mandatory federal spending, in the US
(2017), 101t
mandatory "premium pension," in Sweden,
140
Manichean, "us against them" view, of the
political world, 267
March 2017 Long-Term Budget Outlook (CBO),
88n, 89n
market concentration, changes in the US by
industry, 253t

party elites, more ideologically extreme, 267

pay-as-you-go (PAYG) defined-benefit pension system(s)
  of the defined-benefit type, 121, 126
  of the defined-contribution type, 126
  German, 136
  government promising a replacement rate or a flat benefit which it has to finance, 120
  having a reserve and/or other multiyear balancing mechanisms, 126n
  having budgets as part of the general government's budget, 126n
  lifetime earnings determining the level of benefits, 6n
  linking the older and the younger generation directly, 120
  population and productivity growth determining the rate of return, 119
  reflecting intergenerational distribution between old and young, 117
  replacement rate set by the political process, 129, 130f
  saving more in, 140

PAYG pension system with government subsidies, spillover mechanisms, 136

payment rates, for many parts of Medicare, 99n

payroll taxes
  collection of, 56, 59, 93
  legislating automatic reductions in, 82
  moving with productivity, 92
  percentage of federal revenue from, 92f

Penn World Tables, 154, 232

pension adequacy, 136

pension benefits, 6, 118, 128

pension claiming age, 139

pensioners, number of computed indirectly by MEA-PENSIM, 125

pension payments, effect on the state and local sector, 111n

2015 *Pension Report* (German Federal Ministry of Labor and Social Affairs), 125

pensions, as an important social program, 117

pension systems
  actuarial, 139
  in aging populations, 138

in Europe, 117–42
with flat benefits, 127
maintaining a delicate balance, 117
slowdown in productivity affecting, 118
types of, 119–22, 119f

per capita GDP growth, component analysis of, 33, 34f

personal consumption expenditures (PCE), compensation deflated by, 214n

Peru, 156f, 182t

Philippines, 156f, 157

physical and human capital. *See also* human capital
  accumulation of, 148
  misallocation of in Mexico, 157
  relative levels of, 152, 153f, 154

pluralists, 270

plutocratic class, rejecting parties on the left, 272

plutocrats
  choice of the second-best for, 268–71
  designed state-level policies in Wisconsin, Kansas, and Louisiana, 270
  on the international conference circuit, 269
  opting for populist nationalism, 264
  reaction to the Trump administration, 264
  support for weakening public sector unions, gerrymandering, and stringent voter ID laws, 280
  unappetizing choice for, 271, 279

"pluto-populism," 273, 280

Poland, 18f, 19f, 155, 156f, 182t, 187f, 190t, 196f

polarization, effects of, 269

policies, 9, 257, 259

policy implications, 7, 9–10

policy mix, needed for pension systems, 142

policy rates, changing forward guidance about, 81

political blowback, from the failure of a right-wing populist government to follow through, 275–76

political donors, concentration of, 266

political feasibility, as an issue for optimal policies, 83

political leaders, on the left wary of seeming too friendly to capital, 279

of public K-12 educational services
in the US, 106, 107*f*
pushed up typical and average
compensation in recent decades, 236
rates, US lifecycle estimates of, 46*f*
reaction of interest rates to, 135
recovering somewhat in 2018-19, 54
reduction in recorded, 1–2
reduction in reducing export
competitiveness, 201
relationship to inequality, 246
relationship with compensation
growth, 217, 218*f*, 219*f*
remaining lower over the medium
term, 54
remaining strong at the frontier,
249
shortfall relative to historical
averages, 70
short-term fluctuations in, 231
slowdown, affecting wages across
the board, 99
slowdown, endangering the balance
of pension systems, 118
slowdown, extending well beyond
the US, 69
slowdown, for larger advanced
economies, 16
slowdown, increasing poverty and
Medicaid eligibility will increase
state Medicaid spending, 107
slowdown, in slowing the annual
increase in export competitiveness,
201
slowdown, lowering federal revenue
and increasing spending, 109
slowdown, presenting risks to GDP
growth recovery, 51
slowdown, reducing real bracket
creep, 93
slowdown and rise of inequality
having a common cause, 246
slower, beneficial from a debt-
sustainability perspective, 48
slower, causing rising inequality,
246
slower, effect in the US on federal
outlays and primary deficits, 105*t*

slower, increasing state and local
pension spending, 108–109
slower, increasing the asset-to-GDP
ratio, 112
slower, painful for workers at
the lower end of the income
distribution, 73–74
slower, reducing the extent of real
bracket creep, 74
strong relationship with
compensation growth as compatible
with divergence, 209*n*
substantial variations in, 238
sustained period of lower leading to
changes for tax policy, 71
transmitting to real interest rates via
consumption growth, 19–20
unemployment related to changes
in, 216
in the US, 248*f*
in the US and other advanced
economies, 2*f*
variation across the full set of
OECD countries, 33
growth and inequality, facts about,
247–52
increases translating into compensation
with a lag, 215
labor share and, 233–35, 234*t*
and labor shares, regression results on,
234*t*
literature on the relationship with
compensation, 211–13, 212*f*
low as persistent, 6
lower prolonging the current period of
very low interest rates, 4
and mean-median compensation,
regressions results on, 235*t*
measure of, 213
possible mismeasurement of, 224
projected changes in, 89–90
relationship of emerging-market versus
advanced economies, 164, 165*f*
relationship with compensation, 209,
215
scenarios, impact on export performance,
200–201
slowdown
across countries, 1, 3

telecommunications companies, increasing
    returns to scale, 256
TFP. *See* total factor productivity (TFP)
Thailand, 156*f*, 157, 162, 183*t*
"third rail," pensions as, 117
Third Way, not politically viable in the
    United Kingdom, 272
Thrifty Food Plan, of the Department of
    Agriculture, 104
total factor productivity (TFP). *See also*
    median total factor productivity (TFP);
    productivity
  absolute difference between mean and
    median between 2006 and 2013 in
    selected countries, 196*f*
  annual average change between 1990 and
    2014, 156*f*
  average of five-year median growth
    in emerging-market and advanced
    economies, 149, 150*f*, 151
  computing relative values for, 154–55,
    155*f*
  contribution to changes in GDP per
    worker (1990 and 2014), 162*f*
  correlation of lagged median with
    productivity dispersion indexes, 197*f*
  declining relative to the US, 154–55
  differences in accounting for differences
    in levels of income across countries,
    151
  as the driver of growth in the long run,
    147
  effect of lagged median and productivity
    dispersion indexes, 198*t*
  factors affecting in the long run, 169–74
  gap
      declined in Asia and emerging
        Europe but increased in Latin
        America, 159, 159*t*, 179*t*
      explaining about two-thirds of the
        output gap, 160
      between frontier and emerging-
        market economies, 172
      share of explaining the GDP gap,
        159, 159*t*, 179*t*
      with the US, 148
  growth
      affecting the dispersion of the
        productivity distribution, 198, 198*t*

as a bigger driver of income
    catch-up in periods of growth
    acceleration, 174
  collapse in, 51, 53*f*
  drop in following the global
    financial crisis, 164
  in emerging market economies, 7–8,
    150*f*
  in emerging-market economies, 151
  in emerging market economies, 160,
    174
  impact on export competitiveness,
    200–201, 201*t*
  larger during accelerations, 161–62
  in the US, 1, 2*f*
  widening gap across firms, 172
  as intrinsically difficult to measure, 155
  low, explaining most of the income gap,
    148
  relative to the US, 155*f*
  tending to be procyclical, 165
  for world regions, 159*t*, 179*t*
total factor productivity (TFP) and GDP
    growth in emerging-market and
    advanced economies, 150*f*
total income, share of by top firms, 250*t*
trade, growth of, 168–69
trade barriers, reducing, 10
trade integration, 4, 168
Treasury Inflation-Protected Securities
    (TIPS) yield, 173
Trump, Donald, 269, 270, 273, 275
Trump administration, 272–73, 274, 276
Turkey, 58*f*, 63*f*, 154*n*, 156*f*, 183*t*
typical workers' pay, divergence with
    productivity, 209

Ukraine, 152, 155, 156*f*
unemployment, 216, 220*t*
unionization, 230
United Arab Emirates, 148*n*
United Kingdom
  aging process as considerably slower,
    124*n*
  average compensation and productivity
    in, 228*t*
  basic pension in, 122
  debt-creating flows in, 58*f*
  debt servicing cost, 19*f*

tending to rise with age for many
workers, 74
underestimating compensation growth,
225
weak institutions, related to bad
policymaking, 172
wealth creation, 275
wealth inequality, increasing, 265
wealthy Americans, 265, 268
wealthy people, overestimating the wealth
of others and undervaluing the
benefits of social insurance policies,
269
West Germany. *See also* Germany
average compensation and productivity
in, 228*t*
relationship between average
compensation and productivity, 227,
228*t*
"winner-take-most" markets, increased firm
concentration in, 229
wireless services, increases in concentration
in, 254
women. *See also* female labor force
participation
entry into the labor force, 170–71
work, reducing disincentives for, 77–78
workers
compensation of, 73, 207

facilitating the mobility of, 10
increases in productivity growth of
middle-class, 221
lack of robust wage growth for less-
skilled, 77
limited growth in the earnings of low-
and middle-skill, 74
reductions of bargaining power, 229
workforce aging, reducing TFP growth in
Europe, 59
working longer, as a type of adaptation,
138–40
working population, less tax revenue from,
78
workplace retirement savings plan,
encouraging well-designed, 7
world
changes in five-year-ahead growth
forecasts, 150*f*
labor productivity growth, 52*f*, 67
real interest rate(s), 36
world and advanced economies rates of
growth, 166*f*

year 1973, identified as the beginning of the
modern productivity slowdown, 218
younger generation, paying benefits for the
older generation, 119
young firms, in the US, 255*f*

Other Publications from the
PETERSON INSTITUTE FOR INTERNATIONAL ECONOMICS

POLICY BRIEFS

POLICY ANALYSES IN INTERNATIONAL ECONOMICS SERIES

The Future of World Trade in Textiles and Apparel* William R. Cline
1987, 2d ed. June 1999 ISBN 0-88132-110-9
Completing the Uruguay Round: A Results-Oriented Approach to the GATT Trade Negotiations* Jeffrey J. Schott, ed.
September 1990 ISBN 0-88132-130-3
Economic Sanctions Reconsidered (2 volumes)
Economic Sanctions Reconsidered: Supplemental Case Histories* Gary Clyde Hufbauer, Jeffrey J. Schott, and Kimberly Ann Elliott
1985, 2d ed. Dec. 1990 ISBN cloth 0-88132-115-X/
paper 0-88132-105-2
Economic Sanctions Reconsidered: History and Current Policy* Gary Clyde Hufbauer, Jeffrey J. Schott, and Kimberly Ann Elliott
December 1990 ISBN cloth 0-88132-140-0
ISBN paper 0-88132-136-2
Pacific Basin Developing Countries: Prospects for the Future* Marcus Noland
January 1991 ISBN cloth 0-88132-141-9
ISBN paper 0-88132-081-1
Currency Convertibility in Eastern Europe
John Williamson, ed.
October 1991 ISBN 0-88132-128-1
Foreign Direct Investment in the United States, 2d ed.* Edward M. Graham and Paul R. Krugman
January 1991 ISBN 0-88132-139-7
International Adjustment and Financing: The Lessons of 1985–1991* C. Fred Bergsten, ed.
January 1992 ISBN 0-88132-112-5
North American Free Trade: Issues and Recommendations* Gary Clyde Hufbauer and Jeffrey J. Schott
April 1992 ISBN 0-88132-120-6
Narrowing the U.S. Current Account Deficit*
Alan J. Lenz
June 1992 ISBN 0-88132-103-6
The Economics of Global Warming
William R. Cline
June 1992 ISBN 0-88132-132-X
US Taxation of International Income: Blueprint for Reform* Gary Clyde Hufbauer, assisted by Joanna M. van Rooij
October 1992 ISBN 0-88132-134-6
Who's Bashing Whom? Trade Conflict in High-Technology Industries Laura D'Andrea Tyson
November 1992 ISBN 0-88132-106-0
Korea in the World Economy* Il SaKong
January 1993 ISBN 0-88132-183-4
Pacific Dynamism and the International Economic System* C. Fred Bergsten and Marcus Noland, eds.
May 1993 ISBN 0-88132-196-6
Economic Consequences of Soviet Disintegration* John Williamson, ed.
May 1993 ISBN 0-88132-190-7
Reconcilable Differences? United States-Japan Economic Conflict* C. Fred Bergsten and Marcus Noland
June 1993 ISBN 0-88132-129-X
Does Foreign Exchange Intervention Work?
Kathryn M. Dominguez and Jeffrey A. Frankel
September 1993 ISBN 0-88132-104-4

Sizing Up U.S. Export Disincentives*
J. David Richardson
September 1993 ISBN 0-88132-107-9
NAFTA: An Assessment* Gary Clyde Hufbauer and Jeffrey J. Schott, *rev. ed.*
October 1993 ISBN 0-88132-199-0
Adjusting to Volatile Energy Prices
Philip K. Verleger, Jr.
November 1993 ISBN 0-88132-069-2
The Political Economy of Policy Reform
John Williamson, ed.
January 1994 ISBN 0-88132-195-8
Measuring the Costs of Protection in the United States Gary Clyde Hufbauer and Kimberly Ann Elliott
January 1994 ISBN 0-88132-108-7
The Dynamics of Korean Economic Development Cho Soon
March 1994 ISBN 0-88132-162-1
Reviving the European Union*
C. Randall Henning, Eduard Hochreiter, and Gary Clyde Hufbauer, eds.
April 1994 ISBN 0-88132-208-3
China in the World Economy Nicholas R. Lardy
April 1994 ISBN 0-88132-200-8
Greening the GATT: Trade, Environment, and the Future Daniel C. Esty
July 1994 ISBN 0-88132-205-9
Western Hemisphere Economic Integration*
Gary Clyde Hufbauer and Jeffrey J. Schott
July 1994 ISBN 0-88132-159-1
Currencies and Politics in the United States, Germany, and Japan C. Randall Henning
September 1994 ISBN 0-88132-127-3
Estimating Equilibrium Exchange Rates
John Williamson, ed.
September 1994 ISBN 0-88132-076-5
Managing the World Economy: Fifty Years after Bretton Woods Peter B. Kenen, ed.
September 1994 ISBN 0-88132-212-1
Trade Liberalization and International Institutions* Jeffrey J. Schott
September 1994 ISBN 978-0-88132-3
Reciprocity and Retaliation in U.S. Trade Policy*
Thomas O. Bayard and Kimberly Ann Elliott
September 1994 ISBN 0-88132-084-6
The Uruguay Round: An Assessment*
Jeffrey J. Schott, assisted by Johanna Buurman
November 1994 ISBN 0-88132-206-7
Measuring the Costs of Protection in Japan*
Yoko Sazanami, Shujiro Urata, and Hiroki Kawai
January 1995 ISBN 0-88132-211-3
Foreign Direct Investment in the United States, 3d ed. Edward M. Graham and Paul R. Krugman
January 1995 ISBN 0-88132-204-0
The Political Economy of Korea-United States Cooperation* C. Fred Bergsten and Il SaKong, eds.
February 1995 ISBN 0-88132-213-X
International Debt Reexamined* William R. Cline
February 1995 ISBN 0-88132-083-8
American Trade Politics, 3d ed.* I. M. Destler
April 1995 ISBN 0-88132-215-6
Managing Official Export Credits: The Quest for a Global Regime* John E. Ray
July 1995 ISBN 0-88132-207-5

Visit our website at: www.piie.com; and our bookstore at: http://bookstore.piie.com/

For more information on sales, visit: https://cup.columbia.edu/sales-representation